PRAKṚTI

The Integral Vision

General Editor

KAPILA VATSYAYAN

VOLUME 3

The Agamic Tradition and the Arts

Edited by

Baidyanath Saraswati

Indira Gandhi National Centre for the Arts
New Delhi

D. K. Printworld (P) Ltd.
New Delhi

Cataloging in Publication Data — DK

Prakṛti : the integral vision / general editor,
Kapila Vatsyayan.
Includes bibliographical references.
Includes index.

1. Nature. 2. Cosmology. I. Vatsyayan, Kapila, 1928-

ISBN 81-246-0036-8 (set)
ISBN 81-246-0039-2 (vol. 3)

First Published in India in 1995

Publishers
Indira Gandhi National Centre for the Arts
Central Vista Mess, Janpath, New Delhi - 110001

D.K. Printworld (P) Ltd.
Regd. office : H-12, Bali Nagar, New Delhi-110015

Printed at : D. K. Fine Art Press (P) Ltd., New Delhi

Foreword

In 1986 when the first of the Multidisciplinary and Cross-cultural Seminars was held under the aegis of the Indira Gandhi National Centre for the Arts, there was a trepidation. In my Introduction to the Volume on ***Concepts of Space: Ancient & Modern*** I have shared with the readers the sense of challenge as also of gratification. Then, it was not easy, nor has it been easy in the subsequent years to bring together people from different parts of the world of diverse disciplines and levels of society to speak through a multiplicity of languages to reflect and converse, and have a meaningful dialogue on the fundamental concerns of humanity in the past or present, in science or religion, philosophy and the arts, in civilizations as far apart as Egyptian, Chinese, Greek and Indian, permeating expressions through the written or the oral word, generating a language of myth and symbol which communicates across cultures.

The gathering, the dialogue and the discussion on a single concept of **Space** (***ākāśa***) made it evident that the more fundamental and universal the concept, the greater the probability and possibility of diverse interpretations at multiple levels. The single concept of **Space** had taken us through the journey of the concepts of cavity, cave, aperture, fountainhead, body, air, sky, vacuity, cipher, point and much else. The scientist and the technologist explored the concept through their method of empirical investigation, the philosopher and the metaphysician, artists and the sociologist through perennial questioning and speculation. The two approaches and methods we learnt were complementary and not in conflict. The arts, architecture, sculpture, painting, music and dance enclose, embody and evoke space. Poetry creates vast edifices of space as spatial situations, and evoke the experience of outer and inner space.

The concern with **Space** (***ākāśa***) could not be dissociated from the concern – the concept of **Time** (***kāla***). Two years later, a similar gathering with many familiar faces (who communicated with one another with greater ease) gathered to deliberate upon the many dimensions of **Time** (***kāla***). Once again, the discussions at that Seminar revolved round the micro and macro levels of the single concept, from molecular time to the cosmic time, from the time of biologists to the time of astronomer, from the time of the seer and meditator to the time of the architect, sculptor, musician, dancer and the poet. Besides the familiar faces, there were others who had joined the family of the IGNCA. The enlarged family gave this Seminar a depth and richness, unique and unparalleled. The experiences His Holiness The Dalai Lama articulated in words lucid and resonant, were juxtaposed with the precision and meditation of a scientist – the late Professor D.S. Kothari. The depth of the experience of *Time* in religious traditions, Islamic, Christian, Hindu, Buddhist, Jain and Hebrew, and the embodiment of inner and outer *Time* in poetic language was shared through rapt silence through the voice of the Poet Kathleen Raine.

Logically and naturally, from these two fundamental and universal concepts the next step in our quest for exploration of a single universal theme through diverse paths recalling the Ṛgvedic Verse, **Truth is one; man knows it by different names**, was to explore the concept of the primal elements (five or four) in different civilizations which have governed and determined the evolution of civilization and culture. Perhaps, the first conscious awareness of Man was the fact that his life depended on water, earth, air, fire and, above all, space. Understandably, in all civilizations, at the most sophisticated level as also at the simplest level, the recognition that the primal elements were primary and indispensable for Man, is universal. Myths of the origin of the universe, creation, cosmology and cosmogony, have been developed on the concept of the elements which are four or five. There is a vast body of primary sources and equally extensive and complex a history of critical discourse on the nature of primal elements and their indispensability, not only for Man but for all life on Earth.

The subject was too vast and too monumental to be taken up in a single Seminar. Organizationally, therefore, this time it was decided to hold five successive but interlocked Seminars, one leading to the others, so that they could all culminate in a final international cross-cultural multidisciplinary Seminar. Since cultures, disciplines, and levels of society are not completely autonomous and insulated, there was a planned and understandable overlapping between one Seminar or Workshop and another.

The five Seminars were divided more for facility than the autonomous nature of each area or field. The discussions, therefore, at one Seminar were taken up and did interpenetrate into the next.

Logically, the first of these Seminars focused attention on the articulations of cohesive communities in the world who have lived in harmony with nature and who have communicated with the five elements in a continuous unceasing dialogue. To them the nature of the five elements – water, earth, air, fire and space – is not a matter of intellection or breaking down into separation and division of totality or a whole; instead, it is a question of life here and now. This is manifested in ritual practices which sacralize nature so that man can live as an integral part of the universe, the rhythmic movement of the changing seasons, and the symmetrical punctuation and cycle of seed sprouting, growing, flowering, fruiting, decaying and renewing. In modern discourse this is understood as the need for man to live in harmony with the environment, for an evolution of socio-cultural systems and methodologies for ensuring the maintenance of ecological balances. The lives and lifestyles of these cohesive groups have begun to acquire renewed validity on account of what man has done to pollute, contaminate, desacralize and desecrate the very fundamentals that sustain him and make it possible for him to live on earth. The first Volume is based on the papers submitted at this Seminar.

The Second Seminar moved the emphasis to the textual traditions. There is a vast body of literature in Greek, Chinese and Indian sources where philosophic discourses have been held on the nature of the universe, the nature of matter, the elements and the possibility of transmutation of the gross to the subtle. In India, all branches of philosophic streams have discussed the nature of the *Bhūtas* and the *Mahābhūtas.* The discussion ranges from the earliest articulation on the subject in the *Ṛgveda* to the philosophic schools of Vaiśeṣikas, Vedantins, and the Śaiva *Āgamas.* The old system of *Āyurveda* in India, as much as of medicine in Greece in a very different way, is based on the concept of the *Mahābhūtas* in the constitution of the body itself. The very conception of the five elements constitutes the body. Texts for Indian astronomy, chemistry, metallurgy are replete with discussions on the elements. This discussion cannot be dissociated from a speculation, and discourse of the nature of the universe, cosmology, cosmogony. The Second Seminar delved deep into each of these aspects specially in the Indian tradition – Vedic, Brāhmaṇical, Upaniṣadic and Tāntric. In addition, there was a consideration of the concept of the *Mahābhūtas* in Buddhism and Jainism. This Seminar unfolded the very complex and subtle aspects of the discourse on the nature of the matter, the five-fold organic matter and the five external objects. It also brought forth the many convergences as also divergences of viewpoint between and amongst these different streams of Indian thought as examplified in the textual tradition. The Seminar was hosted by the Department of Sanskrit, University of Poona, Pune. The second Volume of this series is based on the papers and the discussions held at this Seminar.

Logically, the Third Seminar had to and did explore the discussions as also the manifestations of the five elements in the Indian arts, along with their Āgamic background. As is well-recognized, while the *Upaniṣads* provide the basis for speculative thinking, the *Brāhmaṇas* give the methodology of ritual practice (*Yajña* and *Prayoga*). Parallel is the development in early and later medieval India where the texts on *Vāstu* and *Śilpa* provide the frame-work of the abstract principles of creating concrete structures through different media and in different forms. The *Āgama* is the twin which provide the methodology of enlivening, giving life and breath to the concrete structures and forms of art. If monumental architecture, sculpture, painting, music or dance, poetry or theatre, is created on the comprehension of space and time, they are even more built on the system of correspondences first for embodying and then evoking the five elements. The fascinating and unceasing cycle of the movement from the inner experience to the creation of form, which would incorporate the five elements and the employment of a methodology of ritual, is outlined in the Āgamic texts only to achieve the end experience of the transformation of the gross to the subtle. This was the subject of this Seminar. From different vantage points of the architect, sculptor, painter, musician and dancer, the field was re-opened to examine the structure of the Indian arts at its primal level.

Naturally, theories of aesthetics which have emerged from such a viewpoint had to be discussed and many questions asked. The third Volume incorporates the span of the papers presented and the discussions held at this Seminar.

If the arts deal with the process of transmutation and mutation of the subtle to the gross, and the evocation of the subtle from the gross, in other words, the process of the abstract and the concrete suggesting, stimulating and evoking the abstract, then the astrophysicist deals with the nature of primal matter itself. No discourse on the elements could have been completed by excluding the discussion on modern physics of elementary particles and the most recent developments in microbiology. The Fourth Seminar took up the question of the nature and function of matter itself and discussed the theories of the creation of the universe and emergent cosmologies in the modern physics. This was juxtaposed with the consideration on the nature of matter and consciousness. It was obvious that the new developments in science were, perhaps, not all that far remote from the earlier insights in the context of consciousness. The debate between the 19th Century mechanistic science and the modern physics was re-opened. This was juxtaposed with speculations and the philosophic discourses in the Indian philosophic schools. If the second Seminar dealt with the textual traditions and the philosophic schools of *Sāṃkhya, Mīmāṃsā* and the *Vaiśeṣika*, this Seminar looked at these traditions as structuralistic traditions from a scientific point of view. The dialogue created between the method of science and the method of speculation was invigorating. The Fourth Volume comprises papers and discussions at this Seminar.

The fifth and the last Seminar was a coming together of cultures as also disciplines. Coordinators of the earlier Seminars presented brief Reports on each of the Seminars which provided the background and the landscape. The international community, comprising scientists, biologists, philosophers, anthropologists, ecologists and artists shared not only the myth and cosmology of their particular societies but also there was a most meaningful dialogue between those who lived in the awareness of the primordial myths of the elements and those who had employed the tools of science to explore the nature of the phenomenon of matter.

The putting together of the deliberations of the five major Seminars, as a single or a multiple-volume, is a daunting task. Through the combined efforts of the Coordinators of each of these Seminars and, particularly, the Chief Coordinator – Professor B.N. Saraswati and his associates – it has been possible to prepare the five Volumes based on the deliberations of these Seminars as also a companion exhibition which was called "**PRAKṚTI: The Integral Vision**".

It is my hope that these Volumes will provide material for further discussion and dialogue. The perennial nature of the theme and its urgent and contemporary validity will, I hope, make these Volumes significant. As I have said earlier in my Introduction, Man stands today at a moment where he is threatened by the pollution, inner and outer, of his own making. The primal elements and the urgent need for purification through austerity and discipline are not the matters of intellectual discourse alone. Their maintenance and sustenance, and the purity of these that are primary and primal, are the objectives of our life lest death overtakes us.

Kapila Vatsyayan

9th June, 1994

Contents

List of Plates

I. Illustrations P.P. Apte:

Maṇḍalas according to *Pauṣkara Saṃhitā*

II. Illustrations Michael Meister:

Plate 10.4.
(a) Rajim, Madhya Pradesh. Rājīvalocana temple, *ca.* A.D. 600 (drawing: Meister);
(b) Sirpur, Madhya Pradesh. Lakṣmaṇa temple, *ca.* A.D. 600–25, from southeast (photo: American Institute of Indian Studies, Banaras).

Plate 10.5. Sirpur, Lakṣmaṇa temple, pot moulding (*kalaśa*) in *vedibandha* (photo: Meister).

Plate 10.6. Palari, Madhya Pradesh. Siddheśvara Mahādeva temple, *ca.* A.D. 675–700, from east (photo: Meister).

Plate 10.7. *Amala*-fruits (photo: Ajay Sinha).

Plate 10.8. Deogarh, Madhya Pradesh. Gupta-temple *āmalaka*, *ca.* A.D. 500–25 (photo: Ajay Sinha).

Plate 10.9. Nachna, Madhya Pradesh. Pārvatī temple, *ca.* A.D. 450–75. Sanctum doorway (photo: AIIS).

Plate 10.10. Ellora, Maharashtra. Ellora, Kailāsa temple, *ca.* A.D. 750–75. Elephants on *upapīṭha* (photo: AIIS).

Plate 10.11. Amrol, Madhya Pradesh. Rāmeśvara temple, *ca.* A.D. 700. Doorway on east (photo: AIIS).

Plate 10.12. Amrol, Rāmeśvara temple from south (photo: AIIS).

Plate 10.13. Osian, Rajasthan. Harihara temple no. 1, *ca.* A.D. 725–50. North wall, images of Kubera, Mahiṣamardinī Narasiṁha, Brahmā, and Vāyu (photo: Meister).

Plate 10.14. Amrol, Rāmeśvara temple. South sanctum-wall, images of Yama, Gaṇeśa, and *pramatha*; south *kapilī*-wall, image of Agni (photo: Meister).

Abbreviations

AbhiBhā	*Abhinava Bhāratī*
AjitĀ	*Ajitāgama*
BṛD	*Bṛhaddeśī*
BṛUp	*Bṛhadāraṇyaka Upaniṣad*
ChUp	*Chāndogya Upaniṣad*
JaySam	*Jayākhya Saṃhitā*
KKD	*Kriyākramadyotikā*
MakuṭĀ	*Makuṭāgama*
MBh	*Mahābhārata*
MṛgĀ	*Mṛgendrāgama*
NārSam	*Nāradīya Saṃhitā*
NŚ	*Nāṭya-Śāstra*
PārSam	*Pārameśvara Saṃhitā*
PauṣSam	*Pauṣkara Saṃhitā*
PTrīLaghuvṛtti	*Parātrīśikā Laghuvṛtti* (Abhinavagupta)
ṚV	*Ṛgveda*
SātSam	*Sātvata Saṃhitā*
ŚBr	*Śatapatha Brāhmaṇa*
SR	*Saṅgīta-Ratnākara*
SP	*Somaśambhu Paddhati*
SvT	*Svacchanda Tantra*
TĀl	*Tantrāloka* (Abhinavagupta)
TUp	*Taittirīya Upaniṣad*
VāmT	*Vāmakeśvara Tantra*
VātĀ	*Vātulāgama*
YoH	*Yoginī-Hṛdaya*

Introduction

viśvabījaprarohārthaṃ mūlādhāratayā sthitam;
dhartṛśaktimayaṃ vande dharaṇīrūpamīśvaram.

I pay obeisance to the supporting energy of the Lord
in the form of the earth
which remains established as the prime base
for sprouting the seed of the universe.

Abhinava Bhāratī
Maṅgalaśloka (in praise of the first
of the five elements)

Indian Art, both conceptually and in practice, is embedded in a world-view and cosmology, which is based on the fundamental elements (*mahābhūtāni*): earth, water, fire, wind and ether (space). We find a system of correspondences between macrocosm and microcosm, linking the gross and subtle levels, as is evident in the Vedic as well as Āgamic traditions. This conception finds its immediate application in ritual, which can serve as a key to these relationships and to the rich symbolism implied. The correspondences between the elements, in their gross and subtle aspects, sense-perceptions, and human emotive states have been elaborated at all levels of the Indian tradition.

All these conceptions and practices have influenced the Indian aesthetic theories, and have found expression in the different media of the Arts. Taking the *mahābhūtas* as the concrete starting-point, these interrelationships can be examined in the case of each art-form. They appear at different levels: at the level of the material, at the level of the creative process and artistic articulation, at the level of communication and aesthetic receptivity.

Besides the aesthetic and symbolical dimensions of the *mahābhūtas*, their ecological importance should not be forgotten. Man formed by such a tradition lived in harmony with his surroundings and expressed a deep reverence towards the earth on which he dwells, the air he breathes, the water which purifies and gives life, the fire that transforms, and space which gives him the vastness to live. When he draws *maṇḍalas* on the ground, their symbolism of colour and form gives expression to this relationship. When he pours offerings into the sacred fire, he is conscious of the power and manifold nature of the element, and so forth.

The Indira Gandhi National Centre for the Arts has since its beginning been concerned with fundamental themes underlying the Indian Arts, exploring them in all possible directions and thus opening a new and deeper understanding of the artistic traditions. After exploring the concepts of Space and Time,[1] another basic theme has been examined in its various dimensions in several seminars: the concept of the cosmic elements which have been classified as five in the Indian tradition.[2]

A Seminar on *The Role of the Elements* (*mahābhūtas*) *in the Indian Arts and their Āgamic Background* has been held at IGNCA, New Delhi, from March 12-14, 1992, of which the papers are presented in this Volume.

Our life depends on the cosmic elements – earth, water, fire, air and space – but we are rarely conscious of this fact, whether in our own body or in our environment. Any discussion on the elements should lead us to a greater and more immediate awareness of this dependence and to a cosmic sense of responsibility, otherwise it is a futile academic exercise.

The arts, as any human activity which needs a material support, are a sublimation of the elements, "transformation of nature in art", in Coomaraswamy's formulation. Every art-form has its own immediate material, but it uses all the other elements and their transformations in one way or another. It was one of the scopes of this Seminar to explore the relationship between specific art-forms and the elements predominating in them, not only in their material aspect, but in their symbolic function and quality. Water does not only mean the physical element but the quality of fluidity and the symbol of life; fire does not only mean a burning flame, but the quality of intensity, of heat and burning, etc. The texts are full of descriptions of the qualities and symbolic value of the elements.

But the elements or *mahābhūtas* in their gross form are part of a whole cosmology and cosmogony. Their role in cosmogony cannot be discussed here, because it would require a separate treatment. But we have to place the elements in the total scheme of cosmology which is the system of the *tattvas* – whether 25 as in Sāṃkhya or 36 as in the Āgamas. The system of the *tattvas* presents a perfect ecological balance. Ecology in the modern Western sense is limited to nature and remains artificially cut-off from the mental and spiritual dimensions, whereas the system of *tattvas* contains everything: the gross elements (*bhūta*) cannot be separated from the subtle (*tanmātra*), nor from the sense-organs (*indriya*), and beyond them to the subtler mental faculties. Even the latest theories of modern physics have again discovered that the observer cannot be left out of the picture, that the observed is not just an 'object'.

In the system of the *tattvas* the elements are the basis of the pyramid, and the ascent is from gross to subtle and beyond: *sthūla, sūkṣma* and *para* cannot be separated. Thus the theme of this Seminar on the *bhūtas* should not be and has not been understood as a limitation, but as a starting-point. The elements are the very basis of the universe, and any sublimation has to start from them. Or, seen from the other side, there is an evolution from the supreme (*para*) to the subtle and from there to the gross elements.

In another aspect, too, the elements are all-pervading, that is in the symbolic field. Where they are not present materially, they are present symbolically. At all the levels, even the most subtle and spiritual, we find elemental symbolism. As an example we may mention the three yogic *nāḍīs* being identified with sun, moon and fire.

If we agree that the *tattvas* present a complete scheme and an ecological balance, we have to address ourselves to two important issues:

1. In actual practice cosmology becomes manifested in ritual, life-style, festivals and art.
   How are the Indian arts manifesting, expressing, integrating this cosmological scheme in their different media?
   How does the concept take on flesh and form and sound and movement?
   What are the methods of transferring this cosmology into the visual and audible form that we call art?
2. We should not adopt a complacent attitude with regard to the Indian tradition, as if everything were in harmony. We should rather seriously ask ourselves why it is that a tradition with such a wisdom in relation to nature has fallen into such neglect of nature and has allowed an ecological disaster to happen in its own environment. Can our reflections on these inter-relations between cosmology, ritual and the arts be more than a romantic looking back to a lost harmony, and can they create an awareness of the urgent need of the hour? Can the arts, and the theory or philosophy supporting them, become an instrument of integration and ecological awareness, instead of being cut off from their context and used as an isolated act of entertainment for the privileged few?

It is here where the *Āgamas / Tantras* can play a crucial role of mediation, with their integration of the senses and of matter into spirituality.

Here a word of explanation on the limitation and scope of the topic of this Volume is necessary.

There is no doubt that, at least in the Indian context, the arts have grown out of a re-enactment of the cosmos, of human life and of the Divine, which we may call, for lack of better word, *ritual.* Whether it is the Vedic sacrifice,

Āgamic temple-ritual or personal *pūjā*, it always involves symbolic forms like the shapes of the Vedic altars, cosmic *maṇḍalas, yantras*, sculpture, architecture, music, dance, poetry, etc. Thus ritual is all linked with different art-forms and with cosmological conceptions which are basic to all the arts. We could describe it with the symbol of a triangle:

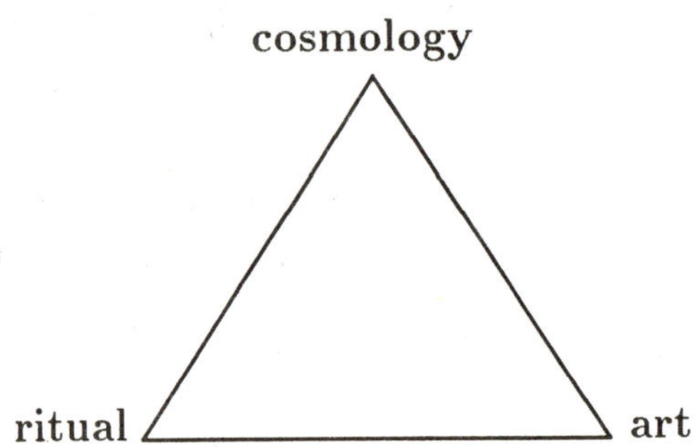

For the sake of a more precise discussion it seemed useful to limit the scope to only one, though very vast, stream of the Indian tradition where this triangle becomes clearly manifest, that is the Āgamic tradition. By *Āgamas* we mean a class of literatures and practice which may be Śaiva, Vaiṣṇava or Śākta (or even Jaina or Buddhist), but which have certain common characteristics. It would have been very tempting to include the *Vedas* in the same discussion, and in not doing so we do not want to emphasize a total separation of the Vedic and Āgamic traditions, on the contrary, we will discover many threads connecting the two. We need not go here into any controversies about the relationship between *Vedas* and *Āgamas* or *Tantras*, this would be besides the scope of our search here. We rather want to find the connecting threads between the three points of the triangle, that is cosmology, ritual and arts, in the context of the Āgamic tradition.

It is an undeniable fact that, when speaking of the elements or *mahābhūtāni*, the cosmological, ritual and artistic dimensions are closely interwoven, but more often than not these are studied in isolation and not in their interconnectedness. Thus it is the aim of this Volume to discover these connections and establish the relationships.

Though the Seminar was primarily concerned with an exploration of the Āgamic tradition in its relation to the Arts, the ecological importance of such an exploration remained constantly in our minds, from the Introduction by the convener to the conclusion by Dr Kapila Vatsyayan. Understanding the tradition should not remain limited to a literary analysis nor to extolling the glorious past when man was in harmony with his surroundings and his activities were integrated in the rhythm of nature. It should rather help us to become more aware of the dimensions we have lost in a fragmented way of life, and to recover some of the attitudes embedded in the tradition, such as respect and reverence for the earth on which we dwell, the air we breathe, the water which purifies and nourishes us, the fire which transforms and heats, and the space which gives us room to live. In this sense this Volume is not merely historical or literary, but directed at the burning issues of present-day ecology.

The aim of the Seminar was to be achieved in five steps, and hence the articles presented here are arranged in five sections, related to the number five of the elements:

1. An exploration of the concepts and practices of the *Āgamas* in relation to the elements, their cosmology, ritual and *Yoga*,
2. An analysis of the aesthetic theories, mainly based on the *Nāṭya-Śāstra* and *Abhinava Bhāratī*,
3. The artistic theories and techniques as found in the *Śāstras* of the Arts,
4. The manifestation of the elements in the different artistic expressions, where each art-form has a special relationship with one or more of the elements, and yet all are present in one way or another, and
5. General questions relating to the Arts and ecology.

These five points are supposed to cover the different levels where the elements underlie the Arts: the level of the material, the level of the creative process and artistic articulation, the level of symbolic relationships and the level of communication and aesthetic receptivity.

In this Introduction I can only give a short survey of the rich material presented in the papers, to show the connecting link.

The *Āgama*, ritual and *Yoga* in relation to the elements was presented from the Vaiṣṇava Pāñcarātra tradition by P.P. Apte, from the point of view of the dualistic and non-dualistic Śaivāgamas by H.N. Chakravarty, S.P. Sabarathinam and S.S. Janaki respectively. From these presentations several common features of these different schools emerged, which are independent of their respective theologies. One of these common features is the importance of ritual purification of the elements in the body, called *bhūtaśuddhi*. Any ritual requires the purification of the worshipper's gross and subtle body which has to go through the five elements, and by which the worshipper's body becomes divinized. This process was clearly described and analyzed by P.P. Apte in the Pāñcarātra tradition, and by H.N. Chakravarty, S.S. Janaki and S.P. Sabarathinam in the Śaivāgamas.

P.P. Apte brought out another important aspect of ritual where the elements are represented in *maṇḍalas* with their corresponding shapes and colours. *Maṇḍalas* are microcosmic representations of the macrocosm, and they combine ritual and art in a unique way.

H.N. Chakravarty gave the philosophical and cosmological background of the elements in the Śaivāgamas, from the point of view of the non-dualistic Śaivism of Kashmir. The five elements are the basic *tattvas* in the Āgamic cosmology comprising thirtysix *tattvas*. The five elements are further understood as forms of Śiva, corresponding to the five Brahmans. The *aṣṭamūrti* conception of Śiva also accords a basic theological importance to the elements.

S.S. Janaki developed the process of *bhūtaśuddhi* in the Śaiva Siddhānta tradition and showed the correspondences of the elements with colours, forms, *mantras*, deities, etc. The yogic correspondences to the subtle centres in the body were also referred to. S.P. Sabarathinam dealt with the *maṇḍalas* in the Śaiva context.

All these presentations of the Āgamic material made it clear that the elements are present at all the levels, from the physical to the subtle and spiritual, and that all these meanings are embedded in a cosmo-theology, whether it is interpreted in a dualistic or non-dualistic way. They are not only instruments of external ritual and inner purification, but they have a definite significance in the ultimate process of divinization of the devotee.

The second section is focusing on the aesthetic theories which have been largely informed by the Vedic and Āgamic traditions. K.D. Tripathi's paper: "From Sensuous to Supersensuous: An inquiry into some terms of Indian Aesthetics" presents a pivotal point of the Volume. Following Abhinavagupta, he went into the very process of creativity and the role of sense-experience in the process of passing from the aesthetic to the transcendent experience. He analyzed the very basic concept of *rasa* in the light of its elemental association with water. The aesthetic qualities of *mādhurya* and *ojas* are related to the watery and fiery elements. In fact, most of the terms of Indian aesthetics can be derived from the essential qualities of the five elements. The paper made it clear that the very process of the aesthetic experience, being a process of universalization or *sādhāraṇīkaraṇa*, is a transformation of the sensuous into the supersensuous. In this, the qualities of the elements are more important than their physical nature.

R. Tripathi discussed the ritual of the Raṅgadaivatapūjana of the *Nāṭya-Śāstra* and the use of the elements and compared the consecration of a temple with the consecration of a theatre. However, the historical question of the dependence on the Āgamic ritual cannot be solved easily, since the textual form of the *Āgamas* is later than that of the *Nāṭya-Śāstra*. However, the symbolism of the elements is essential in the preliminary rituals of theatre.

The third section moves from the *Nāṭya-Śāstra* and the aesthetic theories to the Śāstric theories of the different Arts. Two papers, by Prem Lata Sharma and Mukund Lath, were devoted to *Saṅgīta-Śāstra*. P.L. Sharma analyzed the specific role of the elements and their qualities in music. Some of the elements, such as wind, play a physical role in the production of musical sound, while others are represented by their qualities. The *Saṅgīta-Ratnākara* speaks of the elements in relation to the body and mental faculties in terms of *Āyurveda*, and also in their subtle meaning in terms of *Yoga* and of the *cakras* in the body.

Mukund Lath developed further the idea of "The Body as an Instrument" in the light of the *Saṅgīta-Ratnākara*, and he expanded on the process of sound-production in the human body. From both these papers it became clear that musical theory and practice is intimately linked with the human body, its physical and subtle understanding which consists of the five elements in their gross and subtle form.

My own paper entitled "Lines of Fire, Lines of Water: the Elements in *Śilpaśāstra*" was dedicated to some aspects of the elemental symbolism in *Śilpa-śāstra*, as applied to both, sculpture and architecture. This symbolism is found in the lines of the compositional diagram (*pañjara*), which have certain qualities of the elements: the horizontal is the water-line, the vertical the fire-line, etc. The integration of the apparently opposing qualities of water and fire is found in the hexagram, a basic form of all *yantras*. The images created on the basis of such diagrams share the qualities of the respective elements and their combination. The human figure is also divided vertically in sections attributed to the five elements. In architecture, the symbolism of the elements is part of the general cosmic symbolism of the temple which is applied to its different parts.

Michael Meister, in his paper on "Unity and Gravity of an Elemental Architecture", demonstrated the symbolism of the temple with the help of slides. He summarized the general idea thus: "The temple by intention is poised between elements, always placed near water; built of and on the earth; it is itself the home of fire; its tower the embodiment of air; and its apex of ether."

The fourth section passes on to artistic practice (*prayoga*) in which Ganapati Sthapati gives a summary of his vast knowledge and experience of the conceptions and practice of traditional architecture. He elaborated on Space as the primal element of architecture, and he gave much importance to the *Vāstupuruṣamaṇḍala* in constructing a house or a temple.

Kapila Vatsyayan has related Indian myths and their representations in art to the questions of ecology. She has shown that myth and art have a powerful message for our ecological situation, especially in India, if we know how to read it.

The concluding section starts by a comprehensive survey of "The Cosmic Elements in India; an Agenda of Questions" by A.R. Kelkar. He put the theme in the context of cosmology and gave a survey of different cosmological schemes, comparing them also with other Indo-European cultures, such as the Greek. His semantic analysis of central terms of the theory of art like *rasa*, underlined the thesis proposed by K.D. Tripathi about the elemental origin of these terms. His "agenda of questions" presented a useful survey of possible relationships of the elements with the Arts.

However, the main stress of the last section lies in the emphasis on ecology, a link which had not been sufficiently established in the papers describing the Āgamic and Śāstric traditions. Bryan Mulvihill stressed the need for a "cultural ecology", which is the need of the hour in a world-wide situation of exploitation of the earth, pollution and ecological disaster. All traditional cultures with their wisdom and deep respect for the elemental forces of nature have to teach modern civilization how to deal with their environment. He stated that "perhaps no other society has developed the human interdependence with nature to such a refined and elaborate degree than the cultures of the Indian sub-continent where the relationship with the elemental forces is portrayed on every level of human and cultural expression." Sadly, this harmonious relationship of man and nature is now very much disturbed in India itself. The author also demonstrated his thesis on the elements with the help of a Buddhist *maṇḍala* structure, maybe one of the 'leitmotifs' of this seminar. His appeal was for a greater awareness of the interdependence and relationship with the elements that traditional cultures preserve. He found the reasons for the ecological disaster of our time in a "globally embedded arrogance" and "inflation of the ego", leading to sheer exploitation of the earth.

In her concluding speech, Kapila Vatsyayan also made a poignant appeal to link our traditional wisdom, ritual and art, with the problems of ecology, in India and the world over. Tradition should not remain closed in itself, unaware of the environment, but it should play a crucial role in rediscovering the primordial relationship of man and nature.

The "missing link" between the Āgamic knowledge and ecology could be mentioned as one of the weaknesses of the Seminar, but it reflected faithfully the present state of affairs in India. If we can recognize this weakness and come to a greater awareness of the relevance of the cosmologies propounded in the *Āgamas*, which found their expression in the various art-forms, starting from ritual itself, the Seminar would have served an important purpose.

If at all some conclusions could be drawn, I would dare to make a general remark. It is obvious that such a rich tradition of Āgamic cosmology, ritual, aesthetic theory and artistic practice cannot be exhausted in a few papers. But it is perhaps the sign of a living tradition that it takes the basic elements so much for granted that it is not longer aware of them. Thus, to my mind, the ground on which we stand, the earth element, *pṛthivī* or *bhūmi*, has not been given its due importance. If this basic element alone (though of course not in isolation) could be studied in all its implications, we could come closer to a real Indian ecology.

We are grateful to Professor Kirti Trivedi, Industrial Design Centre, IIT, Bombay, for providing the slides of *maṇḍalas* to illustrate the article by P.P. Apte. These *maṇḍalas* have been created by him in association with Dr P.P. Apte, on the basis of the *Pauṣkara Saṃhitā*.

We thank the American Institute of Indian Studies, Ramnagar, Varanasi, for providing photographs to illustrate the article by Michael Meister.

I also wish to thank the staff of IGNCA, Varanasi, for assisting me in bringing out this volume, for composing and formating the text in the computer and proof-reading. Sri S. Dorai has prepared the line-drawings after the originals provided by the authors.

Bettina Bäumer

Notes

1. Cf. *Concepts of Space*, Ed. by Kapila Vatsyayan New Delhi (IGNCA and Abhinav Publications) 1991, and *Kalātattvakośa*, Vol. II, Ed. by Bettina Bäumer.
2. *Kalātattvakośa*, Vol. III will be dedicated to this theme.

1

Ritual Sublimation of Elements In Pāñcarātra Āgama

Prabhakar P. Apte

The *Āgamas* in general and the *Pāñcarātra Āgama* in particular, have conceived and ritually effected a sublimation of gross and subtle elements (*mahābhūtas* and *tanmātras*) in various areas of regular and occasional rituals. The noteworthy ritual item is found in *bhūtaśuddhi* or elemental purification, a pre-requisite of *bahiḥpūjā* and *mānasapūjā*. It can be compared to an overhauling of a machine. The overhauling in the case of the gross and subtle body is taken to the subtlest layer of elemental composition of the human body. The process of *bhūtaśuddhi* may be described as a psycho-yogic process. The elemental components are made universally pervasive and are then meditatively reduced to ashes with the help of *cidagni* (fire of consciousness) and later on rejuvenated by sprinkling of divine nectar thereover. Thus the gross and subtle elements constituting the body of a devotee are sublimated. In this paper, it is proposed to present a critical appreciation of this unique rituo-yogic procedure in *Pāñcarātra Āgama*.

The elements are also found deified in Agamic rituals and are visualized in some shapes and colours. A note of this contribution is also proposed to be taken in this paper. The third area where the *mahābhūtas* are artistically made use of are the diagrams of *maṇḍalas* in general and *vāstumaṇḍala* in particular. The diagrams are said to be a microcosmic reflection of the macrocosm.[1] It is proposed to place before the scholars the approach towards and treatment of the *mahābhūtas* as found in the *Pāñcarātra Āgama*.

In *Āgamas* five distinct tasks have been assigned to devotees by following which one is able to attain *samādhi* and finally the direct vision of the Lord. These five stages are as follows:

(1) *Abhigamana*, (2) *Upādāna*, (3) *Ijjyā*, (4) *Svādhyāya*, and (5) *Yoga*, are assigned for five tasks.[2] The first covers the period before sunrise, beginning from *brāhma-muhūrta*, i.e., early dawn; the fifth take the earlier portion of the night after the sunset. The second and third accommodate themselves up to noon and the fourth ranges from noon to sunset.

The first, is *abhigamana* or 'approach to the Almighty' with ardent surrender coupled with *japa*, i.e., muttering of the divine name, *dhyāna* or meditation and *stotra* or laudations.[3] Immediately after breaking sleep while about half of the night is yet to pass, the devotee should meditate upon the Supreme Power and offer prayers to purify one's actions throughout the day.[4] The action of *dhyāna* may fall directly under introverts' region; but the *japa* and *stotra* are at least on border. Surrender into the Lord (Viṣṇu)[5] with various names is more important. This period exclusively aims at a direct contact between the God and the devotee; it is a pretty long time when one finds seclusion and solitude coupled with quietude of time and atmosphere. During this period, almost everyone is required to be an introvert at least for a while.[6]

The second portion called *upādāna* is reserved for purely a mechanical activity of equipment of the idol worship. Having done this, the devotee is to embark on the ritual of worship technically called *ijjyākāla*, covering late hours of the forenoon. The *pūjā* especially that in the temple and also that at the time of festivals in renowned shrines is a meticulous process of very many mechanical activities. However, it includes some processes wherein the performer has to shut his eyes so as to yoke his inner faculties. Two such topics which rather form independent units, and which have received a fair treatment in the *Saṃhitās* are the *bhūtaśuddhi* or 'elemental purification' and *mānasayāga* or 'worship-within'. The first comes under *ijjyā* no doubt but actually may be treated as the finishing touch to the *upādāna* activity which has a double mission – collection of materials and their purification even the body purification of the devotee. *Bhūtaśuddhi* aims at purification of the elements which go to form the body. The *mānasayāga* is the first part of the *ijjyā* wherein the entire function is performed with closed eyes with all abstract aid. Having done this, he is eligible to go on with the *ṣoḍaśopacārapūjā*.

Bhūtaśuddhi: Elemental Purification

External bath and cleansing alone does not render the human body completely pure so as to make fit for worship. Evil thought, speech and actions too go on besmearing the body particles with impurities. *Āgamas* provide with a highly scientific and technical process for overhauling the entire body constitution and rejuvenating it every time before the performance of the *pūjā*, since it is a must in accomplishing an atmosphere of purity, piety, sanctity, and serenity in the *sanctum sanctorum*, where the Lord is to be invoked to come and stay. So without the performance of the *bhūtaśuddhi*, the *arcaka* is not recognized to be eligible for the *pūjā*.

The process of the elemental purification may be summarized as under:

The devotee shuts his eyes and open his inner sight to visualize that Lord Viṣṇu is seated on the Supreme Altar. He then gradually elevates Him on way upwards through the right-hand portion of the '*suṣumnā* vein', seeing Him reclining on a 'circular orb' glowing like a cluster of a thousand suns. This seat, as he perceives is made up of *mantras* and resting twelve *aṅgulas* (fingers – a measurement) above the luminous disc (*prabhācakra*) with a substratum made of elements. The devotee further perceives the Lord to assume a body of *mantras* alone.[7]

Just below the seat of the Lord, devotee sees a square shape piece of floor, yellow in colour and possessing the properties of the five elements: *śabda-sparśa-rūpa-rasa-gandha* (sound-touch-colour-taste-odour) and having an emblem of *vajra*. He further sees that the entire creation marked with rivers, islands, cities, forts, etc. surround the earth. At this stage of visualization the devotee chants the *pṛthivīmantra* and finds that the earth enters his body and rests there through the mantric miracle; he allows the earth to pervade the region from foot to knee. With the force of *kumbhaka* wind, it is to be gradually let forth and made to merge into its subtle-element, the *tanmātra*, called *gandhaśakti*.[8] The *gandhaśakti* is then purged out to dissolve into the next element, i.e., *ap* (water) and be deposited in the majesty of Varuṇa; in the same manner all the five elements are to be made to merge back and back ultimately into the *tanmātra* of ether namely *śabda*. Each one should be inhaled with *pūraka*, dissolved into the next one with *kumbhaka* and exhaled with *recaka*. While with *ap*, he meditates on Varuṇa and he sees all storages and reservoirs of water in-drain within his body makes it pervade over the portion between his knee and the thigh. With *dhāraṇāmantra* (i.e., the chant of retention), the entire quantity of water is seen to merge in its *tanmātra* the *rasaśakti*, and that should be thrown out by *recaka*, in the orb of fire, and should be deposited in the majesty of Lord Agni endowed with triangular shape altar. Then the whole empire of Agni, i.e., the lightening, the moon, the sun, the stars, the jewels, etc. gush inside the body of the *sādhaka* when the chanting of the *taijasamantra* commences. This power is absorbed with this *mantra* and it rests in the region from *pāyu* to *nābhī*, i.e., the organ of generation to the navel. This by contemplation, merges into the *rūpaśakti*, the *tanmātra* of light. Then this is purged out to be deposited into the majesty of *Vāyu* or wind. Then he experiences that all sorts of winds enter his body. By the chant of retention they are absorbed within the *sparśaśakti*, or *tanmātras* of touch. Then it should be thrown out and deposited into the *vyoma-vibhava* or the etheric majesty. Then entire space without is contemplated to enter one's body and then by *vyomākhya-dhāraṇāmantra* subtle element should be taken into one's own body, and it should pervade the region between the neck and the *brahmarandhra*. Then he sustains it for sometime in *kumbhaka* and then he pushes it out up from the *brahmarandhra*. Here he experiences that the *jīva* is full of pure consciousness (*caitanya*) and is completely rid of the fetters of the cage made up of the five gross elements – (*pañcamahābhūtapañjara*). Here the individual self, i.e., the *sādhaka* gets a prospective as well as retrospective vision. He can see his entire body as if he is a third party spectator. So does he perceive the Lord seated on the Altar-Divine. The *sādhaka* is then advised to remain in the body made of *mantras* and concentrate on the *samādhi*-stage. Then he leaves that body also, thinking it to be impure and rises still higher and higher. He then visualizes that he is coming out of the nest of his heart as well. He proceeds with the power of wisdom (*jñāna*) alone and drops down the body of the *tanmātras* and reaches the level of the physical vicinity of God. Here he realizes and enjoys the luminous, indescribable state of bliss – the favour of Lord Viṣṇu. Here he experiences that he has resumed to the existence of his 'own'.

Then what he is expected to do is the act of burning down his earthly body by the strength of his will (*icchāśakti*), see to it that the earthly body is completely reduced to ashes leaving of course the *tanmātras* which are already taken out; by the fire which resembles one which is ablaze at the time of the great annihilation of Lord's creation (*yugānta-hutabhuk*). When the function is over the blaze is to be surrendered to the Lord of the *mantras*. Then the *sādhaka* sees that the fire is full burnt and what remains is a heap of ashes. Then he transmits a cyclonic wind to make the ashes scatter away at random, all over. Thus the body disappears totally with no visible trace.

Then the *sādhaka* invokes the disc of *mantras* shining like a full moon and drizzling nectar from the heaven. He should sprinkle this nectar over the remnants whatsoever of his body and lo! he sees that a lotus springs up out of void and gradually the universe evolves in its normal order of creation. He finds that there shines for him a reborn body untainted with any impurities whatsoever. This is a body worth entering which he does by the retreating process and embarks on his worship of the Lord in the form *arcā*, the tangible idol.

By way of resume one could note down following observations:

(i) *Bhūtaśuddhi* is a complete and independent process.

(ii) It is a pre-requisite for the ritual of worship and a *saṃskāra* on the body of the worshipper.

(iii) From spiritual point of view, it is a far difficult process as compared to the mechanism of the *pūjā*. A sincere effort on the part of the devotee to master this process would certainly uplift him on much higher plane; and it is worth giving repeated trials.

(iv) As for the scientific nature, its feasibility and efficacy, only those who are in that line, i.e., the introverts with adequate background alone could say anything.

(v) These various technical terms like the tackling of the *nāḍīs*, the *cakras* and winds present within one's own body. This could be compared by an introvert to the corresponding terms in the *Yoga* school.

(vi) We are told of *layayoga* elsewhere in the *Āgamas* which is the abstract process of absorption of the creation. This might be similar to the *bhūtaśuddhi*.

(vii) We come across some technical processes in metaphysics of the *Upaniṣads*, like *trivṛtkaraṇa, pañcīkaraṇa* and *saṃvarga-vidyā* where one element is absorbed into the other. Those processes have served the source and might have played an important role in the building up of the scheme of elemental purification.

(viii) In any case, the entire process of isolating oneself from the earthly body, reaching the vicinity of the Great Soul, experiencing the discarding of the gross and subtle bodies around oneself, to have a detached visualization of one's own body from a long distance, to set it on fire by one's own fire of wisdom, seeing that it is reduced to ashes, blowing cyclonic hurricane to puff the heap of ashes helter-skelter and further, with the mystic power to the *mantras*, to rejuvenate the body along with the entire Universe with the help of nectar, all this is fascinating for anyone; nay one would be tempted to become an introvert. Naturally, an introvert would rejoice on finding such a fine process to grasp and to practise.

(ix) Even for a devotee having academic interest, this portion would be of great help in tallying various tenets of the *Pāñcarātra* cult, especially those concerning the theories of creation and liberation. And ~~further~~, it is noteworthy that in the form of *bhūtaśuddhi* the tradition could retain the metaphysics of the *Pāñcarātra*; and practising the *bhūtaśuddhi* is making an at-a-glance revision of its metaphysics.

Whatever the merits or otherwise, one may safely announce that here lies an important treasure of our spiritual heritage. Let us not just skip it, or sleep over it, casually dismissing it as impracticable.

The purification of everything from within and without renders the *sādhaka* eligible for the *yāga*, where at the outset he is to perform *mānasayāga* or the 'worship-within' and then alone he may handle the paraphernalia of outer worship (*bāhyayāga*). And *mānasayāga*, too, is an abstract process to be performed with one's eyes shut. This again would form a subject of introvert's special relish.

Mānasayāga: The Worship-Within

There are two names for this *yāga* – *mānasayāga* or *antaryāga* which are same in connotation and hence inter-changeable. They are used as substitutes in the texts of *Śaivāgama, Śāktāgama* and *Vaiṣṇavāgama*. *Mānasapūjā* and *mānasārcanā* are also used to denote the same thing. All these terms indicate a process which may be described as 'Internal worship', 'mental adoration' or 'worship-within'. It is an abstract form of worship. The worship of the Lord is said to be threefold: internal worship, the image worship and the fire-worship – *mānasī, berapūjā ca homapūjeti sā tridhā*. What is common is the object of worship and what varies is the mode. *Āgamas* contemplate no option regarding the choice of one or more forms of worship; but instead they regard all of them to be the essential components of what may be generally called *yāga* or worship. The *mānasayāga* seems to be an unoptional portion of study for those who profess to follow the Āgamic path.

On par with the *mānasapūjā*, there are some other functions wherein the mind plays an important role. There are modes of Vedic sacrifices which can be performed internally and are called *antaryāga*, where instead of the concrete material, only abstract material is used. In various Upaniṣadic passages and other places, descriptions of (1) *manomayī-mūrti* an idol created by one's mental agency; (2) *mānasa-snāna*, i.e., performance of ablution by mind; (3) *mānasa-japa*, i.e., the muttering of *mantras* without the movement of tongue and lips;[9] (4) *mānasa-homa*, i.e., the ritual of fire-worship within one's mind; and (5) *mānasī-sṛṣṭi* mental creation and such other concepts connected exclusively to the sphere of mind are found. It means that the mind has power to create a world of its own – a replica to the outer world. We are familiar with the fascinating picture of the *parāpūjā* and *mānasa-pūjā* offered by Ādi Śaṅkara. The yogic practices, the *bhūtaśuddhi* the *nyāsa*, and such other topics are also allied ones, together forming a category of processes where internal faculties have a predominant role.

The description of the *mānasayāga* may be summarized as follows:

> The devotee takes a *padmāsana* posture and folds his palms close to the navel in an *añjalimudrā*. Having come to a steady physical composure of limbs one recalls the group of senses constantly tending outward, so as to make theme merge in the mind and apply their faculties to the intellect and the faculties of the intellect towards the path of knowledge.[10] With this preparation one proceeds to perform the abstract spiritual rites. Hereafter what is functioning is the mind alone. The interior of the body of the devotee is to serve the purpose of the divine shrine described as *catuścakre navadvāre dehe devagṛhe pure*. The *sanctum sanctorum* stands within one's own heart as a permanent abode of the Lord in the form of the 'Indweller' or *Antaryāmin*. We find a detailed scientific description or the construction of all the components of the temple and the relevant deities presiding over them. In fact, it is not a construction of the scene by the mind in the worldly sense. It is rather a realization of what is already created by the Lord within oneself. All the metaphysical principles, the divinities, the elements, the celestial globes, the sages, the scriptures and the like are invoked to come and take form to receive the worship to be offered. Thereupon one contemplates the process of merger of all these into the body of the Lord. For example, the sacred Ganges is to be visualized to merge in Him in the form *arghya* offered to him. This process is technically called *laya-yāga* or the 'ritual of the worship of merger'. After accomplishing the *laya-yāga* one should start the *bhogābhidha-yāga*. This is just the counterpart of what is called the *ṣoḍaśopacāra-pūjā* in the external worship. It begins with invocation and prayer –
>
> *mānasān jayaśabdāṃśca kṛtvā vijñāpayedidam* |
> *svāgataṃ tava deveśa ! sannidhiṃ bhaja me'cyuta !*
> *gṛhāṇa mānasīṃ pūjāṃ yathārthaparibhāvitām* ||
>
> *PārSam*, IV.134–35

The *upacāras* or the offerings to be presented are not tangible (*sāṃsparśa*) but products of will-power (*saṃkalpajanita*) and their speciality lies in their being immense in size, abundant in quality and they can be gathered from any place of choice out of the seven worlds. Besides they are through and through auspicious, holy, bestowed with finest qualities and undecayable.[11] All is abstract for instance, the fire to be produced is by rubbing the sticks of meditation – *dhyānāraṇiṃ tu nirmathya cidagnimavatārthaṃ ca.* The fire also is not ordinary but a spiritual one. The *nyāsa*, the *mantras*, the *mudrās* all are abstract. Nothing is tangible. The whole performance when accomplished is to be surrendered to the Lord and then the entire paraphernalia is to be withdrawn into one's heart and is to be treasured into one's self, by the power of will or *saṃkalpa.* Then the devotee has to beg permission of the Lord to perform the *bāhyayāga.* The conclusion (*visarjana*) worship-within is not to be done till the completion of the worship-without.

The Āgamic seers promise the performer of the *mānasayāga* various reliefs: from diseases, old age, mortality, bondage of the worldly ties, etc. and further assure him of annihilation of all demerits to his account, thereby granting him 'the eternal bliss'. It is described as the best of the paths and the follower is honoured as the best of the worshippers. It is further assured that the performance of this form of worship, though very hard to practise becomes easy by constant practice.[12] The followers are warned against revealing this to those who have neither faith nor eligibility to perform this.

The first thing that strikes us is the completeness of the process contemplated in the *mānasayāga* as compared to the processes of *mānasajapa, mānasasnāna, mānasahoma*, etc. They are small units in themselves which rather serve as component parts of the abstract worship, while this is a self-sufficient unit.

The *parā-pūjā* or *mānasapūjā* explained by Ādi Śaṅkara, the *bhūtaśuddhi, nyāsa, yoga* and like topics fall under the same category with the *mānasayāga* as noted already. But there are a number of subtle points of difference. In the *mānasapūjā* offered to the Goddesses, we find the *ṣoḍaśopacāra* created and offered by mind alone. In the *parā-pūjā* however, the immense finiteness of the worshipper and his equipments in comparison to 'the Infinite' which is the object of worship seriously strikes the mind of great Śaṅkara and in a mood of ecstacy he expresses his inability to worship the Lord, and going a step further, he says that the action of *pūjā* is impossible due to the identity of the *pūjya* and the *pūjaka.* In the *mānasayāga* on the other hand, no inability is contemplated, nor the identity of the *pūjya* and *pūjaka* at least at the time of the ritual.

In the elemental purification we find a process wherein both psychological and physical agencies are at work. Besides, it is a preparation for the worship and not the body of it. In *mānasa-snāna*, what is aimed at, is the internal purification of the body and mind. *Mānasajapa* is a practice of concentrating on the muttering of the *mantras* or divine names without the help of the tongue and the lips. In the *nyāsa* both the physical as well as the mental activity is at work. In *dhyāna* or meditation, what is required is application of one's mind towards single object.

In the yogic practice, we find that at the stage of *samādhi*, mind has to develop the faculty of concentration (*ekāgratā*) at the first instance and further, in the state of *nirbīja-samādhi* what is contemplated, is the total merger in the object namely the Supreme Self. Besides, the *nāḍī* system is yoked to the yogic feats, which may not be employed in the Āgamic process of the internal worship.

Mānasayāga differs much from the sister rituals mentioned above. Unlike the *Yoga*, it is restricted to mental and abstract functions alone. In *Yoga*, on the other hand, the faculties of mind too are withdrawn in the manner of the limbs of tortoise. In the *mānasayāga* we have to develop the subtle and sublime faculties of mind, since it has to create by realization the entire expanse of the divine enshrinement within and maintain it carefully till the successful accomplishment of the *mānasayāga*. In technical terms, we may say, the mind has to develop the faculty of *samagratva* instead of *ekāgratva*. *Samagratva* may be interpreted as 'concentration on totality'. What we find in that process, is, that the mind has to create the mental image (*manomayī mūrti*), prepare a seat for it by imagination, create the consorts and retinue deities by imagination, instal them at proper places, then collect the proper material for worship, deposit it at proper places and commence the worship, keeping all the while the scene created so far firm and steady by not allowing it to vanish in the least and for even a fraction of a moment. Supposing there occurs some slip, the whole process ought to be repeated *ab initio*. Again the judgement of distance and interspaces of the objects must be maintained very very carefully. No jumble of misplacement would be tolerable if the worship is to be ideal. Keeping this theatrical show intact, the devotee has to proceed for performance, wherein he has to bear in mind the sequence or order of the details of worship, the priority and the posteriority. If by chance some mistake creeps in, the process is to be started again from the beginning. In other words one has to be cautious about the space-perspective and the time-perspective and to effect a harmony of the two (*sthalāvadhānaṃ kālāvadhānaṃ ubhayoḥ sāmañjasyaṃ ca*). It is a collaborative enterprise of the *pūjya, pūjaka, pūjāsthāna, pūjādravya, pūjanakriyā*, i.e., the object of worship, the worshipper, the place of worship, the materials of worship and the process of worship – all being *saṃkalpajanita* or the products of imagination. As such, one may feel that it is many times more difficult a task than cultivation of concentration on a single object (*ekāgratā*).

One more speciality of this worship-within is that, it is independent of means (*sādhananirapekṣa* and *upakaraṇanirapekṣa*) in contrast to the *bāhyayāga* since it requires no tangible material. All the materials as already said are products of imagination or as elsewhere described products of the subtle elements. In other respect, it may be called *śarīranirapekṣa* or independent of the body as well. That is if one achieves skill in its performance, it is immaterial for one whether the body is retained or abandoned, since it can be actuated with the help of the mind and the *tanmātra* or the subtle elements. The process is, however, dependent on attentiveness (*avadhānasāpekṣa*) and not independent of it (*avadhānanirapekṣa*). Indeed, the process of external worship may be done absent-mindedly after a long practice, reducing it to a prosaic mechanical functioning of the body. Mental adoration cannot ever be performed that way. A slight absent-mindedness means invitation to duplication and further repetitions of the entire effort.

As for the comparison of this process, as treated in different *Āgamas*, it may be observed that there is more similarity than difference. In the *Śaiva* and *Śāktāgamas*, we are often told of the maxim *śivo bhūtvā śivaṃ yajet* or *devī bhūtvā tu tāṃ yajet* which aims at the identity of the object of worship and the worshipper. In the *Viśiṣṭādvaita* system this identification is not tolerated or entertained. In other words, differences in philosophical tenets reflect on the details or mental worship. Again, the object of worship varies as per the *Āgamas*, Śiva, Viṣṇu, the Goddess or any other god may assume that place. So would be the case regarding the *mudrās,* the *mantras*, the *maṇḍalas*, the *cakras* and other details of worship. In the process of *mānasayāga* in the left-hand Tāntric practices (*Vāmācāra*) would include the well-known *Pañcamakāras* as the case may be. It might be interesting to observe whether the abstract form of offerings in the Tāntric worship would involve any kind of *hiṃsā* or not. One cannot say whether it would be admissible to the followers of the strict rules of non-violence (*ahiṃsā dharma*). There would be a counter-argument that the mental act of killing or injuring would fetch them worse fruit that accrued through a bodily act of injury. Again they may fear that indulgence in the *makāra* of *madirā-māṃsa-maithuna*, etc. even on a psychological plane may invite a mental degradation by the process contemplated in the *Gītā* verse: *dhyāyato viṣayān puṃsaḥ saṅgasteṣūpajāyate*, etc. leading straightaway to the doom or destruction. Mental contemplation (*mānasacintana*) may prove to be more harmful than actual physical act.

As for the relative superiority and inferiority between the inner and outer worships, it is unanimously declared that the former is superior to the latter. All the same, the two rites are not competitive but complementary ones. The option to prefer the *antaryāga* by an individual devotee in his domestic worship (*gṛhārcā*) may be tolerated. But it is no way an option for the temple ritual.

It is obligatory on the part of a temple priest (*arcaka*) to perform it with accuracy and devotion since he is doing it for the benefit of the devotees at large in a representative capacity. It seems that the *Āgamas* expect of an ideal worshipper, a capacity to perform the *mānasayāga* with perfection. In other words, it may be deemed as a necessary requisite for his eligibility to hold the office. Besides, sincere and devoted accomplishment of the *mānasayāga* paves the way for perfection and liveliness in the otherwise prosaic mechanism of the outer worship, and charge the ritual with spirituality which is automatically transmitted to the minds of the devotees who partake the worship only as spectators having full faith in the priest who actually performs the worship.

The priority and posteriority of the two rituals also is an interesting topic and may create sometimes, a controversy among scholars. In the daily routine, we find that the *mānasayāga* comes first and then comes the *bāhyayāga*. The arrangement of chapters in the texts also testify this. It is however, that it is '*bāhyayāga* that paves the way for the *antaryāga*'. There is an apparent contradiction between the two views before us. Probably the second view is based on the verse from *Vāmakeśvara Tantra* which runs as follows:

> *bahiḥpūjā vidhātavyā yāvajjñānaṃ na vidyate* |
>
> *VāmT*, 51

When we understand the proper position, the paradox will be removed. In the daily worship, the *antaryāga* comes prior and brings perfection, purity and better sense of devotion to the *bāhyayāga* which follows. However, the *bāhyayāga* has its own limits on the path of spiritual progress of the individual aspirants. One day or other he must cry halt to the performance of *bāhyayāga* and it is always desired that the time should come as early as possible and that too before the aspirant is compelled to leave his earthly body. If he gains perfection in performing the *mānasayāga*, before the end of his life, he may continue the worship during the tenure of his further embodiments or inter-embodied states. It would be interesting to note here that individual aspirants have a lattitude of acquiring the proficiency in this ritual even up to the end of this life or failing it in the subsequent embodiments. For an *arcaka*, however, the skill has to come at the initial stage of life. It is just like those who enter the renunciation stage (*sannyāsāśrama*) at the initial stage of life, which for others is a final stage. For this reason, the *arcaka* is rightly praised as *arcako hi hariḥ sākṣāt*.

One more point to be noted about the *mānasayāga* is the purpose behind it. In the *Jayākhya Saṃhitā* of the *Pāñcarātra Āgama*, it is explained that there exist two aspects of the *vāsanās* or the passionic precipitates of the individual self. They are originating from without or within (*bāhyotthā* and *āntarika*). The former are accrued to the soul from the objects around, while the latter go on accumulating even in the absence of objects tempting the senses. The former can be overcome by diverting one's mind from their temptation by yoking the same to the process of outer worship. Nevertheless, that process is ineffective regarding the internal urges (*vāsanās*) that stir the mind from within and are likely to stir the faculties of the body which are restrained by the *saṃskāras* achieved through the *bāhyayāga*. Those *vāsanās* are not an outcome of outer functioning of the senses. They are the sum-total of accumulations of previous embodiments and fresh creations of mind. Even after total annihilation of the external urges (*bāhyotthavāsanā*), the inner ones remain as arrear unremedied for. What one could do, is to close the doors of one's mind for the outer objects and take a fleuroscopic or X-ray search focusing the location of the seeds of the internal *vāsanās* by the help of the power created in him by repeated performance of the mental worship (*mānasayāga*), and burn the seeds reducing them to ashes once for all; and then sterilise one's mind so as to leave no scope for their further germination.

To conclude, it may be observed that the topic of *mānasayāga* in the *Āgamas* is not only interesting and fascinating but is highly scientific as well. It has tremendous appeal to the aspirants, and scholars of an introvert-aptitude. It is a ceaseless challenge to their efforts and perseverance to grasp and master it and an intellectual feast to their scholarly thirst for knowledge.

The third portion of the day is scrutinized and now remain two portions – the *Svādhyāya* and *Yoga*. The period after the meals up to the twilight period in the evening is reserved for self-study, i.e., revision of the religious texts. As stated in the *Āgamas*, the devotee performs his *sandhyāvandanā* at the sun-set and then he becomes ready for the daily yogic practice.[13] This period brings him *Brahmasiddhi* – the attainment of Brahman.

At the outset, the devotee selects a spot fit for concentration of mind, preferably in a sacred but lonely and pleasant atmosphere. Then he has to purify the ground before setting for the venture. He progresses on the path of *Yoga* through its eight climbs, step by step. First of all he follows or rather strictly abides by the rules and regulations, the injunctions and prohibitions or the 'dos' and 'don'ts'. These things bring his physical body under desired results and make it fit for worship.

Then he assumes suitable postures, technically called *yogāsanas*. Different *āsanas* may suit the body constitution of different people.

A comfortable posture helps further tackling of the internal limbs. Having accomplished this, the *yogin* ventures to regulate and dilate his breath, i.e., technically to exercise *prāṇāyāma* by *pūraka, kumbhaka* and *recaka*, the inhaling, retaining and exhaling the breath. This exercise is meant for regulating the five wind-movements.

The fifth stage is *pratyāhāra* process wherein one has to shut out the objects of pleasure in the world and divert the sense-organs towards the internal region. The sixth stage is *dhyāna* or meditation. Lord Viṣṇu is the object of worship. It is followed by *dhāraṇā* wherein, the one achieves the equilibrium of the internal organs. It is equated to the pacification of the waves of the disturbed waters. Here, he concentrates on the 'heart-dweller' (*hārda-paramātman*) along with his consort Lakṣmī. He visualizes the divine couple Lakṣmī-Nārāyaṇa in a direct vision of yogic insight.

When this stage of realization is attained by the *sādhaka*, he is advised to lead the Lord in abstract forms, by his will-power, gradually towards a seat prepared by the *sādhaka*, for the Lord, on the altar in his heart the via media of the right hand outlet to the passage of the *suṣumnā* vein. The devotee perceives by imagination that he has assumed pure physique in the form of the *mantras*. The *yogin* then absorbs the five elements in their proper order (as described in the *bhūtaśuddhi*) within his own body and stand in the immediate presence of the Almighty – the ever-cherished goal of *sādhaka's* life. He then causes the properties of the elements, viz. *śabda-sparśa-rūpa-rasa-gandha* to unite in one and gradually push out of the *brahmarandhra* the apperture opening on the supracosmic region which is said to be situated at the top of the headgear.

At this superb state of *sādhanā* the devotee tries to induce the soul-essence or the *caitanya* out of the cage of the earthly body and transplant it on the *mantraśarīra*. Further, the *mantraśarīra* is also withdrawn and what he receives is the sixfold causal existence, i.e., the *pañcatanmātras*, i.e., the five subtle elements and the *tanmātra* of the mind. This also is to fall back and one receives a body of a luminous disc technically called *prabhācakram*. Resorting to this luminous disc one is led straightaway to the navel of Lord Nārāyaṇa. The *sādhaka* who is completely pure, having realized the Ultimate Truth and having totally severed from the material body, becomes endowed with *cit* the sentient property, the basic characteristic. Like in the *bhūtaśuddhi* process, he burns down his earthly body again to revive it by the help of nectar and enter the newly formed pure body.

Repeated practice of this process finally uplifts the aspirant Yogin to the enviable state of *samādhi* – the total merger in the Supreme Being. The fifth period of the day is utilized for this exercise. The devotee is then free to go to sleep.

That completes the survey of the ideal diary of the *Pāñcarātra* and its literature, keeping in mind, the interest of an introvert as a guiding principle.

Notes

1. See the *maṇḍala* illustrations (Plates 1.1 – 1.25).
2. Vide *JaySam*, XXII.68–69, *NārSam*, XXX.2–4; *Ṛṣirātra* I.1–10 etc.
3. *japadhyānārcanastotraiḥ karmavākcittasaṃyutaiḥ |*
   abhigacchejjagadyoniṃ taccābhigamanaṃ smṛtam ||
   – *JaySam*, XXII.68–69.
4. *samutthāyārdharātre'tha jitanidro jitaśramaḥ |*
   kamaṇḍalusthitenaiva samācamya tu vāriṇā ||
   – *SātSam*, VI.193cd–194ab.
   saṃprabuddhaḥ prabhāte tu utthāya śayanesthitaḥ |
   nāmnāṃ saṃkīrtanaṃ kuryāt ṣoḍaśānāṃ prayatnataḥ ||
   – *PārSam*, II.4.
5. *namo vāsudevāya namaḥ saṃkarṣaṇāya te |*
   pradyumnāya namaste'stu, aniruddhāya te namaḥ ||
   . . . divyānāmavatārāṇāṃ daśānāmatha kīrtanam |
   hariṃ hariṃ bruvaṃstalpādutthāya bhuvi vinyaset |
   . . . namaḥ kṣitidharāyoktvā vāmapādaṃ mahāmate ||
   – *PārSam*, II.6; 10; 17.
6. *Vide AniruddhaSam* Ch. 18, *NārSam*, II.37, *Viṣṇutattva* (iv) – 1, *Pauṣkara*, 20–24, *Viśvāmitra* 10.
7. Besides the verbal meanings, such portion always have mystic, technical and conventional meanings which the aspirants in the same and allied field only are likely to comprehend. Here, the attempt is elementary and aims at highlighting such portions without going much in details.
8. One may trace this process to the *Saṃvargavidyā* of the *Upaniṣads*.
9. *aṃtaryogaṃ bahiryogaṃ. . .*
   – *Amanaskopaniṣad*, II.36.
   manovaijñasya brahmā . . .
   – *BṛUp*, IV.1.6.
   mānasapūjayā japena dhyānena kīrtanena stutyā . . .
   – *Rāghopaniṣad*, I.6.
10. *padmāsanādikaṃ baddhvā nābhau baddhāñjaliṃ dṛḍham |*
    manasyuparataṃ kuryādakṣagrāmaṃ bahiḥsthitam ||
    cittaṃ buddhau vinikṣipya tāṃ buddhiṃ jñānagocare |
    jñānabhāvanayā karmakuryādvaipāramārthikam ||
    – *PārSam*, V.1–2.

11. *saṃkalpajanitairbhogeḥ pavitrairakṣayaiḥ śubhe* |
sāṃsparśaiḥ śaivacārākhyaistathā cābhyavahārikaiḥ ||
mahadrūpaiḥ prabhūtestu saptalokasamudbhavaiḥ |
yathoditestu vidhivadukṛṣṭataralakṣaṇaiḥ ||
– *PārSam*, IV.137–138.

bhāvopanītapuṣpādyairhṛdambhoje śivaṃ yajet ||
– *SP*, III.34.

12. *antaryāgātmikā pūjā sarvapūjottamā priye* |
– *VāmT*.

13. *tato'ṣṭāṅgena yogena pūjayet parameśvaram* |
pañcamo yogasaṃjño'sau kālāṃśo yogasiddhidaḥ ||
– *JaySam*, XXII.72.

2

The Pentadic Universe in the Śaivāgamas

H.N. Chakravarty

In the integral vision of the *Āgamas* the world is seen to be composed of consciousness (*cinmaya*), flooded with light, made of light and permeated with light (*prakāśa*), but though being consciousness in essence a substance is seen and experienced as insentient. The question baffles us why being consciousness in essence it is perceived as insentient. To this question the answer given by the *Āgamas* is that the substance is apparently seen to be insentient in so far as it does not have self-reflection of its own. Only because of the absence of self-reflection some substances are considered insentient and are therefore relegated to the level of matter but some others on account of self-reflection, are raised to the highest excellence of spirit, the sentient beings. In *Āgama*, specially in the non-dualistic *Āgama*, no such dichotomy of spirit and matter exists, rather it sees it as an integrated whole. The *Āgamas* also do not like to classify the whole into *asti, bhāti, priya, nāma* and *rūpa*, like the Vedāntins stigmatizing the world of name and form to be negated, conceiving it to be illusory while accepting only that aspect of Brahman which is being, consciousness and bliss. But the ideal vision of the *Āgamas* is to see everything as the One, not many. It explains *sarvam* of the *Upaniṣad* as the entirety, not multiplicity (*nānā*) because in this integral vision there is no such diversity that is not in essence light (*prakāśaparamārtha*).

With the distinction of perspective the same thing appears to be different according to the view of the onlooker. The one . . . , while remaining . . . , shows innumerable aspects. Even then it does not lose its real nature of fullness, for the very nature of the Full is such that it can assume any form whatever it wills. There is therefore no question of any clash against the phenomenal view of the ordinary people who are accustomed to see only the gross, for it is stated with firm conviction:

> *calitvā yāsyate kutra sarvaṃ śivamayaṃ yataḥ*
>
> *SvT*, IV.313.
>
> When everything is composed of Śiva, then where should you go!

This may seem to be outstepping toward that which is quite unknown to the people of ordinary vision. Viewing everything as Śiva is easy to speak but perceiving it and then realizing it requires *sādhanā.*

śivabhāvanayauṣadhyā baddhe manasi saṃsṛte |
kāṣṭhakuḍyādiṣu kṣipte rasavacchivahematā ||

TĀl, I under 85.

By means of contemplation thought of Śiva as the medicine rightly applied in the mind, while it moves on, transmutes it into gold, like mercury, applied on a log of wood or the walls, transmutes them.

Before going to explain the matter fully we would like to quote an authority here. Śrī Abhinavagupta thought it proper to say that *bhūtas*, the elements are existent because they are seen directly through sense-organs, *bhūtānyadhyakṣa siddhāni* (*TĀl*, I.190), adding further he says that *bhūtas* (the elements) are known by all:

sarvapratītisadbhāvagocaraṃ bhūtameva hi |
viduścatuṣṭaye cātra sāvakāśe tadāsthitim ||

TĀl, I.191.

That which are conceived by all as existing are indeed known as elements (The element is indeed conceived by all as an existing being), for the group of four (that is the earth, water, fire and air) is allowed by the void to occupy a space in their specific temporal existence.

There is no denial of the fact that all the perceptible objects are made of elements, the number of which is five. It may categorically be stated that the entirety of the universe though commonly known in Sanskrit as *viśva* only appears to the seers as *prapañca* (manifestation to be known, *jñeya*) extended in five-fold forms. The *Sāṃkhya* categories are twenty-five in number which is nothing but the number five multiplied by five. In the *Āgamas* the accepted number of principles are thirtysix but even there the scheme of grouping them into five divisions can be possible. So the Āgamic thinkers not only see the presence of five categories in the gross level of their manifestation but also on the subtle level. Therefore, they boldly utter:

pṛthivyāpastathātejo vāyurākāśameva ca |
pañcaitāni tu tattvāni yairvyāptamakhilaṃ jagat ||

Kālottara (quoted in *TĀl*, XI.19)

The earth, the water, the fire, the air and the void – these indeed, are the five principles by which the entire universe is pervaded.

The above five constitute the physical objects, known to all but it is not known to all that they are the manifestation of consciousness. The Supreme consciousness manifests itself or rather extends in five different ways. These ways are five out-lets through which Śiva, the supreme consciousness expresses Himself though basically remaining as being consciousness, bliss, knowledge and activity. These are known to the Śaivas as the five faces of Śiva, the Lord.

The process how consciousness expresses itself and becomes gross, is very subtle and needs a detailed study itself, therefore, we can only give a short hint here in order to clarify the background.

Śrī Abhinavagupta presents a clear picture of the concept in his *Parātrīśikā-Laghuvṛtti.* We have summarized the whole in the lines below.

The universe as it shines before us consists of two aspects – the one is signifier called *vācaka* and the other is *parāmarśa*, the process of cognition manifesting itself in the *vācya*, the signified consciousness. The *parāmarśa* is known to assume the form of the phonemes *a, ā, i, u* and so on to represent *anuttara, ānanda, icchā* and *unmeṣa.* The phonemes *a* and *ā* representing *anuttara* and *ānanda* are considered to be his *antaraṅga* (internal) and the phonemes *i* and *u* representing *icchā* and *unmeṣa* are considered to be the Lord's *bahiraṅga* (external) *śaktis.* As the present paper is mainly concerned with the seed syllables *ya, ra, va, la* which are related to the elements air and so on it seems relevant to explain how they can be the signifying agent to give rise to the signified objects of earth and so on.

> *bahirapi ca somasūryau rātridivasa saṃkocavikāsarūpeṇa tithipañcadaśakasya antaḥ carataḥ* |
> *yaśca asau icchāyāmīśne ca vedyollāsaḥ sa eva pṛthag-bhavan sthūlatayā bhūtapañcakātmā sūkṣmatayā ca tanmātra pañcakātmeti* |
> *daśa tattvāni, pṛthivī jalaṃ tejovāyurākāśaḥ gandho raso rūpaṃ sparśaḥ śabda iti* ||
>
> *PTri, Laghuvṛtti,* p.6.

The phonemes *i* and *a* give rise to *ya*, while *u* and *a* joined together give rise to *va.* Similarly the phonemes *ṛ* and *ḷ* give rise to *r* and *l.* These four, that is *ya, va, ra, la*, have the characteristics of vibration, illumination, nourishing and supporting (*spanda, prakāśana, āpyāyana, dhāraṇa*) respectively.

Even in the external world, the sun and moon, which rule the day and night by their expansion and contraction, move within these fifteen stations.

There now occurs the appearance of knowable objects, which takes place in will (*i*) and domination (*ī*). As knowable objects begin to appear themselves, begin to separate themselves, there occur, on the gross level, the five gross elements, and on the subtle level, the five subtle elements. This results in ten principles, namely, earth, water, fire, air, space, smell, taste, form, touch and sound. This is the manifestation of the knowable objects.

These phonemes are cogitation (*parāmarśana*) by nature characterized by vibration which is nothing but dynamism abiding in the core of all syllables, particularly in the vowels, but externally when this power of *parāmarśa* becomes involved in time, it assumes the form of the moon and the sun causing the night and the day manifested by contraction and expansion and thereby shine in the inner core of fifteen lunar days (*tithis*).

We have mentioned earlier that in the sphere of *icchā* and *īśāna* the knowables remain present in a very subtle way inseparable from the power of cognition *parāmarśaśakti.* The emergence of the knowables occurs grossly as if separating itself from it. It appears in the pentadic form of gross *bhūtas*, the earth and so on, and subtle *tanmātras.* The manifestation of gross and subtle *bhūtas* in the form of knowables becomes possible through the instrumentality of both internal and external sense-organs. The complete picture of the knowable appears with the interaction and the relative evolution of mind, intellect, egoism, primordial *prakṛti* and *puruṣa.* The self-knowingness (*vedana*) born of the void, being manifest, the above group of five comes to the view of *puruṣa*, the self. Therefore, being knowable itself, it remains above them as the knowing subject. In the absence of the self, known as *puruṣa*, all the knowables do not carry any meaning. The knowing subject called *puruṣa*, though limited, serves a great deal for the understanding of knowables. The soul remains bound with the bond of worldliness, attached to the object of its desire, remains plunged in the depth of ignorance, wanders about to perform deeds according to its limited power and becomes the knower of a very little. These powers which are the binding forces are known as four *śaktis*, the *śakti* of earth, water, fire and air. On account of its close relation with these *śaktis*, which keep the soul supported in the middle like the legendary figure *triśaṅku*, it remains between pure consciousness and insentient matter. As it remains bound by the above *śaktis* it is unable to move upward in order to shine in its pristine glory of pure consciousness, nor fall downward as an insentient log of wood. The power of the void serves the soul in two ways. It makes the soul to shine in its pure form of consciousness free from the touch of all knowables on one hand, and on the other allows room for all knowables to shine with their individual distinctions. This void is known as *vimarśa*, reflective consciousness internally inseparable from its very nature. The state of knowableness gradually dwindles. The power known as *ākāśaśakti* helps the limited self to become relieved of the binding forces, with the result, the consciousness shines forth with predominating brilliance. Even then the power of the subtle elements continues to help the limited soul to realize manifestation of consciousness followed by steadiness (*dhṛti*), nourishment (*āpyāyanam*), union with its light (*tatprakāśayogaḥ*), attainment of vibration characterized by supreme freedom and pervasiveness with that.

It is clear that the above *śaktis* which function in the lower sphere as the gross *bhūtas* remain present in this rarefied subtle region and function there as *śaktis*. They are not only pervasive but are the cause to replenish the very nature of the self (*svarūpasya pūrakam*). With this idea in view the *Āgamas* conceive the five Brahmans that is *Śuddhavidyā*, Īśvara, Sadāśiva, Śakti and Śiva to be the subtle forms of earth, water, fire, air and the void, representing Sadyojāta, Vāmadeva, Aghora, Tatpuruṣa and Īśāna, the Supreme Lord.

The form of Śiva consists of five specific divisions which are his head (*mūrdhā*), face (*vaktra*), heart (*hṛdaya*), the secret part (*guhya*) and *mūrti*, the form itself. They are connected with the syllables *kṣa, ya, ra, va, la*, representing five elements respectively. The faces of Śiva that are indicated by them are Īśāna, Tatpuruṣa, Aghora, Vāmadeva and Sadyojāta.

Svacchanda Tantra further adds that *ābrahmarandhraṃ bhrūmadhyāt santi pañcadharādayaḥ*: Five Brahmans abide in the form of the earth and so on in locations from the joint of the eyebrows to *brahmarandhra*.

For the aspirant the form of Śiva should first be conceived as a perpendicular shaft (*daṇḍabhaṅgī*) consisting of five portions made of subtle elements without having any characteristic distinctions. Then this form is to be conceived as a panel of the door (*kavāṭabhaṅgī*) having distinct portions, that is consisting of different directions of the east and so on. Therefore, the face of Śiva occupying the east is Tatpuruṣa, south is Aghora, west is Vāmadeva, north is Sadyojāta and the top is occupied by Īśāna.

In the above context the five faces are conceived as integrated into one but should not be conceived as separate from each other. The method by which this integration is possible is shown below. The aspirant makes use of the seed syllables of the elements thus: *Oṃ laṃ* "I make unification of Sadyojāta face with that of Vāmadeva face uttering *vaṃ*." In this manner all the faces are unified with the face of Īśāna, the Supreme. Thus we see that the elements have their function there.

Purification of the body is performed by bathing in the water. This is known to us but the eightfold bath with eight different materials is recommended by the *Āgamas*. This corresponds to the eightfold form of Śiva. Bath with five gross elements is considered essential for the worshipper to gain competency for the worship of the deity. He makes use of clay, water, sacred ashes, dust emerged from the feet of cows and the water fallen from sky, but though they are considered to be essential for making the body pure, yet they are not so efficacious if not charged with *mantra*. Whatever may be the truth, the *Āgama* presents the view that the eight formed body of Śiva (*aṣṭamūrti*) who is known to have the five elements as his body along with the sun, the moon and the self, plunging into the vast lake (*mahāhrada*) of consciousness one should conceive that verily the self is the Supreme Lord where the entire universe is to be plunged and the aspirant should think himself steadily established there. Thus the one that purifies and the object that is purified become one. This is the highest mode of purification.

In Tāntric literature *bhūtaśuddhi* (purification of elements) is considered to be a common practice generally performed before creation of the pure *śākta* body of the worshipper by means of various *nyāsa* (placement of syllables) in different limbs of the body of the worshipper.

This physical body is made of elements intermixed with one another. Purification of *bhūtas* is nothing else than to separate one element from the contact of another element. The procedure that is followed by the practitioner is *prāṇāyāma* associated with the seed syllable belonging to the respective element. *Svacchanda Tantra* prescribes the method of *udghāta* (forced strike) with the vital air, pressing it to move upward. This *udghāta* for the purification of the earth is five, four for water, three for fire and so on. Finally the worshipper finds himself well-established in the pure elemental form by which the body of his is thought to be made of and which enables him to worship his desired deity.

But the method that is followed by the Tāntric school is different from it. The worshipper makes use of contemplation (*bhāvanā*) first. He conceives a wall of fire created by the seed syllable of fire after encircling him with water. Then seated in the lotus posture and keeping both of his palms on his lap, the right over the left, he conceives the limited self (*jīvātman*) like the flaming bud of fire abiding in the heart. He leads it to *mūlādhāra* from where rises the coiled energy (*kuṇḍalinī*) and associating it (*jīvātman*) with her the worshipper passes through different centres of consciousness through the channel of *suṣumnā* and finally arrives at the thousand petalled lotus which faces downward. He then conceives that all the principles beginning from the earth and ending with *prakṛti* have been dissolved there. Then he makes a *prāṇāyāma* with the seed syllable of the air by which he conceives that the physical body of his has totally been dried up. Then with the seed syllable of fire it is burnt off along with the person representing sin (*pāpapuruṣa*). Then with *prāṇāyāma* associated with the seed syllable of the moon a nectarine flow oozing out from the joint of the eye-brows is to be conceived. The pure body of the worshipper is conceived to be made of all syllables with *prāṇāyāma* by using the seed syllable of water and making it steady by the seed syllable of the earth. From the above description it is evident that all the seed syllables of the elements excluding the void are utilized for the creation of the pure body.

The essence of all the physical objects which are known as the earth and so on, is the subtle elemental form. These subtle elements are called *tanmātras* named *gandha, rasa, rūpa, sparśa* and *śabda* which are presided over by the Lord named differently as Śarva, Bhava, Paśupati, Īśāna and Bhīma. They are not the passive superintendents but the impelling agent to agitate the respective subtle elements through which the gross forms of *bhūtas* come into existence.

The dichotomy between the universe as matter and spirit as the knowing subject is unknown to non-dual *Āgamas*. The considered opinion of the *Āgama* is that the universe composed of five elements is permeated by the divine essence, not only that the basic *mantra* of the divine is made of the divine essence of the deity. Therefore, the *Yoginī-Hṛdaya* commentary quotes from an ancient source –

> *pañcabhūtamayaṃ viśvaṃ tanmayī sā sadānaghe* |
> *tanmayī mūlavidyā ca . . .* ||
>
> *Mantra* section, II.28
>
> The universe is made of five elements. O pure lady, you are always of that nature. The principal *mantra* is also made of your essence.

Therefore it is thought quite relevant to propitiate the desired deity at least with five kinds of offerings, for these articles of offerings which are made of elements have been made manifest by the will of the divine (*bhagavadicchāvijṛmbhitāni*). When they are offered properly to the deity assuming five subtle forms, the deity is believed to be propitiated. One should offer *gandha*, the sandal paste, conceiving it to represent the earth, flowers representing the void, incense representing air, the lamp representing fire, and food representing water.

All these articles are first of all to be conceived and realized as possessed of sweet fragrance having attractive sound, delicate touch, beauty of form and delightful to the taste. Then in the reverse way (*pratyaṅgamukhatayā*) they are thought to rest in the subject, the *pramātā*.

The highest form of sacrifice is that where all the articles expected to be offered to the divine are to be collected in the receptacle of the mind through different sense-organs. There they should be conceived as one's own. It is followed by the conception of oneness of the self with the deity and then each article is offered separately to the deity. This kind of ritualistic offering is really called *mahāmakha*, highest form of sacrifice.

> *indriyagrāmasaṅgrāhyair gandhādyairātmadevatām |*
> *svābhedena samārādhya jñātuḥ so'yaṃ mahāmakhaḥ ||*
>
> *Mukhyāmnāya Rahasya*
> (quoted in *YoH*, III under verse 117)
>
> Self, the Divine, is to be worshipped with sandal-paste and so on after collecting them by the outlets of sense-organs. (It is done) in accordance with the innate mood (*svabhāva*) of one's own. This is considered to be the supreme form of ritual related to the knowing self.

We know the existence of elements in the gross and subtle levels but beyond them they exist as *śakti* or energy and function in the same way as is seen in the gross and subtle levels, but in the level of *śakti* they function differently not to bind the self but helping it to attain liberation.

The elements in their subtle forms are seen to present in *māyā* the delusory power to arrest the soul steadily in its limitation. It acts there as the earth, while *bindu* nourishes the seeker of truth. Thus it is thought to be water. *Nāda* is thought to be born of fire while *śakti* is predominantly of the nature of touch, hence it is born of air. Śiva is without any veil so it is *nirābhāsa*.

We read about the shapes and colours of *bhūtas* in different texts. They are simply centres of consciousness. These centres of consciousness visualized by the Yogin inside the body, are considered to be made of five elements.

The *Yoginī-Hṛdaya* gives an account of four *pīṭhas* designated by Kāmarūpa, Pūrṇagiri, Jālandhara and Oḍḍīyāna representing four elements with their respective shapes and colours thus:

> *caturasraṃ tathā binduṣaṭkayuktaṃ ca vṛttakam |*
> *ardhacandraṃ trikoṇaṃ ca rūpāṇyeṣāṃ krameṇa tu |*
> *pīto dhūmrastathā śveto rakto'rūpaṃ ca kīrtitam ||*
>
> *YoH*, I.42cd–43

Square and circular associated with six dots, the shape of a half-moon, triangular – these are the shapes in their respective order, that is, of the earth, water, fire and air. The colours of them are yellow, smoky, white, red and without any colour. The *pīṭhas*, viz., Kāmarūpa and so on emerge from the principle *bhū*, earth, Parṇagiri consists of the principle water, Jālandhara of fire, Oḍḍīyāna of air. These *pīṭhas* are physically located in different parts of India on one hand, while on the other they are meditated upon as located in *mūlādhāra* and so on.

The shape of the earth is stated to be square and its colour is yellow. The water has white as its colour and its shape is half-moon attached with a white lotus. Fire is red, triangular in shape attached with the mark of a *svastika.* Air is hexagonal dotted with six *bindus* black in colour while the void is circular and transparent in colour if it is proper to call it a colour.

In the context of *nyāsa*, placement of *mātṛkās* or *mālinīs*, the body is conceived as consisting of five elements. This is done when *pañcatattva nyāsa* are necessarily performed there. The body according to the *Mālinīvijaya Tantra* (chap. VI) measures eighty-four digits (*aṅgulas*). From the toe of the feet four digits above the earth pervades, water pervades forty-six *aṅgulas* above it, twenty-two *aṅgulas* above it is pervaded by fire. The air pervades twelve *aṅgulas* above. Thus the total comes to eighty-four. The void remains pervading all.

We have discussed in short about *bhūtaśuddhi*. The truth regarding purification of everything as given by Śrī Abhinavagupta is quite different from that mentioned above. He says that one should deeply contemplate everything as Śiva.

> *pṛthivī sthira rūpāsya śivarūpeṇa bhāvitā |*
> *sthirīkaroti tāmeva bhāvanāmiti śudhyati ||*
> *jalamāpyāyayatyenāṃ tejo bhāsvaratāṃ nayet |*
> *marudānanda saṃsparśaṃ vyoma vaitatyamāvahet ||*
>
> *TĀl*, XVII.103–104
>
> The earth having the steady form contemplated as of the nature of Śiva, verily makes that contemplation steady and thus purifies it, while the comtemplation of water as Śiva gives nourishment to it. The contemplation of fire as Śiva brightens it. The air helps the aspirant to have contact with bliss and the void brings in great expansion of pervasiveness.

To conclude we may say that the *bhūtas* are thought to be the basic elements of the world – the world of pain and pleasure. But to the Āgamic thinkers they should be utilized in a different way in order to attain the ultimate goal of life. We have discussed earlier that the *bhūtas* have gross, subtle and the highest forms. To the aspirant the gross form is the base from which he starts his *sādhanā* and tries to see the dynamic form of it everywhere in order to achieve his aim of Śivahood.

3

Pañcabhūtas in Śaiva Ritual
With Special Reference to Bhūtaśuddhi

S.S. Janaki

The correspondence between the microcosm and the macrocosm worked out and utilized for esoteric and spiritual purposes is much prevalent in the Śaivite system, as in others. These ideas ranging from the gross to the subtle and the supreme aspects and levels are pointed out and explained in the concept of a (i) Śiva temple with its different parts like *gopura, vimāna, dhvajastambha*, and *garbhagṛha*; (ii) the *śivaliṅga*; (iii) the rituals; and (iv) the human being. There is a fund of information on the subject that can be gleaned through the Śaiva Āgamic texts, *Purāṇas* and *Stotras*. Some highlights of such correlations from the viewpoint of five elements are now presented mainly as given in the *Kriyākramadyotikā* (*K.K.D.*) of Aghoraśivācārya (also called the *Aghoraśivācārya Paddhati*) written in twelfth century and commented by Nirmalamaṇi Deśika from Tiruvārūr; this is an authentic text followed by Śaivites in Tamil Nadu even now.

Before taking up the topic of the correlations from the viewpoint of five elements at different levels between the human being and *śivaliṅga*, it should be noted that some Purāṇic texts consider even the many holy *kṣetras* in different parts of India as corresponding to *cakras* like *mūlādhāra, svādhiṣṭhāna* and *ājñā* or the five elements. Thus according to the *Sūta Saṃhitā* (*jñānayoga khaṇḍa*, 11.50-1) the basical *mūlādhāra cakra* near the naval region is Kamalālaya or Tiruvārūr in Tanjore District (*ādhāraḥ kamalālayaḥ*), *anāhata* at the heart is Chidambaram (*cidambaram ca hṛnmadhye*), and the *ājñā* between the eye-brows is Vārāṇasī (*vārāṇasī ca mahāprājña bhruvor ghrāṇasya madhyame*). The principle behind such a description is that the temples in *kṣetras* in different parts of India symbolize and concretize certain *upāsanās* or *vidyās* mentioned in the *Upaniṣads*, local *Sthalapurāṇas* and reiterated in the verses, songs of devotees like Ālwārs, Nāyanmārs, Tyāgarāja and Muttuswāmī Dīkṣita.

Again, following the same principle, the five elements are traditionally considered as being geographically represented in five important temples in Tamil Nadu. Thus 'earth' is associated with Kāñcī, 'water' with Tiruvānaikovil, 'fire' with Tiruvaṇṇāmalai, 'wind' with Kālahasti and 'ether' with Chidambaram.

The *Pṛthivīliṅga* at Kāñcī is Lord Ekāmreśvara for worshipping whom Goddess Kāmākṣī is said to have carved out a *liṅga* out of mud. The *apliṅga* is Śrī Jambukeśvara at Tiruvānaikkovil near Trichinopoly; here the *liṅga* is found always in the water. The *jyotirliṅga* at Tiruvaṇṇāmalai in North Arcot district is well-known. This place is considered so holy that even the very thought of Tiruvaṇṇāmalāī is supposed to lead definitely to salvation (*smaraṇād kaivalyapradam*, as said by Muttuswāmī Dīkṣita). The *vāyuliṅga* is Lord Kālahastīśvara at Kālahasti, approximately 150 km from Madras on the way to Tirupati. It is said that out of the two lamps in the *sanctum sanctorum* in this temple, the upper one seems to flicker as if under the influence of wind.

We saw above that the whole of India was thought of as a macro representation of the all-pervasive Supreme and five or six centres therein were recognized as the *cakras* in His body. In a smaller compass five temples in Tamil Nadu were seen as corresponding to the five elements. In a still narrower conceptualization in the very precincts of the Tyāgarājaswāmī temple at Tiruvārūr, there are five *liṅgas* said to represent the five elements. They are respectively Śrīvalmīkaliṅga, Hāṭhakeśvara, Sadācaleśvara, Siddhīśvara and Ānandeśvara.

From these rather vague traditional ideas we can now move on to the integral association of the five elements in the matrix of Śaivite concepts of ritualistic action (*kriyā*) like the daily *pūjā*, the significance of which could be understood through the Āgamic philosophy (*jñāna, vidyā* or *tattva*). The Śaiva *Āgamas* impress upon the necessity of a Śaivite to be conversant with both *kriyā* and *jñāna* aspects so that he can reach the highest goal of obtaining equality with Śiva (*śivattva*). The fact is that the individual to be liberated (*paśu*) from the worldly bondage as constituted of five elements, is seen as parallel with lord Śiva (*pati*) as represented in the *śivaliṅga*, in more than one way.

The rituals are performed either at home in a special *pūjā* room or at the temple. In either case the entire ritual domain is to be transformed into a suitably pure condition. Of such purifications five are important. They are – the purification of the self (*ātmā*), of the place (*sthāna*), of the *mantras*, of the *liṅga* and of the substances (*dravya*) to be offered. In this paper we are concerned only with the *ātmaśuddhi*, as dealt with in *K.K.D.* Its procedural details are mainly the following:

1. Sitting in a comfortable posture the Śaivite protects the place of worship by creating a wall with *astra* (*Oṃ haḥ astrāya phaṭ*) and *kavaca* (*Oṃ haiṃ kavacāya huṃ*) *mantras* around it.
2. He first imposes the five *brahmāṅga mantras* on the five fingers

in both the hands:
Thumb – *oṃ hoṃ īśāna-mūrdhāya namaḥ*
Pointed – *oṃ heṃ tatpuruṣa-vaktrāya namaḥ*
Middle – *oṃ huṃ aghora-hṛdayāya namaḥ*
Ring – *oṃ hiṃ vāmadeva-guhyāya namaḥ*
Little – *oṃ haṃ sadyojāta-mūrtaye namaḥ*

By the imposition of the above *mantras* related to five faces of Śiva and his five limbs, on to the five fingers in both the hands, the hands are now transformed into Śiva (*śivīkaraṇa*). They become capable of performing all subsequent rites. (See *Fig.* I)

3. To engender *śivattva* in the subtle and gross bodies of the Śaivite *bhūtaśuddhi* is to be performed. In order to do this he imagines that the *suṣumnā*, starting as two branches from the toes and continuing as such till the *mūlādhāra*, combines as a single channel till the *brahmarandhra.* At the regions of heart, throat, forehead, etc. the *suṣumnā* runs parallel with *iḍā* on the left and *piṅgalā* on the right, both of them going till the nostril. From heart onwards the *suṣumnā* is to be specially conceived as a long tubular column and with a lotus-bud turned down. Inside and outside of *suṣumnā* is to be visualized as the supreme *kuṇḍalinī śakti* presiding over the subtle ethereal region and spilling flows of nectar. The blazing *śikhā bīja* of *hūṃ* is to be imagined as located between the *śakti* and *suṣumnā.* Under these circumstances *pūraka* and *kumbhaka* are to be practised, concentrating on *huṃ* syllable at the level of consciousness. At this point the *prāṇa* as *vāyu* moves upward till the *dvādaśānta* level outside. Thus the impure *vāyu* is thrown out. Incidentally by the repeated pronunciation of *huṃ phaṭ* the knots at the lotus-*cakras* at the heart, throat, inside the cheek, between the eye-brows and *brahmarandhra*, are said to be opened out.

Nirmalamaṇi's commentary *Prabhā* adds a critical note here that the respective lotuses at heart, throat, etc. that were originally only buds turned inward, blossom fully due to *pūraka.* They are then restrained by *kumbhaka* and ultimately become upturned by the up-going *vāyu.*

Now the inner Supreme Being is meditated upon as located in the subtle body in the heart-lotus and dazzlingly brilliant. The *mantra* '*oṃ hūṃ hāṃ haṃ hāṃ ātmane namaḥ*' is recited with the necessary inhaling, collecting and exhaling of air. The *saṃhāra mudrā* of the right hand is also shown as moving from *mūlādhāra* to the vacant space above the head, showing the free upward movement of the *ātmā* (in the form of *nāda*) along with *kuṇḍalinī śakti* smoothly through the respective *cakras* and uniting finally with Śiva at the *dvādaśānta* level (*K.K.D.*, p. 57). (See *Fig.* II)

He meditates that his soul, now embodied in the syllable *haṃ* and located on the crown of the syllable *hūṃ* is separated from the subtle body and transmuted into *bindu*, becoming subtle, unitary and free of all defects. This sort of visualization is to be understood from the arrangement of the *ātma mantra* as follows:

oṃ hūṃ hāṃ haṃ hāṃ hūṃ ātmane namaḥ

In the above string of *mantra*-syllables the central *haṃ* stands for *ātman*. It is encased (*samputita*) first by *hāṃ* on either side, *hāṃ* being the *hṛdaya* syllable; it is further emboxed between the outer two *śikhā* syllables, *hūṃ*.

4. In the next phase the subtle body made up of eight constituents (*pūryaṣṭaka*) namely the five *tanmātras* of *śabda, sparśa, rūpa, rasa* and *gandha*, along with *buddhi, manas* and *ahaṃkāra*, is to be purified in order that the *ātmā* can be reinstated in it. This is performed by the thirty-six *tattvas* that constitute the body, visualized as getting back to and merging with their associated sources in the reverse order.

Accordingly, he should visualize earth reabsorbed into odour, water into taste, fire into form, wind into touch, ether into sound and these preceptible qualities (*tanmātras*) into the inert aspect of the ego. He visualizes the active faculties known as mouth, foot, hand, anus, and penis reabsorbed into the animate aspect of the ego, and the faculties of knowledge called ear, skin, eye, tongue, nose, and mind (*manas*) into the wholesome aspect of the ego. He visualizes the ego reabsorbed into the intellect (*buddhi*), that into the qualities (*guṇas*), and the qualities into *prakṛti*. *Prakṛti* along with *rāga* and *vidyā* are reabsorbed into *kalā*. Then he visualizes *puruṣa, kalā*, and *niyati*, as well as *kāla*, reabsorbed into *māyā*.

He then visualizes *śuddhavidyā* reabsorbed into Īśvara, that into Sadāśiva, that into Śakti, that into Śiva, and finally that into the undisturbed *bindu*.

For the visualization of this ritual it will be useful to refer to the following clarifications of the above process by Nirmalamaṇi in his *Prabhā*:

> Firstly, the subtle body here referred to is to be identified with the thirty-six differentiated *tattvas* dispersed throughout the body (see

Fig. III for the *kalās* and *bhūtas* in the human body and *Fig.* IV for the *tattvas* in the *śivaliṅga*).

Secondly, in their differentiated states these *tattvas* are inherently impure. *Tattvas* at the lower levels should ultimately be reabsorbed into the two undifferentiated sources, *māyā* and *mahāmāyā* (or *bindu*). This purity exists in final absorption.

Thus the Śaivite is able to remove a large part of the impurities of the gross body, the *bhūtaśarīra*. As explained in the *Prabhā*, the *bhūtaśarīra*, an invariable assemblage of the five elements, is what constitutes the individual as a human being in this world, associated with name, form, family background, etc. Their purification consists firstly in the formal recognition of their characteristics, shape, nature, presiding divinity, *kalā, maṇḍala*, etc. These details are as follows:

Element	**pṛthivī**	**ap**	**tejas**	**vāyu**	**ākāśa**
Colour	yellow	white	red	dark	crystal-white
Form	square	half-moon	triangle	hexagon	circle
Mark	*vajra*	lotus	*svastika*	six points	*bindu śakti*
Bīja-mantra	*hlāṃ*	*hvīṃ*	*hrūṃ*	*hyaiṃ*	*hauṃ*
Kalā	*nivṛtti*	*pratiṣṭhā*	*vidyā*	*śānti*	*śāntyatīta*
Presiding deity	*Sadyojāta*	*Vāmadeva*	*Ghora*	*Tatpuruṣa*	*Īśāna*
Kāraṇeśvara	Brahmā	Viṣṇu	Rudra	Īśvara	Sadāśiva
Svabhāva	hard	fluid	hot	mobile	void

Of the five elements ether is all-pervasive and cannot be contained by anything else. Earth and wind, water and fire are opposed to each other in many features. Therefore the *guṇas* of earth, for example, like hardness and smell, are considered to have been nullified by conceiving them properly in a yogic-mantric manner so that earth is recognized as though it has got the nature of wind. (*Prabhā*, p. 69)

Similarly water is conceived as having undergone changes so as to be endowed with the features of fire. Of course, this *bhāvanā* is possible only by the yogic ways of *pūraka* and upward *recaka* through *suṣumnā* with the necessary *mantra*-recitation. For example, in the case of *pṛthivī* the *mantra* – *oṃ hlāṃ hlāṃ hlāṃ hlāṃ hlāṃ nivṛttikalāyai haḥ huṃ phaṭ* relating it to the *nivṛtti kalā* is uttered five times along with the Yogic process, in order to get rid of the five *guṇas* of *pṛthivī*, namely *gandha, rasa, rūpa, sparśa,* and *śabda*. Only then it is possible to imagine that the element *pṛthivī* is of the nature of *vāyu*. (*K.K.D.*, pp. 57–58)

Each *udghāta* or upward *recaka* involves three *prāṇāyāmas*. Hence fifteen *prāṇāyāmas* are to be performed for *pṛthivī*, twelve for *vāyu*, nine for *agni*, six for water and three for ether. (*Prabhā*, p. 69)

Now the elements in the body having lost their full capacities, their remnant defects are burnt by the fire emanating from the toes (*pādāṅguṣṭhotthitena agninā*) and with the recitation of *astra mantra.*

By these varied methods, the gross and subtle bodies are converted into a mantric build, worthy of containing within their ethereal cavity, the Supreme Śiva. The *ātmā* in the form of *nāda*, that was taken above the head in the first phase is now brought back to the heart-lotus by *pūraka* along with the recitation of *praṇava.* It is now reinstated in the form of a dazzling light. Its ablution is performed by the flowing nectar as a result of the vibration caused to Niṣkala Śiva. This is shown by the constant recitation of the *mantra oṃ hauṃ śaktaye vauṣaṭ*. (*K.K.D.*, p. 59; *Prabhā*, pp. 75–76)

FIG: I – SUBTLE ANATOMY AND DOMAINS

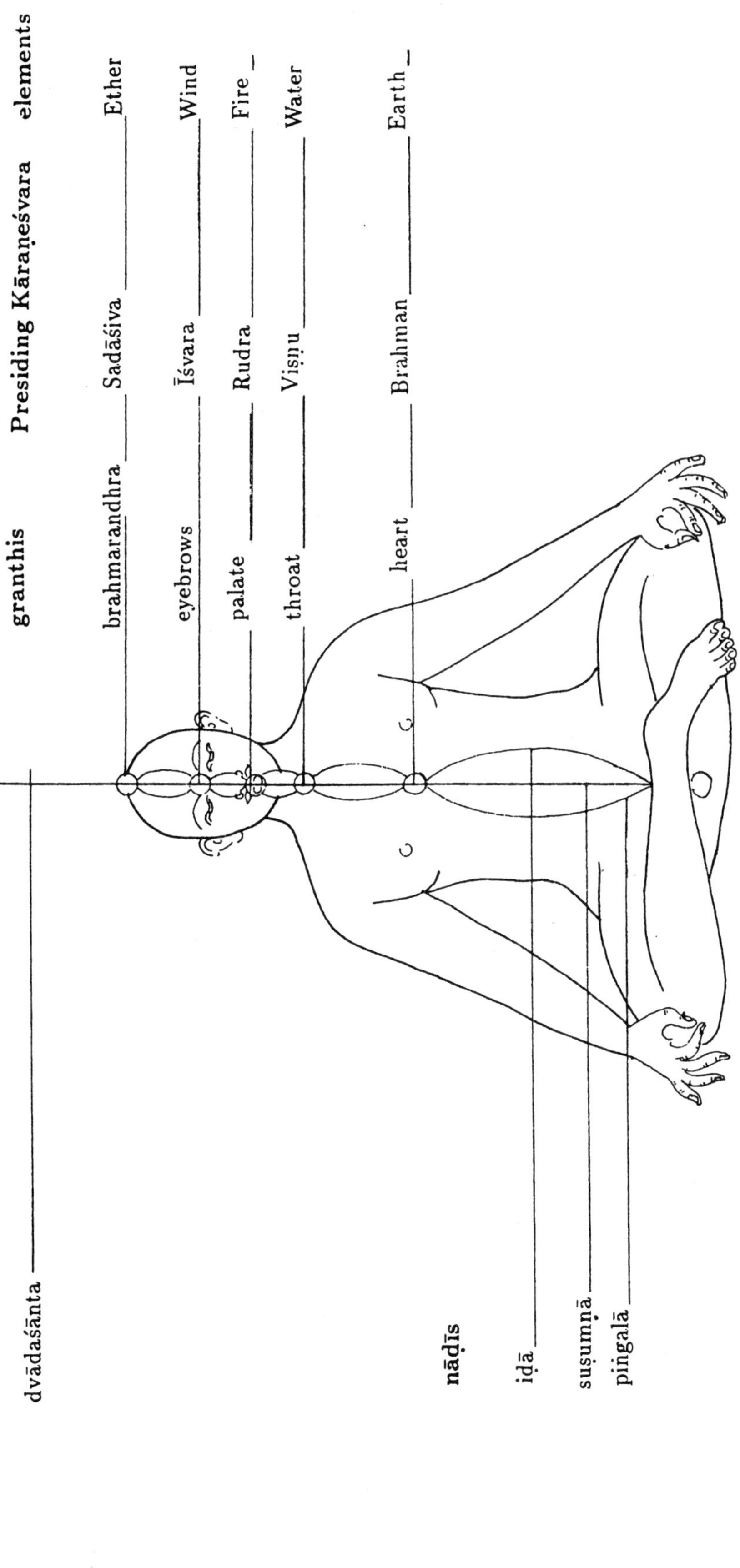

FIG. II - DIRECTION OF BREATH ASCENDING IN SUṢUMṆĀ

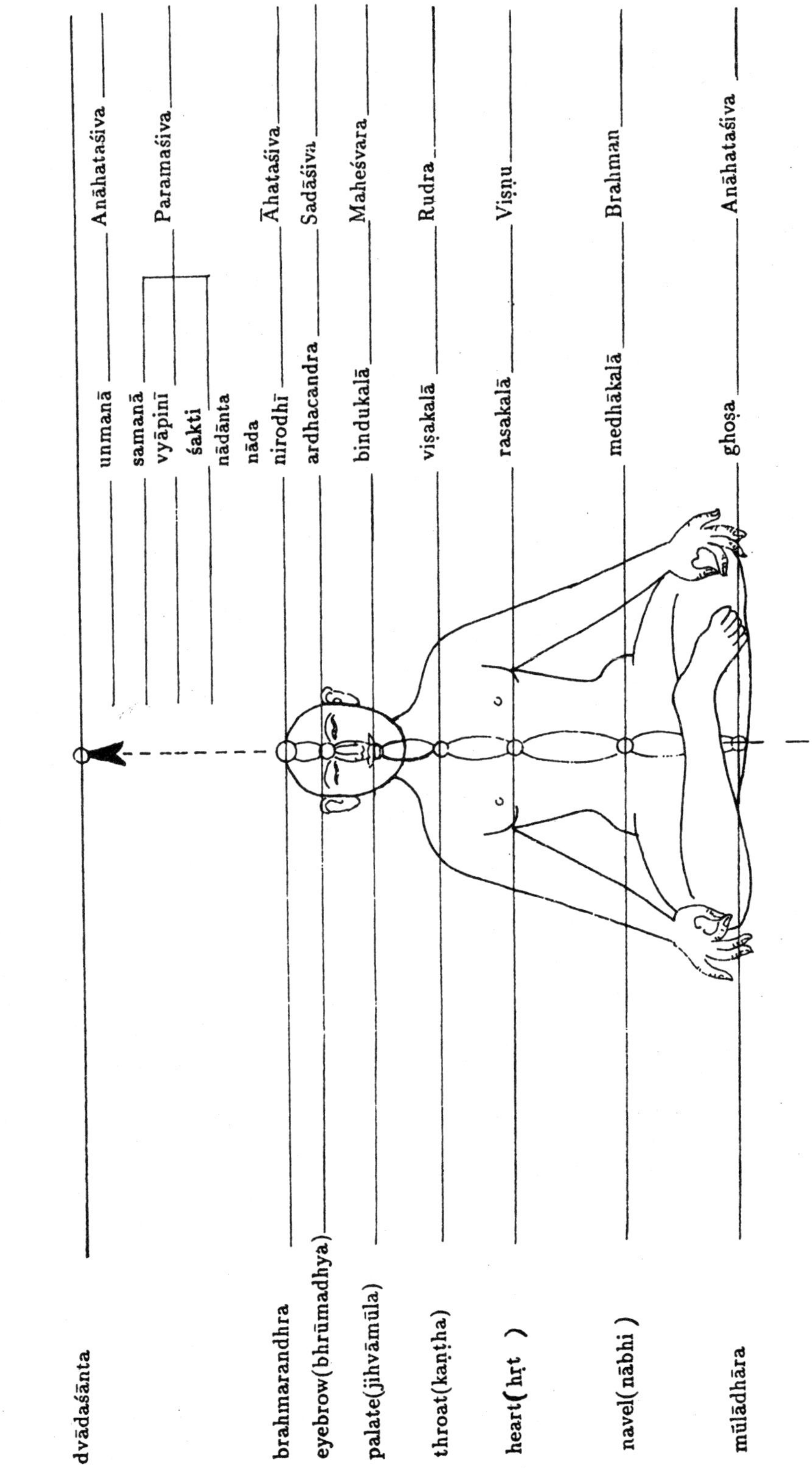

KALĀS AND BHŪTAS IN THE ŚIVALIṄGA — FIG. III — KALĀS AND BHŪTAS IN THE HUMAN BEING

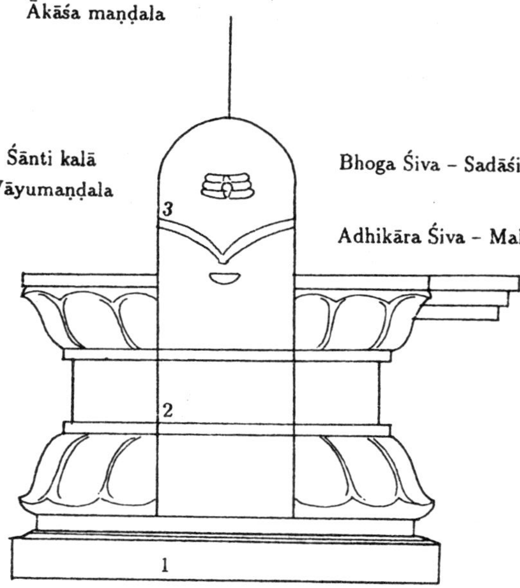

1. Square – Brahmā - Section - Nivṛttikalā – Earth
2. Octagon – Viṣṇu - Section - Pratiṣṭhākalā – Water
3. Circular rod – Rudra - Vidyākalā – Fire

KALĀ	LORD	ELEMENT	MANTRA
Śāntyatīta	Sadāśiva	Ether	Īśāna
Śānti	Īśvara	Wind	Tatpuruṣa
Vidyā	Rudra	Fire	Aghora
Pratiṣṭhā	Viṣṇu	Water	Vāma
Nivṛtti	Brahman	Earth	Sadyojāta

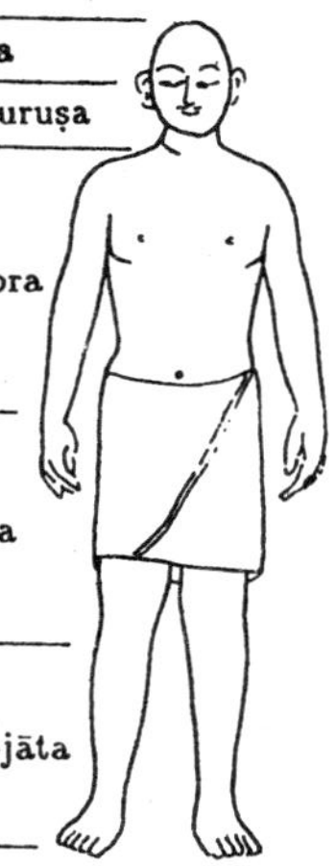

FIG. IV 36 TATTVAS IN ŚIVALIṄGA

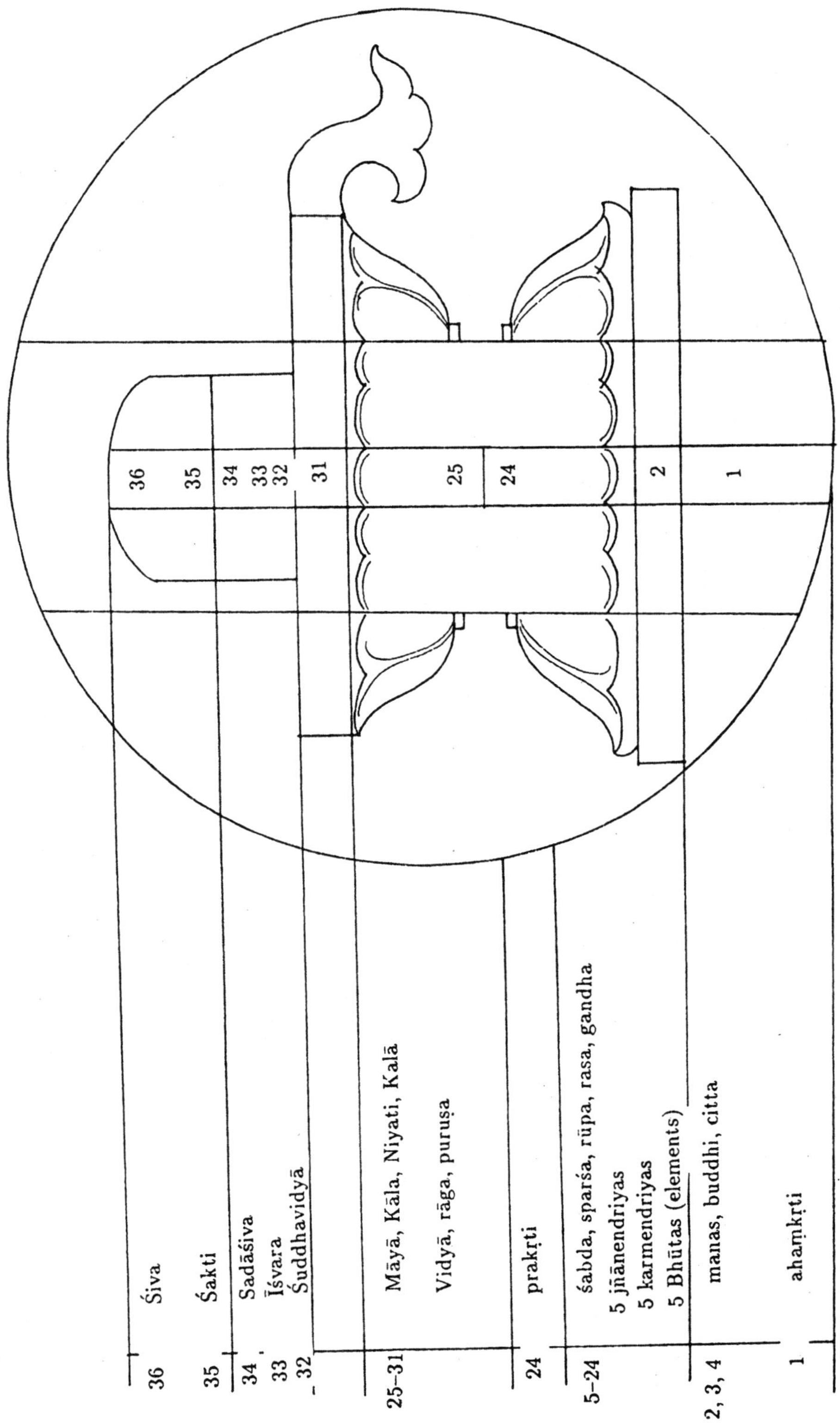

4

Āgamic Treatment of Mahābhūtas In Relation to Maṇḍalas and Arts

S.P. Sabarathinam

The two great master-scriptures which deal with the science of space and forms are the *Āgamas* and the *Śilpa-Śāstras*, corroborative and correspondent to each other. However, we can deduce an element of difference between these two scriptural streams. While the *Śilpa* works set forth the details concerned with structural forms alone, not disowning the concept of mathematical space and time, the Āgamic scriptures copiously deal with both the conceptual and structural forms based on the concepts of space and time.

According to the broader classification of the forms, as found in the *Śaivāgamas*, there are two kinds of forms, one conceptual and the other structural or sculptural. The conceptual forms are strictly meant for the purpose of meditation and intuition alone. They are not subjected to iconographisation.[1] Most of the forms whose lineaments are described in the *Śākta Āgamas* and in the *Āgamas* pertaining to the *Spanda* or *Trika* system are conceptual alone. The *Tantrarāja Tantra* specifically states that the forms of Nityā Devīs and of other Deities except that of Śrī Lalitā or Rājarājeśvarī or Bhuvaneśvarī should not be sculpted and installed. These forms are to be mentally visualized or contemplated based on the respective *dhyāna ślokas*. Even in the *Śaivāgamas* we have this kind of restriction. The *Vātulāgama* states:

> *kartrādikaṃ caturṇāṃ tu sthāpanaṃ na kārayet*
>
> *VātulĀ*, I.118

> The forms of *kartṛ sādākhyam, mūrti sādākhyam, amūrti sādākhyam* and *śiva sādākhyam* are not to be sculpted and installed. These four *sādākhyas* are to be meditated upon by the sages and the *yogins*. To this point we shall refer again in the sequel.

Śiva's Conceptual Forms

ADHVAN-MŪRTI

There are two kinds of conceptual form pertaining to Lord Śiva – one is known as *adhvan-mūrti* and the other is known as *aṣṭa-mūrti*. The concept of *adhvan* is common to South Indian Śaivism, Kashmir Śaivism and Śāktism. In a distorted pattern, this concept figures in some of the *Pāñcarātra* texts also.[2] To dwell upon the philosophical significance and import of the concept of *adhvan* is to go beyond the scope of the present paper and therefore only relevant and important details concerned with the *mahābhūtas* are presented and discussed here.

Mantra, pada, varṇa, bhuvana, tattva and *kalā* are the six kinds of *adhvan* which constitute the cosmic-cum-amorphic body of Lord Śiva.[3] In His *adhvan* form, Lord Śiva assumes *Varṇādhvan* as His skin; *padādhvan* as His head; *tattvādhvan* as His heart; *bhuvanādhvan* as His body-hairs; *mantrādhvan* as His blood, semen, marrow, bone, etc. and *kalādhvan* as His entire limbs. The *Makuṭāgama* states:

> *varṇādhvā ca padādhvā ca tattvādhvā bhuvanādhvakaḥ* |
> *mantrādhvā ca kalādhvā ca sādākhyasya svarūpakam* ||
> *adhvāsthānakramaṃ vakṣye viśeṣāttu maheśvara* |
> *varṇādhvā tu tvagādhāraḥ, padādhvā ca śirastathā* ||
> *tattvādhvā hṛdayaṃ caiva bhuvanādhvā tu romakam* |
> *mantrādhvā rudhirādhāraḥ śuklamajjāsthi rūpakam* ||
> *kalādhvā caiva sarvāṅgaṃ itthaṃ sādākhyarūpakam* ||
>
> *MakuṭĀ*, II.620–23

This cosmic-cum-amorphic form is the very basis of temple rituals. Of these six *adhvans, kalādhvan* is the foremost and dominating one because all other *adhvans* remain included and pervaded by this *kalādhvan. Kalādhvan* is constituted of five *kalās*; *tattvādhvan* comprises thirty-six principles; *bhuvanādhvan* consists of two hundred and twenty-four *bhuvanas*; *varṇādhvan* consists of fifty-one letters; *padādhvan* consists of eighty-one words of esoteric significance; and *mantrādhvan* consists of eleven *mantras*, specifically known as *saṃhitāmantras*. The gross elements (*mahābhūtas*) are characterized by these *adhvans* and this characterization establishes the correspondence between the gross elements and the *adhvan* form of Lord Śiva. All the ritualistic activities concerned with the *adhvan* form have their direct interaction with the gross elements.

An understanding of *kalādhvan* is essential in order to comprehend the significance of *aṣṭa-mūrti* form of Lord Śiva. *Nivṛtti, pratiṣṭhā, vidyā, śānti* and *śāntyatīta* are the five *kalās*, each one pervaded by the succeeding one. *Śāntyatīta kalā* remains unpervaded and ultimate and it is known as primal space (*paramākāśa*) which gives rise to the emergence of *śabda prapañca* and *artha prapañca*. Each *kalā* includes in itself the constituents of other *adhvans* as has been shown pictorially (see the diagram 1).

AṢṬA-MŪRTI

Lord Śiva manifests Himself in the form of earth, water, fire, air, space, sun, moon and individual self. Since earth, water, fire, air and space are the last five principles in the metaphysical scheme of Śaivism and since sun and moon are also considered to be the resultant products of the *taijasa* aspect of certain *tattvas*, it becomes obvious that the *aṣṭa-mūrti* form is directly related to *tattvādhvan*.

Conceptual Form

Adhvan form	*Aṣṭa-mūrti form*
kalā	Earth
tattva	Water
bhuvana	Fire
varṇa	Air
pada	Space
mantra	sun
	moon
	self

(The self, being one of the eight forms of Śiva, realizes and attains its inherent Śivahood or *Śivatva* through the methodic and effective contemplation of *adhvan*-form and *aṣṭa-mūrti* form)

Characteristics of the Gross Elements

All things are the purposeful modifications of the pure and impeccable Śiva. The term *śiva* itself denotes absolute and unsullied purity. The *Vātulāgama* states (I.20):

śuddhatvāt śivam ityuktam

Since all things are to be realized as the modifications of Pure Being, the presence of inertness in the worldly objects and creations is made to vanish during the course of visualizing them through the process of contemplation and synthesis. The scriptures train our mind to look at the worldly objects not as endowed with inertness but as supercharged with divinities.

The *Chāndogya Upaniṣad* (VI.4.4) teaches us how to look at the sun as composed of three primal forms: "Whatever red form the sun has, it is the form of heat, whatever is white, it is the form of water and whatever is dark, it is the form of earth. Thus vanishes the quality of the sun from the sun, the modification being only a name arising from common parlance, while the truth is, that it is of only three forms." "They knew that whatever appeared unintelligible is a combination of just these three divinities (of fire, water and earth)." (VI.4.7)

Keeping this view in mind, let us now proceed to know the characteristics of the gross elements as set forth in the *Āgamas.* Each gross element has a particular form, pertinent symbol and colour. Each gross element is potentialized by a particular letter, activized by a deity and controlled by a supreme Lord.[4]

Gross Elements	*Form*	*Symbol*	*Colour*	*Potentialising letter*	*Activising deity*	*Controlling Lord*
Earth	Square	*vajra*	Gold or yellow	*la*	Brahmā	Sadyojāta
Water	Half-moon	lotus	white	*va*	Viṣṇu	Vāmadeva
Fire	Triangle	*svastika*	red	*ra*	Rudra	Aghora
Air	Hexagon	six dots	black/ smoky	*ya*	Maheśvara	Tatpuruṣa
Space	Circle	point	pure crystal	*ha*	Sadāśiva	Īśāna

Each gross element is related to each one of the five *kalās* as shown hereunder:

Earth related to *Nivṛtti Kalā*
Water related to *Pratiṣṭhā Kalā*
Fire related to *Vidyā Kalā*
Air related to *Śānti Kalā*
Space related to *Śāntyatīta Kalā*

It should be noted here that earth itself is not *nivṛtti kalā* (as some of the modern scholars of *Śaiva Siddhānta* have explained). The gross elements are not to be equated or identified with *pañca-kalās.* The gross elements are functioning regularly as pervaded and induced by *pañca-kalās.*

Concordance and Discordance between the Gross Elements

In the process of purification of the body characterized by the five gross elements, one has to realize the concordance, discordance and neutralism existing between the gross elements. These three modes are denoted by the terms *mitratva, vṛddhatva* and *madhyastha*, respectively.

The nature of concordance exists (i) between earth and water, and (ii) between fire and air.

The nature of discordance exists (i) between earth and air, and (ii) between water and fire.

The nature of neither concordance nor discordance exists (i) between earth and fire, and (ii) between water and air.

The only element left out in this analysis is space. Since the space (*bhūtākāśa*) is the principle of accomodation and since it gives room for the movement and existence of all objects, space is in concordance (*mitra svabhāva*) with the other elements.

Śrī Nirmalamaṇi Deśika, the celebrated commentator on the *Dīkṣā Vidhi* (*Kriyākramadyotikā*) of Aghoraśivācārya explains this theory of concordance and discordance thus:

> *bhūmipavanayoḥ jalānalayośca eṣāṃ caturṇāṃ bādhya-bādhaka bhāvena parasparam avasthiteḥ śatrutā | bhūmijalayoḥ pavanā-nalayośca anyonyāṃ poṣakatvān mitratvaṃ | jalapavanayoḥ kṣitya-gnyośca parasparaṃ na śatrutvabhāvamiti madhyasthvameṣāṃ | ākāśasya tu vārivāyuśikhikṣitīnāṃ avakāśadāyatvena mitratvamiti ||*

Pervasion of the Gross Elements through Aṣṭa-mūrti

In his conceptual form known as *Aṣṭa-mūrti*, Lord Śiva assumes different forms and names.[5]

> *Pṛthivī-mūrti* is known as Śarva
> *Jala-mūrti* is known as Bhava
> *Vahni-mūrti* is known as Paśupati
> *Vāyu-mūrti* is known as Īśāna
> *Ākāśa-mūrti* is known as Bhīma
> *Candra-mūrti* is known as Mahādeva
> *Sūrya-mūrti* is known as Rudra
> *Yajamāna-mūrti* is known as Ugra

The gross elements are elevated to the higher realms of metaphysical principles by Śarva, Paśupati, Īśāna and Bhīma.[6]

	36 *tattvas*	
	1. *pṛthivī*	
	2. *ap*	
	3. *tejas*	
	4. *vāyu*	
	5. *ākāśa*	
	6. *gandha*	
	7. *rasa*	
	8. *rūpa*	
	9. *sparśa*	
	10. *śabda*	
	11. *upastha*	
	12. *pāyu*	
	13. *pāda*	
	14. *pāṇi*	
	15. *vāk*	
	16. *nāsā*	
(1) Earth-elevated	17. *jihvā*	*aśuddha māyā*
by Śarva up to *rāga*	18. *cakṣu*	or
	19. *tvak*	*aśuddhādhvan*
	20. *śrotra*	
	21. *manas*	
	22. *ahaṅkāra*	
	23. *buddhi*	
	24. *prakṛti*	
	25. *puruṣa*	*miśra māyā*
	26. *rāga*	or
		miśrādhvan
(2) Water-elevated	27. *vidyā*	
by Bhava up to *kāla*	28. *kalā*	*miśra māyā*
	29. *niyati*	or
	30. *kāla*	*miśrādhvan*
(3) Fire-elevated	31. *māyā*	*miśra māyā*
by Paśupati up to *śuddha vidyā*	32. *śuddha vidyā*	

(4) Air – elevated by Īśāna up to *īśvaratattva*	33. *īśvaratattva*	*śuddha māyā* or *śuddhādhvan*
(5) Space – elevated by Bhīma up to *śivatattva*	34. *sādākhya*	
	35. *śaktitattva*	
	36. *śivatattva*	

The individual self, though it is bodily confined to impure *māyā*, is capable of being in touch with the principles of mixed and pure planes only through the grace of Lord Śiva, who manifests Himself as Śarva, Bhava, Paśupati, Īśāna and Bhīma correspondent to earth, water, fire, air and space respectively.

Gross Elements and Letters (*mātṛkā-akṣara*)

It has already been stated that each gross element gets potentialized by a particular letter. Apart from this, the *Vātulāgama* provides an interesting classification of *mātṛkā-akṣaras* in relation to the five gross elements.[7]

1. Letters belonging to *pṛthivī varga* (earth)
   kṣa, la, ha, sa, ṣa, śa, va, la, ra, ya (10)
2. Letters belonging to *jala varga* (water)
   ma, bha, ba, pha, pa, na, dha, da, tha, ta (10)
3. Letters belonging to *vahni varga* (fire)
   ṇa, ḍha, ḍa, ṭha, ṭa, ña, jha, ja, cha, ca (10)
4. Letters belonging to *vāyu varga* (air)
   ṅa, gha, ga, kha, ka, aḥ, aṃ, au, o, ai (10)
5. Letters belonging to *vyoma varga* (space)
   e, ḹ, ḷ, ṝ, ṛ, ū, u, ī, i, ā, a (11)

The vowels are shared by the gross elements as follows:

Earth	–	*aḥ, aṃ, au*
Water	–	*o, ai, e*
Fire	–	*ḹ, ḷ, ṝ, ṛ*
Air	–	*ū, u, ī*
Space	–	*i, ā, a*

Irrespective of these classifications, the *Vātulāgama* expatiates the supremacy of the letter *ha* and of the space over the other letters and elements.[8] That is why the sound of *ha* gets associated with most of the *mantras* during the ritualistic processes. The science of space, as dealt with in the *Śaivāgamas* has not yet been accorded due attention and diligent study.

Gross Elements and the Forms of *Sādākhya*

Mention has already been made about four forms of *sādākhya*. *Sādākhya* is the name applied to Lord Śiva when he assumes the state of *adhikāra* at the plane called *sādākhya*, the third principle in the process of evolution.[9] Owing to his boundless compassion towards the bound souls, Lord Śiva gradually comes down to the lower planes of evolution and assumes various forms corresponding to the nature of the planes (See the diagram 2).

(i) At the point of implosion, *parāśakti*, also known as *śāntyatīta*, the primal energy inseparable from Śiva, releases one-tenth of her force or power and this force assumes the form known as *Śiva Sādākhya*. This form is very subtle, flashing forth like a lightning in the sky. It presents itself as the most effulgent form. This form is the source of all *tattvas*, (*tattvānām akhilālayam*).

(ii) *Ādiśakti*, also known as *śānti*, who manifests as one-thousandth part of *Parāśakti*, releases one-tenth of her force and this force assumes the form known as *Amūrti Sādākhya*. This is in the form of *liṅga* with an effulgence of one crore of suns (*sūrya*). This *liṅga* form is also known as *jyotistambha, divya liṅga* and *mūlastambha*.

(iii) *Icchāśakti*, also known as *vidyā*, who manifests as one-thousandth part of *Ādiśakti*, releases one-tenth of her force and this force assumes the form known as *Mūrti Sādākhya*. Only at this stage, Śiva assumes a form endowed with one face, three eyes, four hands and feet.

(iv) *Jñānaśakti*, also known as *pratiṣṭhā*, who manifests herself as one-thousandth part of *icchāśakti*, releases one-tenth of her force and this force assumes the form known as *Kartṛ Sādākhya*. At this stage, Śiva's form becomes endowed with four faces, twelve eyes, eight arms and two feet.

(v) *Kriyāśakti*, also known as *nivṛtti*, who manifests herself as one-thousandth part of *jñānaśakti* releases one-tenth of her force and this force assumes the form known as *Karma Sādākhya*. Only at this stage Śiva manifests Himself in Sadāśiva form having five faces, ten arms and two feet. Only this *Karma Sādākhya* is to be represented as the combination of *liṅga* and *pīṭha*.

Having explained in detail all these manifestations, the *Vātulāgama* succinctly states (I.67–69):

liṅga pīṭha prakāreṇa karma sādākhya lakṣaṇam
nādaṃ liṅgam iti jñeyaṃ bindupīṭhamudāhṛtam
nādabinduyutaṃ rūpaṃ liṅgākāram iti smṛtam
catvāri kartṛ rūpāṇi kevalaṃ nādamīritam.

The *liṅga* form typifies the principle of causal and primal sound and the *pīṭha* typifies the principle of *bindu*, the point of cosmic evolution and involution. Śivaliṅga is the structural form of the combination of *nāda* and *bindu*. The four forms of *kartṛ, mūrti, amūrti* and *Śiva sādākhyas* are representative of *nāda* principle only. (They are not associated with the *pīṭha* portion; they are not to be iconographized).

The fifth *sādākhya*, namely, *karma sādākhya* is installed and consecrated in the *sanctum sanctorum* of a temple. *Karma sādākhya* which also becomes known as Sadāśiva *mūrti* is endowed with five faces – Īśāna, Tatpuruṣa, Aghora, Vāmadeva and Sadyojāta, each one associated with particular form, colour and function.[10] Of these, Sadyojāta facing west is directly related to *nivṛtti kalā* and indirectly related to the sphere earth (*pṛthivī maṇḍala*); Vāmadeva facing north is directly related to *pratiṣṭhā kalā* and indirectly related to the realm of water; Aghora facing south is directly related to *vidyā kalā* and indirectly related to the realm of fire; Tatpuruṣa facing east is directly related to *śānti kalā* and indirectly related to the realm of air; and Īśāna facing upwards is directly related to *śāntyatīta kalā* and indirectly related to the *maṇḍala* of space.

The *Bṛhajjābālopaniṣad* states that *pṛthivī* arises from *sadyojāta* and *nivṛtti kalā* arises from *pṛthivī* and all other gross elements water, fire, air, and space, having evolved from Vāma, Aghora, Tatpuruṣa and Īśāna, give rise to *pratiṣṭhā, vidyā, śānti* and *śāntyatīta* respectively.[11] (I.10–15)

This concept may seem to be discordant with the Āgamic theory of *pañcakalā* and *pañcabhūta*. But in reality, there does not prevail any contradiction between these theories. What the *Bṛhajjābālopaniṣad* sets forth is the theory of *bimba* and *pratibimba*. This is explained as follows:

No.	*Primal source*	*Primary emanation*	*Secondary emanation*	*Reflected emanation*	*Cosmic cow (product of reflection)*
1.	Sadyojāta	*Nivṛtti*	*Pṛthivī* (Earth)	*Nivṛtti*	Nanda (*Kapila Varṇa*)
2.	Vāmadeva	*Pratiṣṭhā*	*Udaka* (Water)	*Pratiṣṭhā*	Bhadra (*Kṛṣṇa Varṇa*)
3.	Aghora	*Vidyā*	*Vahniḥ* (Fire)	*Vidyā*	Surabhi (*Rakta Varṇa*)

No.	*Primal source*	*Primary emanation*	*Secondary emanation*	*Reflected emanation*	*Cosmic cow (product of reflection)*
4.	Tatpuruṣa	*Śānti*	*Vāyu* (Air)	*Śānti*	Suśīla (*Śveta Varṇa*)
5.	Īśāna	*Śāntyatīta*	*Ākāśa* (Space)	*Śāntyatīta*	Sumana (*Citra Varṇa*)

The five cosmic cows symbolize purification, nourishment and totality of divinities. The ultimate source for these emanations is *karma sādākhya* or Sadāśiva.

In the process of manifestation, Lord Śiva appears himself as Maheśvara as one-thousandth part of *karma sādākhya* and according to the needs and necessities, Maheśvara assumes twenty-five forms known as *Maheśvara mūrtis.*[12]

Gross Elements under the Context of Rituals

ĀSANAS

In the ritualistic process of *śivārcana*, Lord Śiva is invoked and installed on a mystic pedestal known as *śivāsana* which itself is constituted of five *āsanas* known as *anantāsana, siṃhāsana, yogāsana, padmāsana* and *vimalāsana*. Each *āsana*, with an attributed form represents a gross element.[13]

	Āsana	*Form*	*Element represented*
1.	*Anantāsanam*	triangle	Earth
2.	*Siṃhāsanam*	square	Water
3.	*Yogāsanam*	octagonal	Fire
4.	*Padmāsanam*	circle	Air
5.	*Vimalāsanam*	hexagon	Space

(i) In the process of invocation (*āvāhana*) Lord Śiva is contemplated as seated on *Yogāsana*.

(ii) In the process of holy bath (*abhiṣeka*) he is contemplated as seated on *siṃhāsana*.

(iii) In the process of offering of flowers (*arcana*) he is meditated upon as seated on *padmāsana*.

(iv) In the process of offerings (*naivedya*) he is meditated upon as seated on *vimalāsana*.

(v) In the process of praising, singing and dancing, he is contemplated upon as seated on *anantāsana*.[14]

Basically, each *āsana* is composed of a *tattva* or a group of *tattvas* and on the whole *śivāsana* is nothing but a mystic pedestal composed of thirty-six principles (*tattvas*). The *pīṭha* part of *śivaliṅga* is to be identified with *śivāsana*.[15]

INSTALLATION

When an image is duly installed in a temple, it is imputed with the cosmic force through the process of *nyāsa*. The five gross elements are identified with the lower portion of the image.

YĀGAŚĀLĀ

Every construction is to be strictly based on *vāstu puruṣa-maṇḍala*. Longevity, auspiciousness, strength and beauty could be accomplished to any construction only through *vāstumaṇḍala*. Satish Grover seems too harsh in commenting that in the *Vāstuśāstras* there is much that is deliberate esoteric mumbo-jumbo.[16] He has utterly failed to realize the intrinsic validity and significance of the *vāstu puruṣa-maṇḍala*, the confluence of cosmic forces.

Needless to mention that temple construction is based on *vāstumaṇḍala*. *Yāgaśālās* also are constructed at the time of consecration and of other auspicious functions based on *vāstumaṇḍala* (either *maṇḍūka* or *paramaśāyi*). These *yāgaśālās* represent both *adhvan* form and *aṣṭa-mūrti* form of Lord Śiva.

Śrī Pañcākṣara yogin, the author of *Śaiva-Bhūṣaṇa* states that the term *maṇṭapa* itself denotes the presence of five gross elements – *ma* meaning earth, *ṇa* meaning water, *ṭa* meaning fire, *pa* meaning air and *m* (*makāra* with *bindu*) meaning space.[17] The eight fire-pits constructed inside the *yāga maṇṭapa* represent the eight forms of Lord Śiva.

The entire space covered by the *yāga maṇṭapa* represents the supreme *kalā*, namely *śāntyatīta*, the entrance in the east – *śāntikalā*; entrance in the south – *vidyākalā*; the entrance in the west – *pratiṣṭhākalā*; and the entrance in the north – *nivṛttikalā*. (Here again, confusion is to be avoided. Basically, *nivṛtti* (*sadyojāta*) is always to be ideated so as to be in the west and *pratiṣṭhā*, to be in the north. Here they are interchanged to effect interaction and interplay between the gross elements).

Since *pañca-kalās* are related to *pañca-bhūtas*, it becomes evident that the gross elements are represented by the *yāga maṇṭapa*.

Gross Elements and the Fire-pits (*kuṇḍas*)

Inside the *yāga maṇṭapa*, nine fire-pits are to be constructed along the *mānuṣa-pada* of the *vāstu maṇḍala*, four in the main directions, four in the intermediate directions and the one (*pradhāna kuṇḍa*) between east and north-east.

(i) The fire-pit in the form of a square which is in the east represents earth.

(ii) The fire-pit in the form of a circle which is in the west represents water.

(iii) The fire-pit in the form of a *yoni* which is in the south-east represents fire.

(iv) The fire-pit in the form of a hexagon which is in the north-west represents air.

(v) The fire-pit in the form of an octagonal which is in the north-east represents space.

(Here again, it is to be noticed that the forms related to the gross elements get altered except the element air.)

For other details, see the diagram (4).

Gross Elements and the *Maṇḍalas*

With an emphasis on certainty, it can rightly be claimed that the most aesthetic aspect of Indian rituals is *maṇḍala*. Almost all religious systems of India are employing *maṇḍala* as a device in their ritualistic activities. In fact, in Buddhism, the science of mystic device – *maṇḍala* – has become the main core.

Being an artistic device, *maṇḍala* incorporates in itself all the significant aspects of symbols, sounds, forms, colours and divinities, with a stronghold on metaphysical and ontological principles. The *Āgamas* excel all other scriptures with their elaborate and effective details and descriptions of various *maṇḍalas*. In the Śaivāgamic group, the *Kiraṇāgama* is held in high esteem owing to its copious details and directions on the mechanism of *maṇḍalas*. Besides its separate chapter on *maṇḍala-vidhi* it prescribes *vaktra-maṇḍala* for the worship of Sarasvatī and *kalaśa-maṇḍala* for the worship of Lord Mṛtyuñjaya, the details of which are not to be seen in any other *Āgama*.

Maṇḍala is an aesthetic and mystic design in which the combination and intersection of various forms related to the gross elements and to the deities concerned have their full play. The correspondence of colours, the distribution of letters (*mātṛkā akṣaras*) and the esoteric significance enhance the mystic value of *maṇḍalas*. Each *maṇḍala* has its own principal deity and attendant deities directly or indirectly related to the five gross elements. So the rituals which involve *maṇḍala-pūjā* are highly efficacious in energizing and sanctifying the environment conditioned by the gross elements. Because of such importance, the *Śaivāgamas* have specifically set forth the details of *maṇḍala*-worship in connection with monthly festival.

In the month of *meṣa* (April-May), *sarvatobhadra-maṇḍala* should be worshipped.

In the month of *bṛṣabha* (May-June), *svastika-maṇḍala.*

In the month of *mithuna* (June-July), *navanābha-maṇḍala.*

In the month of *karkaṭa* (July-August), *sarvatobhadra-maṇḍala.*

In the month of *siṃha* (August-September), *svāyambhuva-maṇḍala.*

In the month of *kanyā* (September-October), *subhadrā-maṇḍala.*

In the month of *tulā* (October-November), *gaurīlatā-maṇḍala.*

In the month of *vṛścika* (November-December), *sarvatobhadra-maṇḍala.*

In the month of *dhanu* (December-January), *svastika-maṇḍala.*

In the month of *makara* (January-February), *umākānta-maṇḍala.*

In the month of *kumbha* (February-March), *padma-maṇḍala.*

In the month of *mīna* (March-April), *svastika-maṇḍala.*

Apart from these, there are numerous *maṇḍalas* such as *ananta vijaya, ṭaṅka, prākāra, latāliṅga*, etc.

In the Āgamic texts, it has been declared that square is the basis for both, fire-pits (*kuṇḍas*) and *maṇḍalas.*

The symbolism and correspondence of colour is the essential aspect of *maṇḍala*. *Ācārya* or *upāsaka* is to be acquainted with the infallible knowledge of colour correspondence. In the science of *maṇḍala*, white represents water, *kṛta yuga, sattvaguṇa, buddhi tattva*; red represents fire, *tretā yuga, rajoguṇa, kalā tattva*; black represents air, *dvāpara yuga, tamoguṇa, niyati tattva*; yellow (gold) represents earth, *kali yuga, śuddha vidyā tattva*; pure crystal represents space, *avyakta tattva* and Śiva *tattva*.

For other details of *maṇḍala*, see the diagram (5).

Gross Elements and *Kumbha*

Inside the *yāgamaṇṭapa*, especially at *brahma-sthāna*, the main altar (*vedikā*) is to be constructed. At bottom part of *vedikā*, and *upavedikā* is to be made. On the surface of the main altar (*vedikā*), paddy, rice, sesamum, parched-rice and other grains are to be placed in order.

Once arranged in this pattern, the *vedikā* becomes representative of *śivāsana* which includes in itself five *āsanas* as has already been explained.

Upavedikā	–	*anantāsana*	–	*pṛthivī-maṇḍala*
Mahāvedikā	–	*siṃhāsana*	–	*jala-maṇḍala*
Paddy	–	*yogāsana*	–	*vahni-maṇḍala*
Rice	–	*padmāsana*	–	*vāyu-maṇḍala*
Sesamum	–	*vimalāsana*	–	*ākāśa-maṇḍala*

The *kuṁbha* which is placed on the grains represents Lord Śiva.[18]

Gross Elements and Five Causal Sounds

The *Ajitāgama* (XX.259) lays down the rule that in the fourth quarter (*yāma*) of the night, the great *śabdas* should be made with *śaṅkha* and *dundubhi*. The *Kāraṇāgama* also enjoins that the five great causal sounds should be made at the termination of night. The five great causal sounds are related to the five gross elements.

Sound born of wooden instruments (*dāruja*)	–	earth
Sound born of conch (*śaṅkha*)	–	water
Sound born of metal instruments (*lohaja*)	–	fire
Sound born of flute, etc. (*vaṃśa*)	–	air
Sound born of songs (*geya*)	–	space

rātrāntake viśeṣeṇa sarvadaivapriyārthakam |
kuryāt – pañcamahāśabdaṃ tato'śubha nivṛttaye ||
dārujaṃ pṛthvī jātaṃ śaṃkhajaṃ cāpyamucyate |
āgneyaṃ lohajaṃ proktaṃ vāyavyaṃ vaṃśajaṃ bhavet ||
geyaṃ gaganajātaṃ syāt pañcaite śabda ucyate |

I.31.34–37a

These five causal sounds related to the gross elements are to be sounded to ward off inauspiciousness and to please all the deities.

Gross Elements in Relation to Music and Dance

There are sixteen kinds of *upacāras* offered to the Lord at the end of the *pūjā*-process. These *upacāras* are classified into five in relation to the five gross elements. In the course of these *upacāras*, the fourteenth is *geya* or music and the fifteenth is dance (*nṛtya*). These two are related to the space element. Just as there is no greater element than space so also there is no *upacāra* more effective and auspicious than music and dance. The Āgamic scriptures prescribed particular *rāgas* for the particular divisions of a day.

In the early morning, songs set on *gāndhāra rāga*
In the next division, songs set on *mālava rāga*
In the midday, songs set on *takka rāga*
In the next division, songs set on *kauśika*
In the evening, songs set on *indola*
In the night, songs set on *pañcama*

These songs should be followed by *nṛtya* as enjoined in Bharata's *Nāṭya-Śāstra*.[19] The following varieties of *nṛtya* and their appropriate time and place of performance are mentioned in the *Āgamas*.[20]

samapāta, bhujaṅga, maṇḍala, daṇḍapāda
bhujaṅgatrāsa, kuñcita, bhujaṅga lalita.
ākuñcita, ūrdhvapāda

(from *bhujaṅga* to *ūrdhvapāda* – from east to north east)

Here we see how the Temple rituals give rise to aesthetic and fine arts. Impressed by the early and significant development of ritual behaviour in Greek life, Jane Harrison concludes that art had its origin only in rituals. This theory is equally applicable to Indian Arts also.

Conclusion

The way in which the gross elements have been explained and inter-related in the *Āgamas*, seems to be unique and significant. In order to restructure ourselves, we are trained to destructure the gross elements in such a way as to look at them as not invested with inertness but as invested with divinity and as charged with symbols, colours and sounds. All the ritualistic activities have their direct effect on the gross elements. The study of *Āgamas* and *Śilpa-śāstras* is sure to award the reader with a sound knowledge of the interaction between the rituals, images and the elements.

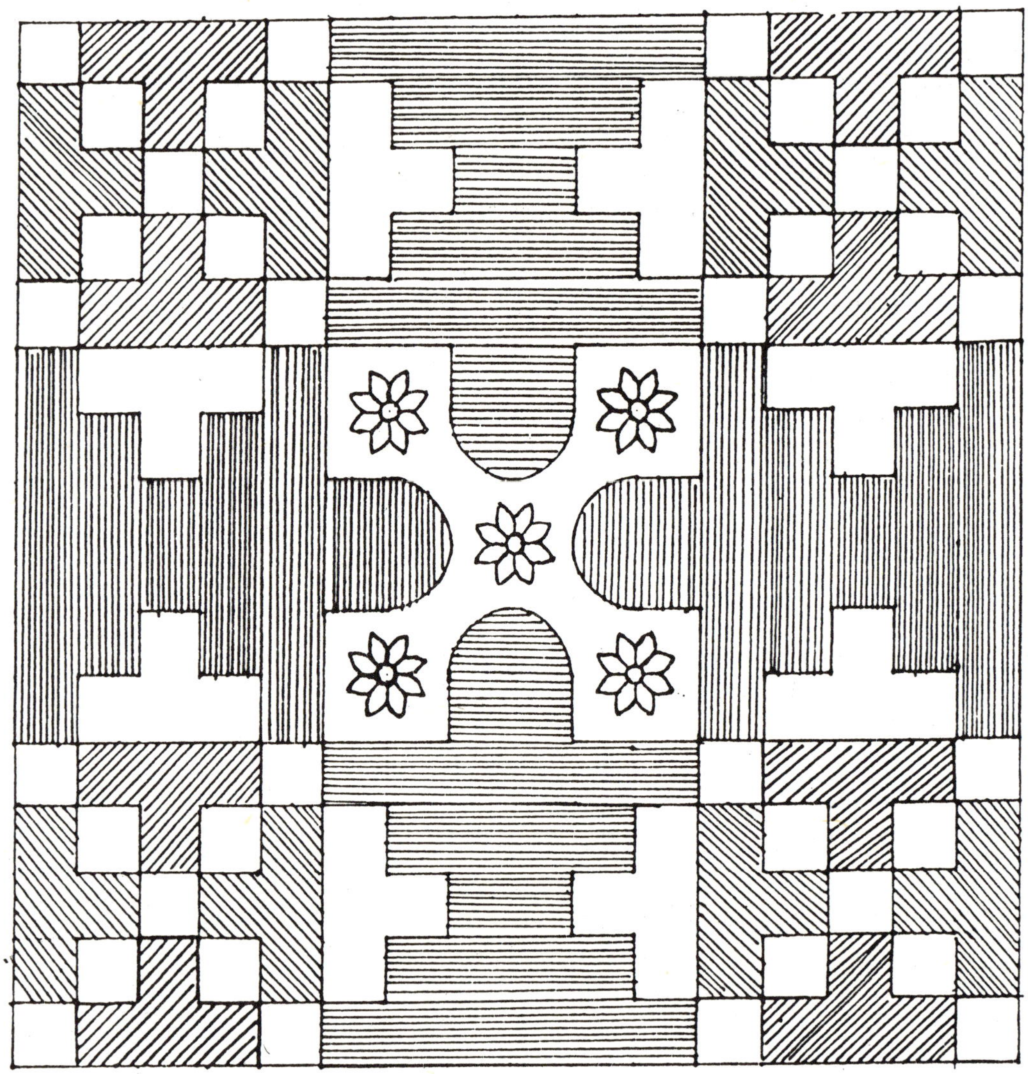

Gaurīlatāmaṇḍala
The five lotuses in different colours represent the five elements.

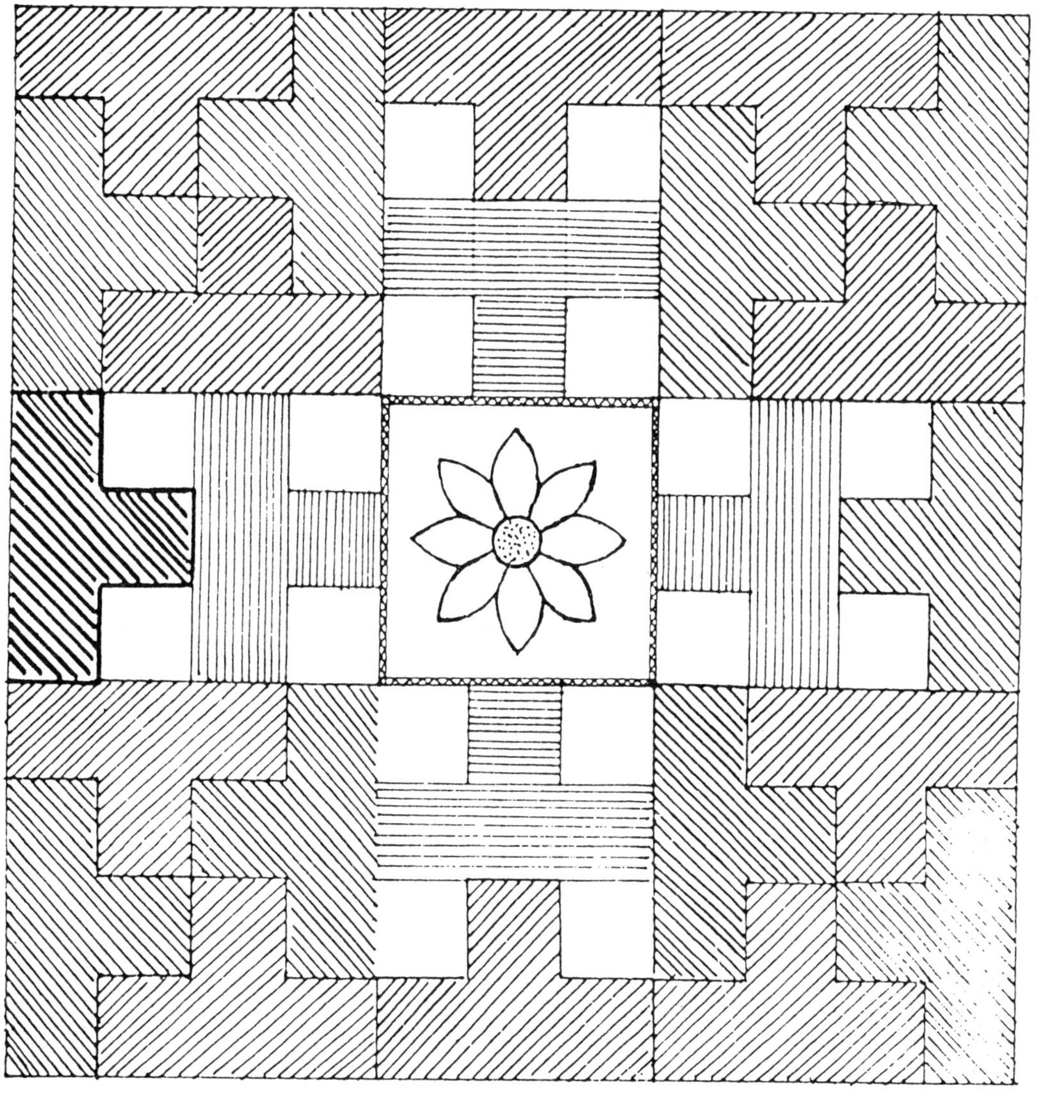

Sarvatobhadramaṇḍala

Notes

1. This sort of conceptual form, designed for meditation alone, figures largely in Buddhism also. "Instead of multiplying and projecting Buddha images, the goal of the adept is often to 'visualize' them" – W.Randolph Kloetzli, *Buddhist Cosmology* (Delhi: Motilal Banarsidass 1989) p. 107.
2. For example, see the *Padma-Saṃhitā* and the *Śrī Praśna-Saṃhitā.* They postulate *kālādhvan* dealing with time and its fractions, omitting the *kālādhvan.*
3. There are some references in the *Vedas* to this *adhvan* concept. *"Adhvanāṃ pataye namo namaḥ" "Pathīnāṃ pataye namaḥ"*, etc., occurring in the *Rudrādhyāya* of the *Yajur-Veda* refer to the *adhvanmūrti.*
4. See *Kāmika Āgama*, IV. 66b–76.
   The rationale behind the correspondence between the gross elements and their form, symbol, colour etc., has been explained in my commentary on the *uṇmai viḷakkam.*
5. For further details with regard to the descriptions of the forms of Śarva, Bhava, see the works *Pratiṣṭhā Aṣṭādaśa Kriyāvali* and the *Śivaliṅga Pratiṣṭhā Vidhi* of Aghoraśivācārya.
6. See the *Siddhānta Śārāvalī*, IV.33.
7. See the *Vātulāgama*, Ch. 2 and Ch.4.
8. *Ibid.*, IV.22–30 for the varied theories of relationship between the gross elements and the letters, proposed in the system of Kashmir Śaivism, see Abhinavagupta's *Parātrīśikāvivaraṇa.*
9. *Laya, bhoga* and *adhikāra* are the three states assumed by Lord Śiva; the *laya* state corresponds to *śivatattva, bhoga* state corresponds to *śaktitattva* and *adhikāra* state corresponds to *sādākhya* or *sadāśiva tattva.* For further details see the *Pauṣkarāgama, Mṛgendrāgama* and *Mataṅga Pārameśvara Āgama.*
10. For other details, descriptions, and significant meanings, see the *patipaṭala* of the *Pauṣkarāgama* and of the *Mṛgendrāgama.*
11. The *Bṛhajjābālopaniṣad*, I.10–15 and also the *Pañcabrahmopaniṣad*, 5–21.
12. For further details of 25 forms, see the *Vātulāgama*, I.122–34.
13. *Sakalāgamasāra Saṅgraha*, p. 81.
14. *Kāraṇa Āgama*, *pūrva*, 30.53b–55.
15. *Anantāsana* which is in the form of triangle represents earth. But, we have already seen that earth is represented by a square *maṇḍala.* These theories are not to be confused. These are to be understood against the background of esoteric significance.
16. Satish Grover, *The Architecture of Indian Buddhist and Hindu*, New Delhi: Vikas Publishing House, 1980 p. 172.

17. See the *Śaiva-Bhūṣaṇa* of Pañcākṣara yogi, verse, 192.
18. *Ibid.*, verse, 229.
19. See the *Kāraṇāgama*, *pūrva* 31.102b–104a.
20. See the *Mahotsavavidhi* of Aghoraśivācārya.

5

From Sensuous to Supersensuous
Some Terms of Indian Aesthetics

K. D. Tripathi

The traditional Indian holistic and cosmocentric vision governs the entire Indian view of arts and aesthetics. Therefore, an inquiry into the Indian view of time, space, direction, universal, substance or elements, numbers, relation and action etc., is an imperative for the clear understanding of Indian arts and aesthetics, as is the inquiry into the nature of *ātman*. The concept of *mahābhūtas* may be taken to be the starting point for a better understanding of the world of differentiation – the universe of name and form, reflected in all art-forms.

But the metaphysical question of going beyond the knot of the ego-sense in the form of limited 'I' and 'mine', which has been the central problem in almost all the schools of Vedic and non-Vedic philosophy, is also linked with the Indian view of creative process and aesthetic experience. Postulating the Being as pure unity and non-differentiation in order to explain the profound correlation of objective and subjective aspects of reality culminates in the aesthetic theory of unified experience of *rasa*.

The system of correspondences between macrocosm and microcosm, linking the gross and subtle, sense perception and human emotive states, paves the way for such an aesthetic experience of unity.

The multiplicity of name and form and the imaginative participation with and celebration of colour, sound, touch and smell does not simply stop there. It goes further to the unity of Being through the impersonalization of emotive states. It is a journey from sensuous to supersensuous for an aesthete and a reverse process from unity to multiplicity for an artist in the creative expression.[1]

The Vedic as well as Āgamic traditions offer a firm background for such an aesthetic theory.

The manifestation of the unmanifest is an act in which the entire cosmos is involved. "It is neither a merely divine affair, nor a purely human endeavour, nor a blind cosmic process, it is human, divine and cosmic all in one."[2] This reveals the inter-relation and the unity of the cosmos.

The Vedic view of the human body and its senses, the microcosm, in its relation to the parts of the universe, namely space, the elements, fire (*agni*), light (sun), water, earth and moon, in short, the cosmos and the converse process, where it is seen that the fire becomes speech, entering the mouth; wind becomes breath, entering the nostrils; the sun becomes sight, entering the eyes; the quarters become hearing, entering the ears; the annual herbs and regents of the forest become hairs, entering the skin; the moon becomes mind, entering the heart; death becomes vital air, going downward and entering the navel; and the water becomes seed entering the organ of generation, have been very elaborately dealt with by Dr Kapila Vatsyayan in her brilliant paper entitled "Indian Arts: Background and Principles".[3] She has also examined the question of the relationship of parts to the whole, of a multiple to the one, and of the finite to the infinite and the question whether any of the parts can have an independent existence, and she answered that they are all interdependent and in their single state they are incapable of comprehending the whole. Man acquires special significance not because he is best and conquers nature but because he is one amongst the many with a capacity for consciousness and transcendence of pure physicality through psychical discipline. He has been viewed as a biological-psychical unity and finally, there is he who transcends both the physical and psychical to achieve the state of *ānanda* or bliss. Going deeper into the imagery of the Vedic *Saṃhitās* and *Upaniṣads*, Dr Kapila Vatsyayan shows that "senses and sense perception play an important role, both in themselves and as vehicles of communicating the *arūpa* and *pararūpa* (the formless and the form supreme)."[4]

Āgamas also share this Vedic view of universe and man and emphasize the *śakti* or *kriyā* aspect in order to explain the riddle more satisfactorily and in a more intelligible way. For example, the primal creative act has been explained in the following words in Non-dualistic Kashmir Śaivism – "Śiva intent on creativity in the form of expansion by means of the energy of the great *mantra* of supreme primal word, viz., the perfect 'I' in union with *śakti*, in whom the urge of expansion is implicit, and in whom abounds the bloom of compactness of their energy, becomes engaged in the act of creative expansion."[5]

Abhinavagupta's *Parātrīśikā Vivaraṇa* offers a deep insight into the process of aesthetic experience also: "Now whatever enters the inner psychic apparatus or the outer senses of all beings, that abides as sentient life-energy (*cetana-rūpeṇa-prāṇātmanā*) in the middle channel, i.e., *suṣumnā* whose main characteristic is to enliven all the parts of the body. The life energy is said to be *ojas* (vital lustre) that is then diffused as enlivening factor in the form of common seminal energy (*vīrya*) in all parts of the body. Then when an exciting visual or auditory perception enters the percipient, then on account of exciting power, it fans the flame of passion in the form of the seminal energy."[6]

According to Abhinavagupta, the celebrated author of *Parātrīśikā Vivaraṇa*, "whatever is taken in, whether in the form of food or perception (e.g., sound, visual awareness of form, savour, contact etc.,) is converted first in the central channel in the form of *ojas* (vital energy); then this *ojas* is converted into seminal energy (*vīrya*) which permeates the whole body. All reproductive and creative functions are performed by this energy. Whether it is the enjoyment of good food, beautiful scenery, sweet music, entrancing poem, the embrace of a dear one, everywhere it is this energy that is at play. It is the representative of the divine energy (*khecarī*) on the physical plane. Even passion, anger, grief owe their life to that divine energy."[7]

When that energy is used as a distinct form of mere physical, chemical, biological or psychic energy, then it is *khecarī-vaiṣamya*, the heterogeneity, the disparateness of *khecarī*. When everything is viewed and used as a form of divine energy then it is *khecarī-sāmya*, the homogeneousness of *khecarī*. This *khecarī-sāmya* leads to liberation.[8]

Thus the *Āgamas* explain the process of mundane as well as aesthetic and spiritual experience satisfactorily in terms of *śakti* or potentiality and energy.

Creation and creativity, being activity, may be explained in terms of Vedic *yajña* (sacrifice) also.

As the one becomes many through the primordial act of sacrifice, the lost unity may be regained through the same sacrificial act freeing the self from the spatial and temporal limitations. This happens in the sphere of aesthetic experience too. The *sahṛdaya* (aesthete) of the traditional Indian art, literature and theatre attains repose in his deeper self for a moment and experiences *rasa* after having transcended the duality of relationship spread over the temporal and spatial differentiations.

The experience drawn from the art-form emanating from the awareness of either affirmation or negation of the specific relationship is somewhat different. It is mainly in terms of 'understanding', although this way of 'understanding' of the life and the self may be distinguished from that which is acquired through other means.

Art-forms in which one has to transcend the temporal and spatial differentiation manifested in the world of relationship offer a very different aesthetic experience. Although in such art-forms too, the beginning is from enunciation of the *vibhāva* (the causes or the determinants), *anubhāva* (the effects or the consequents) and the *sañcāribhāva* (relatively fleeting emotions) and of course, the *sthāyībhāva* (lasting or permanent emotions), yet the point of culmination is *sādhāraṇī-karaṇa* (universalization) in which these *vibhāva* etc., do not appear belonging to or not belonging to the aesthete or belonging to or not belonging to others (either an enemy or someone quite indifferent). For there is neither affirmation nor negation of the specific relationship at that stage.

This point may be a little elaborated. In our ordinary mundane life, emotions and feelings are evoked by someone and by the accompanying situations. Such evocatives (particular-person-*āśraya* or the substratum of emotion and the surrounding situations – the stimuli) are taken to be 'causes' to the given emotions (*bhāvas*). Emotions, feelings and dispositions are, again, sometimes permanent such as love and anger etc., and sometimes relatively fleeting emotions such as blushfulness and envy etc. It is difficult to determine which one is permanent and which one is fleeting. Therefore, Bharata's verdict has been taken to be final in such matters by the tradition. The permanent emotions are called *sthāyībhāvas* and the fleeting emotions are named as *sañcārībhāvas*. The *sthāyībhāvas* are only eight or nine, while *sañcārībhāvas* are thirty-three in number. The *bhāvas* are known to others through the gesture, language and facial expressions etc., which are the 'effects' of the emotions.

Now when depicted in, for instance, a play the 'cause' is known as *vibhāva*. The substratum of emotion is called *ālambana-vibhāva* and the stimulating surroundings etc., as *uddīpana-vibhāva*. The effect such as gesture, facial expressions etc., as *anubhāva*. In our life a dominant emotion is, ordinarily, mingled with various fleeting emotions. A pervasive portrayal of life can never have only one sentiment. It will be always an interweaving of one dominant emotion and various fleeting emotions. Even where there is the portrayal of a narrower aspect of life and there is the depiction of only one dominant or fleeting emotion explicitly, other relevant accompanying emotions may be implicitly present. Therefore an artistic portrayal of life is a depiction of *vibhāvas, anubhāvas, sthāyībhāvas* and *sañcārībhāvas*, but it always culminates into the absolute unity, which is *rasa*.

The means of attaining this unity is *sādhāraṇī-karaṇa* or universalization of *vibhāva* etc., leading to transcending the specificity of relationship. This is the reason why it paves the way to transcending time and space and thereby merging into one's own deeper self which is 'consciousness' (*cit*) and 'bliss' (*ānanda*). This is *rasa*.

The fact of unity between sensuous and supersensuous is further demonstrated by the profuse employment of the terminology with the connotation of elements to designate the supersensuous aesthetic experience of unity.

Sensation proper to the sense of taste and related to the element *āpaḥ* (water), almost devoid of noetic representation, has been taken to designate the aesthetic experience or *rasa*. *Nāṭya-Śāstra* of Bharata enunciates the aesthetic concept of *rasa* in the context of *nāṭya*, the highest form of art, which appeals to sight and hearing simultaneously. The senses of sight and hearing only are capable of rising above the boundaries of the limited 'I' according to some thinkers. In drama, sight and hearing both collaborate in rousing in the spectator, more easily and forcibly than the other forms, a unique state of consciousness conceived intuitively as a quintessence, juice or flavour, called *rasa*.[9] The total nature of the aesthetic experience, though supersensuous, includes psychic and sensuous things as its subordinated parts and has its effects felt on the body as well. It is remarkable that the pervasive as well as the quintessential nature of this aesthetic experience is designated by the term *rasa*, which reminds of its cosmic and spiritual connotations in Vedic cosmogony and metaphysics.[10] For the enjoyment aspect of this experience, the terms employed are *āsvāda*, *rasanā* and *carvaṇā* and they are equally rooted in the sensation proper to sense of taste related to *āpaḥ* (water).

The substance of drama and poetry is *rasa*, which is qualified by *guṇa*. As the quality always inheres in a substance and the two can never be separated, *rasa* always appears qualified by some *guṇa*. *Guṇa* is thus the transformation of mind (*citta*) in the process of aesthetic sublimation culminating into repose in the Self. This transformation means, at the first place, purification and clarity of mind and relates to the lucidity in sound and sense also. It is a quality common to all sentiments and all kinds of compositions. Hence this quality has been understood primarily relating to the suggested sense only.[11]

When the feeling depicted is delicate, love or sorrow, for example, the words and the sense delineating poetic passion are equally soft and heart-melting. When the feeling concerned is fierce, harsh like anger or courage, the expression also becomes likewise fiery. The quality of delicacy is called *mādhurya* and that of fieriness *ojas*. But both are only different expressions of gradual freedom from the finiteness of the self. This disappearance of the limitation paves the way for an experience of the totality and unity, which is *rasa*. The basic emotive states merely colour this experience of unity. Paṇḍitarāja Jagannātha defines this state of *rasa* experience as accepted by Abhinavagupta and Mammaṭa etc.

> *bhagnāvaraṇa-cidviśiṣṭaḥ sthāyī*[12]
>
> This aesthetic experience is analogous to highest spiritual experience – *brahmāsvāda*.

The concept of *guṇa* as explained by Ānandavardhana and Abhinavagupta and accepted by the later critics like Mammaṭa is really the concept of purification of mind in the aesthetic experience according to some modern scholars of Sanskrit poetics. This concept of purification has been distinguished from the *rasa* itself as effect from the cause. Dr Shri Krishna Mishra observes: "Indian critics very clearly distinguish every stage of the poetic process or experience. Thus they clearly point out that *rasa* is a stage of poetic experience higher than that of *guṇa*. And even in *rasa*-experience, the experience of primary *śāntarasa* is the apex. Again, just as they measure these immeasurable heights so finely, they best explain the descent of the divine Muse in the tangible form of words and meaning. *Guṇa* is the connecting link between the spiritual intuition (*rasa*) and the material conception (*rīti*) in the poet's experience and between *dhvani* and *alaṃkāra* in the poet's expression."[13]

Thus it is clear that the terms *prasāda, ojas* and *mādhurya* related to *ākāśa, tejas* and *āpaḥ* respectively, designate not only the different modes of beauty at the sensuous level, but the one at the intermediary level between sensuous and supersensuous also.

Ākāśa and similar *spatial* terms have been employed symbolically in spiritually or esoterically oriented context. Dr Javier Ugaz Ortitz in his paper entitled: "The spatial vocabulary of the interior experiences in Indian esoterism" has demonstrated it in an elaborate manner. Likewise in the aesthetic terminology of *rasa*-experience also, a core term *hṛdaya* is deeply related to *ākāśa*. Abhinava's concept of *hṛdaya* (heart) is that of microscopic inner sky which has been defined in the following words:

> O Aspirants who have reached the stage, that in which the entire universe shines, that which (by itself) shines everywhere, that sparkling light (which is both *prakāśa* and *vimarśasphurattā*) alone is the highest reality.[14]

Sahṛdaya is one who is endowed with this *hṛdayākāśa*, the inner central space of consciousness, which is at the same time 'Sparkling Light' or *sphurattā*. Space is seen as light and light endowed with vibration – initial, e.g., *vimarśa-sphurattā*. Here it is again a case of deriving the term from 'spatial' terminology for a very deep spiritual as well as aesthetic experience.

As the 'spatial' terms have been employed to express religious and aesthetic experience, so the terms pertaining to sound such as *nāda* and *dhvani* have been taken to designate spiritual as well as aesthetic states.

The theory of *dhvani* is a landmark in the history of Sanskrit poetics. Ānandavardhana and Abhinavagupta expressly refer to their debts to grammarians. Ānandavardhana states: "This designation (*dhvani*) was first devised by the learned and that it has gained currency in a haphazard fashion. The foremost among the learned are grammarians because grammar lies at the root of all studies. They indeed, refer to articulate letters by the term *dhvani* or suggester. In the same way, since the element of suggestion is common (to both) not only the word and its meaning but its essential verbal power and also that which is usually referred to by the term poetry has been given the same designation, viz., *dhvani* by the other learned men whose insight into the fundamental truth about poetry was profound and who were followers of the principles laid down by grammarians." (K. Krishnamurty (tr.), *Dhvanyāloka*, pp. 27–29)

Abhinava specially refers to Bhartṛhari and maintains that the word *dhvani* has four meanings according to various ways of grammatical formation. They are the suggestive word, suggestive meaning, the power of suggestion, and the suggested meaning. The poem with such words and meaning is also called *dhvani*. Mammaṭa also maintains that the grammarians employed the term *dhvani* as the suggester of *sphoṭa*, and their followers (*dhvanivādins*), then employed the term for both – the word and meaning capable of suggestion by subordinating the literal meaning (*vācya*)."[15]

There is ultimate unity of word and meaning. Differentiation of word and meaning becomes explicit at the stage of *madhyamā vāk*. But even at this stage word and meaning are inner realities. *Vāk* as consciousness is the *paramaṃ jyotis* (Supreme Light) and *akrama* (above temporal sequentiality). Audible external speech in time, therefore, manifested in temporal sequentiality. The audible external word reveals the inner word (*madhyamā nādātmaka āntara sphoṭa*). *Sphoṭa* is *vyaṅgya* (revealed) and the audible *varṇa* (letter) is the *vyañjaka*. *Varṇa* as *dhvani* (external sound) reveals *sphoṭa*, the inner word. This *dhvani* has another quality of resonance. It reaches our ears through resonance. The power of revealing or suggesting things on the one hand and the process of resonance on the other offer a sound foundation of the aesthetics of suggestion. The process of resonance as it is seen in the case of sound, may be equally seen in the echo of other levels of meaning. This *dhvanana* or *anusvāna* or *anuraṇana* is basically a quality of sound, but it has been further expanded to explain the nature of aesthetic experience. In terms of manifesting the unmanifest, it is called *vyañjana* or suggestion. *Anuṣvāna* or *anuraṇana*, i.e., resonance further elaborate the process. As the sound and words go on producing another sound and word and sound-waves and the word-waves gradually reach our ears, so the *vācaka*, *vācya* etc., go on manifesting other levels of meaning. Beauty consists in the process of resonance on the one hand and suggestion or revelation of the unmanifest on the other.[16]

Beauty and the experience of beauty, as *dhvani* is, thus, deeply rooted in the concepts of *vāk*, *nāda* and *śabda*.

The term *camatkāra* designates flash and wonder of aesthetic delight, which comprehends all poetic elements from *guṇa* and *śabdālaṃkāra* to *rasa* and *dhvani*. According to Dr Raghavan the concept of *camatkāra* came into *Alaṃkāra-Śāstra* from the *Pāka-Śāstra*. Its early history is indistinct and dictionaries record only the later meanings, the chief of which are 'astonishment' and poetic relish. According to Dr Raghavan originally the word was as onomatopoeic word referring to the clicking sound we make with our tongue when we taste something snappy, and in course of its semantic enlargements, *camatkāra* came to mean sudden fillip relating to any feeling of pleasurable type.[17]

"Nārāyaṇa, an ancestor of the author of the *Sāhitya-Darpaṇa*, interpreted *camatkāra* as an expansion of the heart, *citta vistāra* and held all kinds of *rasa*-realization to be of the nature of this *camatkāra* or *citta-vistāra*, of which the best example was *adbhuta rasa*" – informs Dr Raghavan. But *camatkāra* occurs in *Dhvanyāloka* and *Locana* as all-comprehensive for *literary relish* according to Dr Raghavan. *Agni Purāṇa, Kavi Kaṇṭhābharaṇa* and *Sāhityamīmāṃsā* also refer to this term. Viśveśvara in his *Camatkāra-Candrikā* maintains that *camatkāra* is *sahṛdaya*'s delight on reading a poem and *guṇa, rīti, vṛtti, pāka, śayyā, alaṃkāra* and *rasa* are seven *ālambanas* in a poem. Hari Prasad, the author of *Kāvyāloka* calls *camatkṛti* the soul of poetry.

R. Gnoli maintains that probably Utpaladeva was the first in the Kashmir Śaivite tradition to use this term in a technical sense.[18] It is a fond term of Abhinavagupta in his Āgamic works. The term *citta-camatkāra* has been translated as 'self flashing of light' by Dr Dasgupta refers Gnoli.[19] Dr Dasgupta appears to be correct in taking *camatkāra* in the sense of 'flash'. This meaning is preserved in Prākṛta *camakkai* for *camatkaroti*. Hindi also preserves this meaning. The sudden flash of lightning etc., causes wonder and it appears to be quite natural that the sense of 'wonder' and 'relish' are an addition to the original meaning of 'flash'.

Thus it is apparent that aesthetic delight designated by *camatkāra* does have the connotation of 'flash' and 'light'. *Pratibhā* is another such term with the connotation of 'light' and 'flash'.

It may be noticed that the three terms *rasa*, *dhvani* and *camatkāra* designating the supersensuous and the core aesthetic experience have been evolved with the background of the elements *āpaḥ*, *ākāśa* and *tejas* respectively, but there is no such term with the background of the remaining two elements to designate the core experience. However, there are such terms either for defining the intermediary process of *rasa* experience or to designate the very general aspect of beauty. For example, *bhāva* is made to derive from *bhū-* intended in two different meanings, that is 'to cause to be' (viz., to bring about, to create, etc.,) and 'to pervade'. Here *bhāvitam* has been explained as *vāsitam* (pervaded)[20] and according to this meaning *bhāvas* are so-called because they pervade, as a smell, the minds of spectators of drama. Here *bhāvanā* or *vāsanā* has a clear connotation of smell, which is a quality of earth. This intermediary act of pervading of mind by *bhāva* has been designated by a term with the background of the earth-element.

Terms employed for beauty[21] have the background of different elements from the very beginning. For example, the terms *Śrī, madhu,* and *supeśas* have the background of *tejas, āpaḥ* (water) and *rūpa.* The adjectives such as *vibhāvarī, śukra,* and *śociḥ* have the background of *tejas. Sūnarī* has been linked with the later word *sundara* by Peterson. If it is correct, then *sūnara* may also be linked with *āpaḥ,* for the etymology of *sundara* appears to be *suṣṭhu, undaṃ kledanaṃ rāti* – that which brings about melting.

Mādhurya and *lāvaṇya* too, are very apparently linked with *āpaḥ, śobhā, kānti* are associated with *tejas.*

Cāru is a term so common for beautiful. Etymologically it appears to be derived from *car-* to move. Thus *cāru* is that which moves, which vibrates in the heart. Movement and vibration are the qualities of *vāyu* (wind).

Thus it may be concluded that as there is a correspondence between macrocosm and microcosmic body, external and internal sense-organs, vital air and speech, there is a correspondence between sensuous and aesthetic as well as religious spiritual experience. Beauty is the experience of unity of the sensuous and supersensuous. It is an experience of totality. This experience has also been designated by terms with the elemental background.

Notes

1. Ānandavardhana hinted at the *rasa* experience of the poet artist in the process of creative expression and Abhinava elaborated the point in his *Locana.*

   kāvyasyātmā sa evārthastathā cādikaveḥ purā |
   krauñcadvandvaviyogotthaḥ śokaḥ ślokatvamāgataḥ ||
   (*Dhvanyāloka,* I.5)

   na tu muneḥ śoka iti mantavyam | evaṃ sati tadduḥkhena so'pi duḥkhita iti kṛtvā rasātmateti niravakāśaṃ bhavet | na ca śokasantaptasya eṣā daśeti | evaṃ hi carvaṇocitaśokasthāyibhāvātmakakaruṇarasa-samuccalana-

svabhāvatvāt sa eva kāvyasyātmā sārabhūtasvabhāvo'paraśabdavailakṣaṇya-kārakaḥ | (*Locana, Dhvanyāloka*, I *uddyota*, p. 160)

2. *The Vedic Experience*, R. Panikkar, p. 73, M.L.B.D. Delhi, 1983.
3. "The Indian Arts: Background and Principles" Kapila Vatsyayan in *Rūpa-Pratirūpa*, Ed. by Bettina Bäumer, p. 16, Biblia Impex Pvt. Ltd., New Delhi, 1982.
4. *Ibid.*, p. 13.
5. *śivo hi paravāṅmayamahāmantravīryavisṛṣṭimayaḥ parameśvarīvisṛṣṭyā tad-vīryaghanatātmakaprasūnanirbharayā sṛṣṭyā yujyate* | *Parātrīśikā Vivaraṇa*, Text, p. 15, Dr Jaideva Singh, Ed. by Bettina Bäumer, p. 42, M.L.B.D. Delhi, 1988.
   Cf. also
   paravāṅmayamantrātmavīryasargamayaḥ śivam |
   svavīryaghanatārūpedantāsphuraṇrūpayā ||
   yujyate satataṃ sṛṣṭyā svīyaśaktivisṛṣṭayā |
   adeśakālakalitaspandātmānuttarābhidhaḥ ||
   (Rameshvar Jha, *Purṇatāpratyabhijñā*, 17.18 p. 6, R.V. Joshi & Brothers, Varanasi, 1984.)
6. *tathā hi sarveṣāmantarbahiṣkaraṇānāṃ yat yat anupraviśati tattat madhya-nāḍībhuvi sarvāṅgānuprāṇanasārāyāṃ prāṇātmanā cetanarūpeṇa āste-oja iti kathyate* | *tadeva sarvāṅgeṣu anuprāṇakatayā tadavibhaktavīryarūpatvena tato'pi punarapi nayanaśravaṇādīndriyadvāreṇa bṛṅhakarūpaṃ rūpaśabdādi anuprāviśat bṛṅhakatvādeva tat vīryakṣobharūpakāmānalaprabodhakaṃ bha-vati* || *Ibid.*, p. 42
7. *Ibid.*, p. 52.
8. *Ibid.*
9. *The Aesthetic Experience According to Abhinavagupta*, Introduction, p. xiv, R. Gnoli, III Edition, Chowkhamba Sanskrit Series Office, Varanasi, 1985.
10. "*atha yaiteṣāṃ saptānāṃ puruṣāṇāṃ śrīḥ, yo rasa āsit tamūrdhvaṃ samudauhan-stadasya śiro'bhavat* | *yacchriyaṃ samudauhan stasmācchiraḥ* | *tasminnetasminprāṇā aśrayanta* | *tasmādvevaitacchiraḥ* | *atha yatprāṇā aśrayanta tasmādu prāṇāḥ śriyaḥ* | *atha yatsarvasminnaśrayanta tasmādu śarīram* ||"
    "*atha yaścite'gnirnidhīyate – yaivaiteṣāṃ saptānāṃ puruṣāṇāṃ śrīḥ, yo rasaḥ – tametadūrdhvaṃ samudūhanti tadasyaitacchiraḥ – tasminnetasmintsarve devāḥ śritāḥ* | *atra hi sarvebhyo devebhyo juhvati* | *tasmādvevaitacchiraḥ* ||"
    (*ŚBr*, VI.1.1.4,7)

"*asadvā idamagra āsīt | tato vai sadajāyata | tadātmānaṃ svayamakurūta || tasmāttatsukṛtamucyata iti | yadvai tatsukṛtam | raso vai saḥ | rasaṃ hyevāyaṃ labdhvānandī bhavati | ko hyevānyāt kaḥ prāṇyāt | yadeṣa ākāśa ānando na syāt | eṣa hyevānandayāti | yadā hyevaiṣa etasminnadṛśye'nātmye'nirūkte'nilayane'bhayaṃ pratiṣṭhāṃ vindate | atha so'bhayaṃ gato bhavati | yadā hyevaiṣa etasminnudaramantaraṃ kurute | atha tasya bhayaṃ bhavati | tattveva bhayaṃ viduṣo'manvānasya | tadapyeṣa śloko bhavati* ||" (*TUp*, II.7)

11. *Dhvanyāloka*, II.10, *Vṛtti* and *Locana*, pp. 212–13, Ed. by Pattabhirama Shastri, Chaukhamba Sanskrit Series, Varanasi - Vikrama Samvat, 1997.
12. *Rasagaṅgādhara*, Ed. by Durga Prasad, Edition IV, Kāvyamālā, 12, Bombay, 1930. ref.1.
13. *Coleridge* and *Abhinavagupta*, Shri Krishna Mishra, p. 545, Mirzapur, Darbhanga, 1979.
14. *yatrāntarakhilaṃ bhāti yacca sarvatra bhāsate |*
    sphurattaiva hi sā hyekā hṛdayaṃ paramaṃ budhāḥ ||
    (*Parātrīśikā Vivaraṇa*, Text, p. 99).

    yathā nyagrodhabījasthaḥ śaktirūpo mahādrumaḥ |
    tathā hṛdayabījasthaḥ jagadetaccarācaram ||

    iha asat na tāvat kiñcit ityuktam | viśvaṃ ca viśvātmakamiti | tataśca yathā vaṭabīje tatsamucitenaiva vapuṣā aṅkuraviṭapapatraphalāni tiṣṭhanti, evaṃ viśvamidaṃ hṛdayāntaḥ | evaṃ parijñānameva asandigdhā nirvāṇadīkṣā || (*Ibid.*, Text, pp. 92–93.) (Tr. by Dr Jaideva Singh, *Parātrīśikā*, p. 260).
15. *Kāvya-prakāśa*, Ed. by Vamana Jhalakikara, p. 19, Pune, 1950.
16. *Locana, Dhvanyāloka*, Ed. by Pattabhirama Shastri, pp. 340–41.
17. *Studies in some concepts of Alaṃkāra Śāstra*, Dr V. Raghavan, p. 269, Adyar Library, Adyar, 1942.
18. *Aesthetic Experience According to Abhinavagupta*, Introduction, pp. xlv–vi.
19. *Ibid.*, p. xlvi.
20. "*bhū iti (ṇyantaḥ) karaṇe dhātuḥ, tathā ca bhāvitaṃ vāsitaṃ kṛtam ityanarthāntaram* ||"
    Nāṭyaśāstra, Vol.I, Fourth revised edition, Ed. by Dr K. Krishnamurti; Oriental Institute, Vadodara, 1992, p. 338.
21. Cf. D.H.H. Ingalls, "Words for Beauty, in Classical Sanskrit Poetry", In *W. Norman Brown Felicitation Volume*, pp. 87–107.

6

The Cosmic View of Raṅgadaivatapūjana
The Question of its Āgamic Background

Radhavallabh Tripathi

The third chapter of *Nāṭyaśāstra* (*NŚ*) describes the ritual of *Raṅgadaivatapūjana*. This ritual was meant to be performed for the consecration of a newly built *Nāṭyamaṇḍapa*. Abhinavagupta refers to some *ācāryas* who uphold the desirability of its performance before each and every dramatic presentation.

Raṅgadaivatapūjana comprises worship of gods enshrined on the *raṅga* or stage. Metaphorically, it has also been termed as *raṅgapūjā* (*NŚ*, II.105) and the word *bali* has also been used synonymously for it (*NŚ*, III.46).

After the construction of the *nāṭyamaṇḍapa* (theatre), it was left to be resided by cows and brāhmaṇas for a week. Then the ceremony of the installation of the gods was performed by the *nāṭyācāryas* or *sūtradhāra*. Before proceeding, he was required to purify his body by sprinkling holy water and fasting for three days. He put on new garments and kept his senses under control (*NŚ*, III.2, 3). The *pūjā*-ritual then was performed in the following order:

1. Preparation of the *maṇḍala* and installation of the gods on it,
2. Worship of the gods enshrined on the *maṇḍala*, with specific *bali* (offering) respectively to each one of them with the invocatory verse,
3. *jarjarapūjā*,
4. *homa*,
5. The *udyotana*-ceremony, which is like the *āratī* done in the temple worship even now-a-days. According to Abhinavagupta, the other word current for *udyotana* during his days was *nīrājana*. This *nīrājana* was done by a burning lamp called *darbholmuka*. This *ulmuka* was lighted from the fire burning on the altar for *homa*,

7. Lightening the theatre from the *dīpikās*, sprinkling holy water on the body of the king and the danseuses and the *nāṭyācārya's* address and benediction to them, and

8. Playing of various *ātodyas* (musical instruments) and enactment of fights.

The list of gods to be worshipped during the course of *raṅgapūjā* has been cited thrice in the *Nāṭyaśāstra* in this very context with slight variations. The following points are to be noted in connection with the order in which divine and non-divine figures have been mentioned here:

1. Mahādeva has been held as the Supreme Deity, the Creator of all the worlds (. . . *sarvalokodbhavaṃ bhavam*, *NŚ*, II.4). He is to be saluted first; Brahmā, Viṣṇu and Indra are to be worshipped thereafter.

2. The extensive list of gods to be worshipped in *raṅgapūjā* comprises some of the gods belonging clearly to the Vedic pantheon. They are – Indra, Marutaḥ, Aśvinau, Mitra, Agni, Medhā and Dhṛti. Association of *Nāṭyaveda* with the Vedic worldview is quite evident in invoking and offering salutations to them through the ritual of *raṅgapūjā*.

3. Some of the divine figures to be worshipped through *raṅgapūjā* are originally Vedic gods, but are more prominently associated with Āgamic or Purāṇic traditions. Viṣṇu and Sarasvatī can be named from the list in the *Nāṭyaśāstra* as examples.

4. Quite a number of gods contained in the list of *Nāṭyaśāstra* can be identified with the Āgamic or Purāṇic traditions only. They are – Mahādeva, Pitāmaha, Guha, Lakṣmī, and Mahāgrāmaṇī (who, according to Abhinavagupta, stands for Gaṇapati).

5. Some of the properties, weapons, etc. belonging to a particular god have also been incorporated in the list. They are Mṛtyu, Niyati, Kāladaṇḍa (the sceptor of Yama), the Weapon of Viṣṇu (*Viṣṇupraharaṇa*) and Vajra.

6. The list also includes natural phenomena (the sea and the lightening), semi-divine beings, like *gandharvas*, *yakṣas*, *guhyakas* as well as *bhūtas*, *piśācas*, *daityas* and *rākṣasas*.

7. The last but not the least, this list has attained a unique character with the inclusion of *nāṭyavighnas* and. *nāṭyakumārīs*, as they can figure only

in the practice of the *Nāṭyaveda*. The *Nāṭyakumārīs* have been named as *Nāṭyamātṛkās* in the subsequent versions. (*NŚ*, III.30, 67)

The list of gods as given in the beginning of the chapter III of the *Nāṭyaśāstra* is not exclusive and Bharata has suggested a flexible framework by remarking that other gods can be included. (*NŚ*, III.10) The subsequent references to the gods in connection with *raṅgapūjā* in the same chapter itself include Nandin, Dakṣa, Garuḍa, Viśvedevas, the *munis* and the *devarṣis*, which have not been mentioned in the original plan. (*NŚ*, III.26–32)

The whole ritual of *raṅgapūjā*, beginning from the *bhūmi-parīkṣā* or examination of the site for construction, has a certain affinity with the *Āgama*-tradition, particularly the tradition of the *Śaivāgamas*.

The *Āgamas* categorize temples into three types in accordance with their size – *uttama, madhya* and *kanīyas*. (*AjitĀ*, I.XII.15) *Nāṭyaśāstra* has also given exactly the same classification for theatre-buildings. (*NŚ*, II.21,22) After the selection of the site, the soil should be levelled equally and it should be tilled by a plough. (*Ibid.*, I.7.3, 11) *Nāṭyaśāstra* confirms this practice. *Ajitāgama* also prescribes sowing of the seeds of *tila, brīhi* and *mudga* to confirm the fertility of the land. *Nāṭyaśāstra*, however, is silent about it.

Such similarities (or dis-similarities) are superficial, and both *Āgama*-tradition and the *Nāṭyaśāstra* might have borrowed them from the regional practices of the *Vāstu*-tradition. However, the similarities with regard to the system of *pūjā* seem to indicate deeper levels of correspondence between the *Āgama* and *Nāṭyaśāstra* traditions.

Both *Āgama*-literature and the *Nāṭyaśāstra* prescribe *pūjā* after *bhūmiparīkṣā* and before laying the foundation. This *pūjā* involves the offering of food and salutations to the brāhmaṇas. (*AjitĀ*, I.7.26, *NŚ*, II.32) *Nāṭyaśāstra* prescribes chanting of benedictory verses and sprinkling the earth with holy water. *Ajitāgama* however, rules for its purification by *pañcagavya*. (I.VI.26)

It is clear from the following table that the range of common ground between the ceremony of the consecration of a newly built temple or *yāgamaṇḍapa* as described in the *Āgamas* and the consecration of a newly built theatre as described in the *Nāṭyaśāstra* comprises several minute details as well as certain obvious features that are the parts and parcels of every type of *pūjā*:

Consecration of a temple or Yāgamaṇḍapa	*Consecration of a theatre*
(i) The consecration rites are to be performed by the *ācārya* clad in new white garments which have not been washed. (*MṛgĀ*, I.8.8–10)	(i) The consecration rites are to be performed by the *nāṭyācārya*, who should wear new clothes that have not been washed. (*NŚ*, III.3)
(ii) The *ācārya* chants the *mantras* to make Śiva enshrined within himself.	(ii) The *nāṭyācārya* takes the *dīkṣā* for the performance of consecration rites.
(iii) The gods are invoked and enshrined in the *maṇḍala*. Brahmā is enshrined at the centre. (*AjitĀ*, I.8.22)	(iii) The gods are invoked and enshrined in the *maṇḍala*, which is a square of 16 *hastas*, with four doors on the four directions. Brahmā is enshrined at the centre and gods are given their respective places according to the *kakṣyāvibhāga* – (division of space in imaginary zones). The following articles are used for the *niveśa* of the gods – *yava, lāja, akṣata, śālitaṇḍula*, powder of *nāgapuṣpa, vituṣa, priyaṅgu*. Two horizontal and vertical lines are drawn in the middle of the *maṇḍala*. (III.18–24)
(iv) A *kumbha* full of water is placed in the middle of the *maṇḍala*. (*AjitĀ*, I.9.32) This *kumbha* is also to be worshipped and some of the *Āgamas* give a very detailed account of *kumbhapūjā*.	(iv) The *kumbha* full of water is placed at the centre of the *maṇḍala*. No account of *kumbhapūjā* is available in the *Nāṭyaśāstra* while the ceremony of *kumbhabhedana* is described. Abhinava says that this ceremony is performed after the worship of *kumbha*. (*NŚ*, III.88–90 and *AbhiBhā*)

(v) Worship of each god with a different set of articles has not been specified. *Gandha* (incense), flowers, *dhūpa* and *dīpa* are commonly used, while *māṣa, godhūma, masūra, śyāmaka* and *niṣpava* have also been prescribed for *pūjā* by *Ajitāgama* (XXII.33–37) and some other *Śaiva Āgamas.*	(v) Worship of each individual god has been prescribed with a different set of articles each time. Flowers, *dhūpa* and *dīpa* are common here also. The cereals prescribed in the *Āgamas* are not mentioned. Brahmā is to be offered *madhuparka*; Sarasvatī *pāyasa*; Śiva, Viṣṇu, and Indra *modakas*; Agni *ghee* and rice; Soma and Arka *guḍa* and rice; the *munis*, Viśvedevas and *gandharvas* are served with honey and *pāyasa*; Yama and Mitra with *apūpa* and *modakas*; Pitṛs and Piśācas with *ghee* and milk and so on.
(vi) *Homa* is to be performed after the *pūjā*. *Homavidhi* has been described in detail.	(vi) *Homa* is a part of *raṅgadaivatapūjana* as well. No description of *homavidhi* is given in the *Nāṭyaśāstra.*
(vii) Musical instruments are played after the ceremony. There is no mention of the enactment of fights.	(vii) Musical instruments are played after the ceremony and fights are enacted.

These similarities cannot lead to establish that the ritual of *raṅgadaivatapūjana* bears direct and sole influence of the *pūjā*-system as given in *Śaivāgamas.* Such similarities can be found in almost all Vedic and non-Vedic rites in this country, and the motifs of the invocation of gods and their placement on the *maṇḍala*, offering of flowers, *gandha, dhūpa*, etc. are always common. The system of *pūjā* as given in *Vaiṣṇava* or *Pāñcarātra Āgamas* can lead to the same type of comparison as given above.

Besides, the ritual of *raṅgadaivatapūjana* differs from the Āgamic *pūjā* system on several points and the dissimilarities between the two give a unique character and distinct identity to the former. The worship of *Nāṭyamātṛkās* or *Nāṭyakumārīs* and the *Nāṭyavighnas*, the worship of *Jarjara* and the enactment of fights after the ritual – these are some features which establish the ritual of *raṅgadaivatapūjana* as a theatric ritual.

F.B.J. Kuiper finds the ritualized consciousness of Vedic *Yajña* embedded within the ritual of *raṅgadaivatapūjana* (*Varuṇa and Vidūṣaka*, pp. 110–16). Dr N.R. Lidova refutes any connection or correspondence between the two, insisting that the origin of *raṅgapūjā* as described in the *Nāṭyaśāstra* should be 'studied in the context of *pūjā*-dominated Hinduism' in contrast to the 'Yajña-dominated Vedism' (Abstracts, VIIIth World Sanskrit Conference). She has based her thesis on the idea of 'an opposition' between Vedic and non-Vedic cultures, between *yajña* and *pūjā* and between the *Nigama* and the *Āgama* traditions (*Ritual Sources of Sanskrit Drama*, p. 86), and also on the misconception that *yajña* ritual was simply dominated by 'animal slaughter' and that women and people belonging to the lower castes were debarred from participating in it.

Dr Lidova thus proceeds to establish the foundations of the ritual of *raṅgadaivatapūjana* in the Āgamic *pūjā*-tradition *ipso facto*. However, many of the lines of comparison drawn by her between the Āgamic and the *Nāṭyaśāstra*-ritual can be dismissed as mere coincidents; and seeing a correspondence between *dhvaja-pūjā* of Āgamic tradition and the *jarjara-pūjā* in the *Nāṭyaśāstra*-ritual is also far-fetched. There is apparant similarity between the raising, worshipping and lowering down of *jarjara* as described in the *Nāṭyaśāstra* (*NŚ*, III.12–14, 73–75) and the ritual of raising, worshipping and lowering down of the *dhvaja* as described in the *Āgamas*. (*AjitĀ*, I.XXVII.26,42–76) The *jarjara* and *jarjara-pūjā* are definitely linked to Indra and his weapon, and the purpose of *jarjara-pūjā* is quite different from the purpose of *dhvaja-pūjā*. Besides, the question of the authenticity of the *Āgama*-texts as available in print[1] will have to be taken into account in drawing any such comparison.

A totally different view of the ritual of *raṅgadaivatapūjana* has been advanced by some modern scholars. According to them, the whole ritual is simply an appendage. R.V. Jagirdar thinks that the whole of the chapter III of *Nāṭyaśāstra* is an interpolation (Introduction to Bharata's *Nāṭyaśāstra*, pp. 9–10), while Pramod Kale finds in *raṅgadaivatapūjana* 'a defence structure' 'which was needed perhaps to counter the attacks of Phillistines and puritans' (*Theatric Universe*, p. 4)

'Sanskrit Drama has least to do with religion and religious rites' Jagirdar concludes – '. . . it is the work of people treated as anti-Vedic'. (*Drama in Sanskrit Literature*, pp. 35–36) Like Dr Lidova's thesis, such refutation of the inter-relationship between *yajña* and the *Nāṭyaśāstra* is also based on a misconception, overlooking the fact (as Dr Kapila Vatsyayan rightly puts it) that 'Ritual is invariably accompanied by gestures and in it we find the seeds of *abhinaya* as it was to develop later. The ritual practices of *Yajurveda* must have provided the actor and the dancer with unique material which was as profound as it was symbolic and beautiful, as it was stylized and technical. . . . In all the sacrifices, the puntiliousness with which hands and feet are placed in different directions, or figures are used, are indicative of a sense of perfection and consciousness of an artist and a mathematician combined." (*Classical Indian Dance in Literature and Arts*, p. 155) The ritual of *raṅgapūjā* must therefore be viewed in this background where *yajña* and theatre thrived on a common platform. (Lectures on the *Nāṭyaśāstra*, pp. 34–45)

The insistance on a sole Āgamic background based on the idea of a dichotomy between Vedic and non-Vedic cultures therefore is not acceptable, and *raṅgadaivatapūjana* must be viewed as a ritual having Vedic worldview at the core, with *yajña* and *pūjā* fused together to form a theatric ritual. *Nāṭyaśāstra* itself adjusts this ritual as an *ijyā* and *iṣṭi* also and Abhinava calls it *devayajana.* (*AbhiBhā*, Vol.I, p. 46)

Note

1. This question was raised by Dr Kapila Vatsyayan during the discussion on this paper.

References

Ajitāgama; Ed. by N.R. Bhatt, Pondicherry, 1964 (*AjitĀ*).

Jagirdar, R.V., *Introduction to the Study of Nāṭyaśāstra*, Bombay, 1966.

Kale, Pramod, *The Theatric Universe*, Bombay, 1974.

Kuiper, F.B.J., *Varuṇa and Vidūṣaka: On the Origin of Sanskrit Drama*, Amsterdam-Oxford-New York, 1973.

Lidova, N.R, *Raṅgadaivatapūjana in the Nāṭyaśāstra and the Āgamic Rituals, Summaries of the papers of VIIIth World Sanskrit Conference*, University of Vienna, 1990.

Lidova, N.R, *Ritual Sources of Sanskrit Drama, Indian Traditions Through the Ages*, New Delhi, 1990, pp. 85–106.

Mṛgendrāgama; Ed. by N.R. Bhatt, Pondicherry, 1962.

Nāṭyaśāstra, with Abhinavabhāratī, Vols. 1–4, Baroda.

Rauravāgama; Ed. by N.R. Bhatt, Pondicherry, 1961.

Tripathi, Radhavallabh, *Lectures on the Nāṭyaśāstra*, Centre of Advanced Study in Sanskrit, Poona, 1991.

Vatsyayan, Kapila, *Classical Indian Dance in Literature and Arts*, New Delhi, 1968.

7

Mahābhūtas in Saṅgīta-Śāstra
With Special Reference to Yoga and Āyurveda

Prem Lata Sharma

> You are the Sun, You are the Moon, You are Air, You the Fire (*hutavaha* – the one who carries that which is put in the sacrificial fire). You are Water, You are Space, You are Earth and You are the Ātman. Those who have taken refuge in you may use the above speech that is thus limited. We do not know any entity that is not your Manifestation.
>
> *Śivamahimnastotra*, 26

The five elements have been said here to be the manifestation of Śiva, the Supreme Being.

An enquiry into the role of *Mahābhūtas* in Music is essentially a quest for the relationship between the 'outer', 'inner', and what is beyond the two. Roughly, the human organism is the 'inner', whatever is outside the body is the 'outer' and both are closely interrelated. That which permeates both of them and is yet intangible is beyond them. In understanding the 'inner', both Yoga and Āyurveda have made a deep study of the psycho-physical centres in the human body as well as the physiological structure of the body in terms of the *Mahābhūtas*.[1] The unity of the 'inner' and the 'outer' has been established by expounding that the sense-organs, their objects and their functions are all manifestations of the *Mahābhūtas*. The following passage from *Saṅgīta-Ratnākara* makes this very clear.

The *Saṅgīta-Ratnākara* (I.2.56c–71b) describes the structure and functions of the human body in terms of the five *Mahābhūtas* as follows:

> The body is a composite of the (five) great elements (*Mahābhūtas*) and has therefore acquired their qualities (as herein described):
>
> (i) *Ākāśa* – Sound, the faculty of hearing, porosity, individuation, intelligence and hollowness are derived from *Ākāśa*.

(ii) *Vāyu* – Touch, the sense-organ for touch, five types of motion, viz., upwards, downwards, contraction, linear movement and expansion have been derived from air.

The ten modifications of air (breath in the body) viz., *prāṇa, apāna, vyāna, samāna, udāna, nāga, kūrma, kṛkara, devadatta* and *dhanañjaya* and *rūkṣatā* (roughness caused by the scarcity of oily matter) as well as lightness are derived from air.

Of these (ten) *prāṇas*, that which is the most important is stationed below the root of the navel and it operates through the mouth, the nostrils, the navel and the heart and (thereby) causes the verbalization of speech, the inhalation and exhalation of breath and also sneezing and coughing.

Apāna is stationed in the anal region and the genitals, waist, legs, abdomen, the root of the navel, the groin, thighs and the knees. Its function is to discharge urine and excretion etc., (from the body).

Vyāna dwells in the eyes, ears, ankles, waist and the nose and its function is to draw in, hold and to push out breath.

Samāna pervades the whole body; and running through the 72,000 nerve-channels of the body accompanied by the (digestive) fire, helps to nourish it by carrying essence of lymph-chyle (*rasa*) of the food and drink (to the tissues) and distributing it proportionately.

Udāna abides in the hands, the feet and the joints of the limbs; its function being the lifting of the body upwards and breathing the last, i.e., dying etc.

Presiding in elements such as skin etc., are the five (other) modifications of the vital breath such as *nāga* etc., performing the function of eructation (such as spitting) etc., sneezing etc., lassitude etc., and swelling respectively.

(iii) *Agni* – From fire, the body acquires sight, *rūpa* (colour and form), bile, digestion, lustre, wrath, sharpness, heat, vigour, splendour, valour and intellectuality.

(iv) *Jala* – From water (it derives) the sense of taste, relish, coolness, *sneha* (roughly, viscidity), fluidity, perspiration, urine etc., as well as softness.

(v) *Pṛthivī* – From the earth, (it acquires) the sense of smell, odour, stability, fortitude and heaviness (weight[1]), beard, hair

(on the head etc.,) nails, bones and such other hard materials.
(tr. by R.K. Shringy and Prem Lata Sharma)

All this is from the point of view of Āyurveda which itself is not dissociated from Yoga. With reference to Yoga, *SR*, I.2.120–148 and I.2.149–163b sets forth the point of view of Yoga, specially *Haṭhayoga*.

Ten *Cakras* (psychophysical centres):

1. *Ādhāra-cakra* and *kuṇḍalinī*: Situated in-between the anus and the genitals is the basic psychic centre called the 'foundational cycle' (*ādhāra-cakra*), a four-petalled lotus as it were. The petals named *īśāna* etc., are invested with the fruits of supreme bliss, spontaneous happiness, heroic joy, and the divine unity respectively.
   In the centre of the foundational cycle lies the creative power of the Supreme Being called *kuṇḍalinī*, which in the event of being unfolded bestows immortality.
2. *Svādhiṣṭhāna-cakra*: Situated at the root of the genitals is the six-petalled lotus, the psycho-physical centre called 'self-abiding cycle' (*svādhiṣṭhāna-cakra*). The consequent fruits of (concentration on) the eastern and the other petals are respectively said to be courtesy, cruelty, freedom from pride, stupor, disrespect and distrust. This is the seat of passion.
3. *Maṇipūraka-cakra*: The ten-petalled lotus, the psycho-physical centre called the 'navel cycle' (*maṇipūraka-cakra*) is located around the navel. The results flowing out of (meditation on) the eastern and other petals respectively are dreamless sleep, craving, jealousy, fault-finding nature, boastfulness, fear, hatred, stupidity, impropriety and dejection. This centre is the seat of a particular *prāṇa* called *bhānu*.
4. *Anāhata-cakra*: In the heart is located the psycho-physical centre called the 'cycle of the unmanifest' (*anāhata-cakra*) with twelve petals which is considered to be the place of worshipping Śiva in the form *oṃ*.
   The consequences meeting the mind concentrated upon eastern and other petals respectively are freedom from fickleness, clear thinking, repentance, hope, light, worry, desire for warding off evil, equanimity, vanity, mental instability, discernment and will.

5. *Viśuddhi-cakra*: The psycho-physical centre with sixteen petals, called the 'cycle of purity' (*viśuddhi-cakra*) is situated in the throat-larynx and is known as the abode of Bhāratī, the goddess of learning. Contemplation on the eastern and other petals offers the following results respectively: *praṇava, udgītha, huṃphaṭ, vaṣaṭ, svadhā, svāhānamaḥ*, nectar, the seven tones *ṣaḍja* etc., and poison.

6. *Lalanā-cakra*: The psycho-physical centre called *lalanā* with twelve petals is situated in the back of the neck. The consequences emerging out of (concentration upon) the eastern and the other petals respectively are – arrogance, haughtiness, affection, sorrow, agony, greed, disenchantment, emotional excitement, the basic urge for living, devotion, satisfaction and cleverness.

7. *Ājñā-cakra*: The psycho-physical centre called the 'cycle of supreme command' (*ājñā-cakra*) having three petals is located in-between the two eye-brows. The results of (contemplating upon) the various petals respectively are the manifestations of the three *guṇas* – *sattva, rajas* and *tamas.*

8. *Manas-cakra*: Even higher than that is situated the psycho-physical centre called the 'cycle of the mind' (*manas-cakra*) having six petals. The consequences attendant upon the eastern and other petals respectively are dreams and the palatal enjoyment, olfactory sensation and the perception of form, touch and sound.

9. *Soma-cakra*: Over and above that is located the psycho-physical centre called the 'cycle of the moon' (*soma-cakra*) with sixteen petals enshrining the sixteen phases (of the moon). The consequences, for the individual, attendant upon the eastern and other petals respectively are: grace, forgiveness, straightforwardness, forbearance, detachment, patience, cheerfulness, mirth, horripilation, tears of fixed gaze, stability, profundity, endeavour, purity of heart, generosity and one-pointedness.

10. *Sahasrapatra-cakra*: 'The thousand-petalled lotus' (*sahasra-patra*) which is the source of nectar is located in the cerebral aperture (*brahmarandhra*). Spilling innumerable streams of ambrosia, it nourishes the body.

11. Meditation of *cakras* as related to the cultivation of music. The embodied soul established in the (contemplation of) first, eighth, eleventh and the twelfth petals of the 'cycle of the unmanifest' (*anāhata-cakra*) attains proficiency in music etc., while (by concentration on) the fourth, sixth and tenth of the petals one destroys one's capacity for music etc.

    In the 'cycle of purity' (*viśuddhi-cakra*) contemplation on eight petals from the eighth onwards leads to success in musical arts etc., while the sixteenth petal is destructive for the purpose.

    The tenth and the eleventh petals of the psycho-physical centre called *lalanā* bestow success in the musical arts, while its first, fourth and fifth petals are known to be detrimental.

    The embodied soul whose attention is focused in the aperture of the upper cerebrum, being immersed in ambrosia, finds fulfilment and should therefore cultivate the musical arts with great excellence.

    The embodied soul cannot in any way accomplish anything (worthwhile) in the field of musical arts by concentrating on any other petals or psycho-physical centres.

    Brahma-granthi: Two finger-length above the base and two finger-breadth below the genitals in the space of one finger-breadth is the centre of the body, shining like molten gold.

    There is located a slender flame of fire at a distance of nine fingers from that centre, and it is there that the life-source of the body is found, four fingers in elevation as well as in extension. This has been called *brahma-granthi* by the ancients.

    Right in its centre is situated the 'cycle of the umbilicus' (*nābhi-cakra*) with twelve spokes, and like the spider caught in (its own) net, yonder there wanders the self-conscious being.

    Suṣumnā and other *nāḍīs*: Mounted upon the vital breath, the self-conscious entity, through the *suṣumnā* keeps on ascending to the cerebral aperture and descending back, moving like a tight rope dancer.

    From the life-centre to the cerebral aperture the *nāḍīs*, surrounding the *suṣumnā* and enmeshing the life-centre by their network, enlarge the body by developing their branches.

    These *nāḍīs* are in a large number; but fourteen out of them are important, viz., *suṣumnā, piṅgalā, iḍā, kuhū, sarasvatī,*

> *gāndhārī, hastijihvā, vāruṇī, yaśasvinī, viśvodarā, śaṅkhinī, pūṣā, payasvinī* and *alambuṣā*. The first three of these again are considered to be most significant.
>
> *Suṣumnā* is the supreme among these three; with Viṣṇu as its presiding deity, it leads to the pathway of liberation. It is established in the centre of the life-source and is flanked by *iḍā* on the left and *piṅgalā* on the right. The vital breath moving through *iḍā* and *piṅgalā* is called moon and the sun, for they determine the movement of time; but *suṣumnā* destroys time.
>
> *Sarasvatī* and *kuhū* are on the either sides of *suṣumnā*. *Gāndhārī* and *hastijihvā*, are respectively situated behind and in front of *iḍā*, while *puṣā* and *yaśasvinī* are similarly situated with respect to *piṅgalā*.
>
> *Viśvodarā* lies in the midst of *kuhū* and *hastijihvā*, and *vāruṇī* likewise is in the midst of *kuhū* and *yaśasvinī* exists between *gāndhārī* and *sarasvatī* and *alambuṣā* is in the midst of the life-centre.
>
> Now, *iḍā* and *piṅgalā* (extend) up to the tips of the left and the right nostrils respectively, and *kuhū* to the front of the genitals. *Sarasvatī* extends up to the tongue, while *gāndhārī* is set by the back (of the body). *Hastijihvā* runs from the left eye to the toes of the left foot; while *vāruṇī* pervades the entire body; on the right other hand, *yaśasvinī* extends from the toe up to the right foot; while *viśvodarā* pervades the whole body. *Śaṅkhinī* extends up to the left ear and *pūṣā* up to the right eye, while *payasvinī* is extended to the extremity of the right ear. *Alambuṣā* stands coiled around the root of the anus.
> (tr. by R.K. Shringy and Prem Lata Sharma)

Sound, tonal and syllabic, constitutes the body of music. The production, travel and perception of sound is a physical phenomenon, but perception also involves the mind. In the carrying of sound, air is the best known medium. In the process of sound-production in the human body, air is not only the medium of carrying the sound but is also the instrument of sound production as it strikes the various locations. The *Nāṭyaśāstra* combines all this while saying that sound is made of air or is of the nature of air.[2]

After *Nāṭyaśāstra*, *Bṛhaddeśī* introduces Agni (or the kinetic energy in the body) as the element that propels the air as well as *pṛthivī* that forms the base for this action of the fire and the air and *ākāśa* that provides space for all this movement.[3]

Thus, four elements, viz., *ākāśa* or space, air, fire and earth have been spoken of in the context of the production of sound in general and musical sound in particular. The role of air and fire is direct, that of the earth is figurative and that of space is implied or implicit (rarely pronounced).

The *Śikṣā* texts also deal with the production of sound in the human body in similar terms.[4] The close similarity between the description of the process of sound production in the texts of *Śikṣā* and *Saṅgīta-Śāstra* is notable, though their subtle nuances are also interesting.[5] The process is the same in relation to speech and music. That the two have been taken to be integral constituents of the totality of human expression through the aural medium is also clear from the fact that three basic words are common to them. These are:

Word	*In Speech*	*In Music*
Svara	Vowel	Tone
Varṇa	Syllable	Primary melodic unit
Pada	Word (Primary semantic unit)	Lexical or non-lexical textual unit, melodic phrase, sub-section of a composition or *ālāpa*

In language, it is the vowel that embodies interval (high, low tone), and duration (long and short) and the consonant merely holds their reflection. It is impossible to separate tone from syllable. Tone cannot be manifested without the association of syllable at least *ākāra* (the *ā* sound) will unavoidably accompany the production of any musical sound by the human organism. In musical instruments, the 'stroke' part of the sound produced has invariably been identified with consonants of language in the Indian tradition and the 'resonance' part has been identified with vowels to which nasalization is sometimes suffixed. Similarly, linguistic communication is not devoid of pitch (albeit irregular), loudness, timbre and duration. The holistic approach of the Indian tradition takes due cognizance of the basic unity of linguistic and musical expression. In music text and melody form combinations of numerous varieties, according to the degree of emphasis on one or the other at any given time.

Both *Pāṇinīya Śikṣā* and *Saṅgīta-Ratnākara* speak of the 'will to speak' arising in the *ātman*, although the former is dealing with language and the latter with music. The concept of unity between the two has been discussed above. The subtle difference between the two has, however, been pointed out by Abhinavagupta in *Tantrāloka*. That (*vāk*) which is made of *nāda* and is beautiful with patterns of *svaras*, that is verily the gross *paśyantī* on account of the non-differentiation of syllables and the like. The potency (*śakti*) in the form of being one with non-differentiation is called *mādhurya*. The concrete state (of this *vāk*) comes into being on account of the friction between *sthāna* (location in the body or on an instrument) and air and that is the *pāruṣī śakti* (potency taking the form of harshness).[6]

Hence, the state of merging in this (*vāk* taking the form of *nāda* is attained immediately (on its perception) on account of its similarity with *saṃvit* brought about by the fact of its being of the same category (*sājātya*). Those who do not attain this state of merging or identification, they do not know the state of the merging of the body and the like and are *ahṛdayas* (as distinct from *sahṛdayas*) and their *saṃvit* is subdued or submerged. Whatever sound is produced on instruments covered or fastened with membrane and the like, that is both concrete and non-concrete and is hence *madhyamā* (*vāk*) in its gross form. *Raktatā* or the state of being red or delightful comes about on account of the existence of the aspect of non-differentiation present in *madhyamā*. Where there is *svaramayī* (*vāk*) characterised by non-differentiation, that (rendering on the drum-instruments) is the bestower of delight. Non-differentiation leads to bliss, which could be seen to be experienced. In the recitation of the *tāla*-syllables, one gets delight from the inarticulate sound (in which the syllables are couched).[7]

That (*vāk*) which is the cause of the manifestation of articulate syllables, is the gross *vaikharī* from which is born the expanse of the sentence and the like. The *anusandhāna* (lit. planning or aiming at, here mental image accompanied by self-consciousness) that constitutes the beginning of these three forms of gross *vāk*, is distinct in each of the three forms and is given the name *sūkṣma* or subtle. 'I am making *ṣaḍja*' or 'I am producing *svaras*', I am playing (on the drums) and 'I am speaking a sentence, these three forms that *anusandhāna* (self-conscious will) takes are experienced as being distinct.[8]

The form of these three that is free from *upādhi* (attribute or qualification) is the *para* or ultimate state where there is Śiva, the embodiment of *paracit*. (*Tantrāloka*, III 237c–248b)

Abhinavagupta speaks of the desire to produce *ṣaḍja*, i.e., a musical note or *svara*, to play on drums and to speak. These three aural expressions have been identified with three manifestations of *vāk* in its gross form, as follows:

Aural Expression	*The gross form of vāk.*
1. Rendering of melody with the voice or on chordophones or aerophones	*Paśyantī*
2. Rendering on drums	*Madhyamā*
3. Speaking	*Vaikharī*

The above three forms of expression gradually proceed from the subtle towards the gross.

The will or self-consciousness of the performer/speaker is the subtle (*sūkṣma*) form of the above three levels of *vāk*. The unmanifest or ultimate form of these three is called *parā*.

Ātman or *Puruṣa* is the Ultimate Reality that is beyond the *Bhūtas* which in turn are manifestations of the same. The desire to speak or produce a sound arises in the *Ātman*, i.e., the mind, fire, air, etc., start functioning at the behest of the *Ātman* or *Puruṣa*. In other words, the 'action' of the *Bhūtas* is actuated by the *Ātman* or *Puruṣa*.

The mind is the element that propels the fire or kinetic energy. It is said to be *annamaya*, equated with *anna*, the Upaniṣadic word for 'food'. Primarily, food is the object of oral assimilation by the body and secondarily, it stands for all the objects of sense perception that are 'consumed' or 'taken'. In its primary meaning, *anna* is directly equated with *pṛthivī* and in its secondary meaning with all the five elements. As for water, *rasa* being the ultimate determining factor of propriety (*aucitya*) in all creative activity and aesthetic delight or enjoyment, bearing analogy with the sense of taste, its presence is all-pervading.

In instrumental music also, the mind, the kinetic energy as the 'acting agent' the air as the carrier or even producer of sound, the latter in the case of wind instruments like flute, are in operation.

Thus, the mind as a direct 'associate' of the earth is not only responsible for image-making in music or any other art, but is also the propelling agent that activates the kinetic energy in the body for sound production through the voice or through an instrument. The earth functions through the mind and also as the base for all activity, psychological or physical. The mind in turn is the agent or *karaṇa* (instrument) of *Ātman*, the other two instruments being *vāk* and *prāṇa*. In music, all these three agents are directly active. In visual arts, *vāk* is implicit, but in music, *manas* (mind), *prāṇa* (not only vital air but all physical and physiological activity) and *vāk* (articulate and inarticulate sound or syllabic and tonal sound) are all explicitly involved. Mind embodies the beginning, *prāṇa* comes in the middle and continues and *vāk* is the product that is arranged in structures of *svara, tāla* and *pada.*

When the *bhūtas* are talked of as being three, instead of five, then *manas* is identified with *anna* or *pṛthivī, prāṇa* with water and *vāk*[9] with *tejas* or *agni.* In this scheme of three *Mahābhūtas* viz., *agni*, water and earth, water is identified with *prāṇa* or air, and *ākāśa* is accepted as being implicit.

The figurative representation of the *Mahābhūtas* in the delineation of the impact of sound, as available in *Saṅgīta-Śāstra* is very striking and remarkable. It reveals the psychic process that comprehends the 'inner' and 'outer' in one stroke. Some examples will illustrate this point:

1. High and low in *svara* is generally termed as *tāra* and *mandra.* But they are also called *dīpta* (lit. brilliant) and *prasanna* (lit. clear, secondarily happy)[10]. Brilliance is related to *Agni* and clarity to water. Empirically, higher notes have an association of warmth and lower notes that of coolness both for the performer and the listener. *Mṛdu* is another name for lower notes, its literal meaning is soft. Softness, primarily, pertains to the sense of touch which is related to air but secondarily, softness could also be associated with water.

2. *Madhura* (sweet) as an adjective and *mādhurya* (sweetness) as an abstract noun is a very basic quality of musical sound. Sweetness is directly related to water as the sense of taste and the object of taste, both are derived from water or are attributes of the same.

3. *Snigdha* is an adjective derived from the noun *sneha* which is difficult to translate in English. *Sneha* is the basic quality of oil, butter or other similar substances. It is considered to be the opposite of *rūkṣa* or dry. In the English language 'dry' stands both for that which is devoid of water or oil, butter and the like. But in Sanskrit, there are two different words, viz., *śuṣka* for the former and *rūkṣa*, for the latter. *Sneha* also means love and thus the quality of butter is transferred to the mind. *Sneha* is an attribute of water and butter, oil and the like are said to have an element of *tejas* or *agni.* Hence this quality is related to both fire and water. *Ślakṣṇa* (lit. continuous like the vertical flow of oil) is another quality of the voice, that bears the association of water and fire.

4. *Ghana* (dense) as an adjective of the voice or musical sound is associated with the earth which embodies density.

5. *Rañjaka, rakta* (red and delightful) as adjectives and *rañjakatā, rakti* as abstract nouns are all derived from the root *rañja* which means 'to colour'. Primarily, colour pertains to visual perception and secondarily, it has been applied to aural perception. The sense-peception of colour has been transferred

to the psychological realm as delight. Colour (*rūpa*) is an attribute of *Agni*.

6. *Pracura* (full) as an adjective of voice stands for the fulness or richness of tone like density (*ghanatā*). This also is associated with the earth. *Gāḍha* (lit. closely knit) is another quality that bears association with the earth.

7. *Ujjvala* (lit. bright) or *chavimāna* (lit. lustrous) as qualities of the voice are again related to *Agni*.

8. The five categories of musicians spoken of in *Saṅgīta-Ratnākara* include a triad of *rañjaka*, the one who brings about *raṅga* or colourfulness, *bhāvuka* or *bhāvaka*, who delineates *bhāva* and *rasika*, who expresses *rasa*. The first one is mindful of the interest or taste of the audience, the second one also pays some attention to the expectations of the audience, but the third one is completely oblivious of the audience.[11] *Raṅga* or colour is related to fire, *bhāva*, having been figuratively equated with smell, is related to the earth and *rasa* to water.

Music, being directly related to aural perception and this perception being an attribute of *ākāśa*, is primarily related to the same. Conceptually, this relationship is complete in itself. But in the production, communication and enjoyment of musical sound, the other four elements, specially earth, fire and air, have their definite roles. Water is related to the *gestalt* of music. The qualities of the musical voice have been given figurative names that bear close affinity with one or the other of the five elements.

Saṅgīta-Śāstra has attempted to discover the essential unity between the 'inner' and the 'outer' and the Ultimate Reality that permeates both of them.[12]

Notes

1. It is notable that not only physical or physiological organs, functions, objects etc., have been said to be derived from the five elements, but psychological qualities like intelligence, wrath sharpness etc., have also been enumerated in this context.
2. *NŚ*, XXXIV.28a *vāyvātmako bhavecchabdaḥ. . .*
   Sound is made up of air or is of the nature of air.
3. "*yaduktaṃ brahmaṇaḥ sthānaṃ brahmagranthiśca yaḥ smṛtaḥ |*
   tanmadhye saṃsthitaḥ prāṇaḥ prāṇād vahnisamudgamaḥ ||
   vahnimārutasaṃyogānnādaḥ samupajāyate |
   nādādutpadyate bindurnādāt sarvaṃ ca vāṅmayam ||
   kandasthānasamuttho hi samīraḥ saṃcarannadhaḥ |
   ūrdhvaṃ ca kurute sarvāṃ nādapaddhatimuddhatām || "
   nakāraḥ prāṇa ityāhurdakāraścānalo mataḥ ||
   nādasya dvipadārtho'yaṃ samīcīno mayoditaḥ || (20)

*anu.*1
tatrādau tāvad dehāgnipavanasaṃyogāt puruṣaprayatnaprerito dhvanirnābherūrdhvamākāśadeśam ākrāman dhūmavat sopānapadakrameṇa pavanecchayā'nekadhārohannantarbhutapūraṇapratyayārthatayā catuḥśrutyādibhedabhinnaḥ pratibhāsate. . .

"That which is spoken of as the location (*sthāna*) of *Brahman* and which is known as *brahma-granthi, prāṇa* is seated in it, *vahni* (fire) arises from *prāṇa*; *nāda* is born of the combination of *vahni* (fire) and *māruta* (air)."

"From *nāda* is formed *bindu* and from *nāda* all *vāṅmaya* (whatever is made of speech or language) is born."

. . . the air arising from the location of *kanda* (lit. bulbous root, here *brahma-granthi* or the centre of energy in the human body situated below the navel) and moving about up and down, produces the intense course of *nāda*. (*Bṛhaddeśī*, three verses quoted in the text after verse 19).

"The letter *na* is spoken of as *prāṇa* (air) and the letter *da* is known as fire; this is spoken of by me as the meaning of the dual verbal component (*pada*) of *nāda*."

". . . There in the beginning on account of the combination of the *dehāgni* (lit. bodily fire, battery of energy) and air, the sound propelled by the effort of the *puruṣa* (*ātman*), attacking the *ākāśa* (space) above the navel, ascending in many ways, in steps of a ladder like smoke, according to the will of the air, appears to be different by way of being composed of four *śrutis* etc. through being comprised of the inherent *pratyaya* (assured consciousness) of filling up with air. . ." (*Ibid.*, Anu. 1)
ātmecchayā mahītalād vāyurudyannidhyāryate |
nāḍībhīttau tathākāśe dhvanī raktaḥ svaraḥ smṛtaḥ ||
"By the will of the *ātman*, the *vāyu* (that is) moving upward from the base of the 'earth' (*nābhi*, navel) (and) is held on the 'wall' of the *nāḍīs* and in the space, is known as *svara*, the delightful sound." (*Ibid.*, verse quoted after Anu. 15)

The architectural image suggested in the above verse is striking. The centre below the navel has been equated with the earth, the air rising upwards strikes against the 'walls' of *nāḍīs* (tubular vessels) and raises its head in *ākāśa* (space), represented by the cerebral region, during sound that is gradually rising in pitch.

4. *ātmā buddhyā sametyārthān mano yuṅkte vivakṣayā* |
manaḥ kāyāgnimāhanti sa prerayati mārutam ||
mārutastūrasi caran mandraṃ janayati svaram |
prātaḥ savanayogaṃ taṃchando gāyatramāśritam ||
kaṇṭhe mādhyandinayugaṃ madhyamaṃ trairṣṭubhānugam |

tāraṃ tārtīyasavanaṃ śīrṣaṇyaṃ jagatānugam ||
. . .*vaktramāpadya mārutaḥ* |
varṇāñ janayate. . .

(*Pāṇinīya Śikṣā*, 6–9)

"*Ātman*, having gathered or put together the content, *artha* (of sound) with *buddhi* (intellect) activates the mind with the will to speak.

The mind strikes the fire in the body. The fire propels the air. The air, moving in the chest-region, throat and cerebrum manifests low, medium and high sound respectively. Reaching the mouth cavity, the air manifests the *varṇas*."

5. Comparison of the description of the process of sound-production in the human organism as given in the *Pāṇinīya Śikṣā, Bṛhaddeśī* and *Saṅgīta-Ratnākara*, brings to light the following subtle nuances:
1. Instead of *ātman* that is mentioned as the substratum of the desire to 'speak' in *Pāṇinīya Śikṣā* and *Saṅgīta-Ratnākara, Bṛhaddeśī* mentions *puruṣa. Puruṣa* is the collection of twenty-four elements viz., *buddhi* (sixfold perception as associated with the five sense-organs and mind), the ten *indriyas* (viz., five sensory and five motor organs), mind, the six objects of perception and the ultimate repository of the above twenty-three elements, i.e., *ātman*, according to *Āyurveda.*
2. In *Pāṇinīya Śikṣā* and *Saṅgīta-Ratnākara* the first step is the will of the *ātman*, but in *Bṛhaddeśī* the combination of 'fire' and 'air' is spoken of as the first step, without the mention of any activating agent. The *puruṣa* is mentioned in the second step as the agent that propels the air upwards. A citation in the name of Kohala, quoted in *Bṛhaddeśī*, reproduced in note No. 4 above, does mention the will of the *ātman* as the first step.
3. In *Pāṇinīya Śikṣā*, *buddhi* is mentioned as an agent that 'gathers' the content of speech. This is absent in *Bṛhaddeśī* and *Saṅgīta-Ratnākara*; the reason could perhaps be that in musical sound the differentiation of the form and content (meaning) of sound is not pertinent.
4. In *Bṛhaddeśī* mind has not been mentioned at all. The mention of *pratyaya* (assured consciousness), however, does bring in the mind, but it is related to the process of hearing in the speaker. (Based on Vimarśa, p. 155 *BṛD*, Vol.I) Whatever the differences, the direct involvement of 'air' and 'fire' is accepted by all.

6. The resonant quality of *svara* is called *mādhurya* here and the 'attack' constituting the concrete nature of musical sound is called the *pāruṣī śakti* (harsh potency).

7. The rendering on drums is accompanied with an explicit or implicit recitation of the syllables that represent identification of the strokes on the instrument concerned. These syllables are differentiated or articulate, but the non-differentiated tonal component of the rendering on drums does give delight, i.e., is *rakta*.

8. Jayaratha's commentary on verse 246 gives the name *jigāsā* for the first, *vivādayiṣā* for the second and *vivakṣā* for the third. Texts of *Saṅgīta-Śāstra* have not taken this distinction into account and have thus emphasised only the unity of the process of sound-production in speech and music.

9. *annamayaṃ hi saumya manaḥ | āpomayāḥ prāṇāḥ | tejomayī vāk ||*
(*ChUp*, VI.7.6)

"O gentle one the *manas* is made of *anna*. The *prāṇas* are made up of water and the *vāk* is made up of *tejas*."

10. *Abhinava-Bhāratī* on *NŚ*, XXIX.35 equates *dīpana* or the act of making *dīptā* with highness of notes and *prasāda* or clarity with *mandratā* or lowness. The words *dīpta* and *prasanna* have been used profusely in *NŚ* in this chapter.

11. *śikṣākāro'nukāraśca rasiko rañjakastathā |*
bhāvukaśceti gītajñaḥ pañcadhā gāyanaṃ jaguḥ ||
anyunaśikṣaṇe dakṣaḥ śikṣākāro mataḥ satām |
anukāra iti proktaḥ parabhaṅgayanukārakaḥ ||
rasāviṣṭastu rasiko rañjakaḥ śrotṛrañjakaḥ |
gītasyātiśayādhānādbhāvukaḥ parikīrtitaḥ ||
(*SR*, III.19–21)

Five types of vocalists are recognised by the vocal experts viz., *śikṣākāra, anukāra, rasika, rañjaka* and *bhāraka*. One who is capable of imparting flawless instructions is considered by the wise to be *śikṣākāra* (the educator). The imitator of another's style is called *anukāra* (the imitator). One who gets absorbed in the aesthetic delight (*rasa*) is *rasika* (the aesthete), and one who entertains the listeners is *rañjaka* (entertaining), and one who is extremely expressive in the delineation of the song is known as *bhāvaka* (the inspirer of emotion).

12. "Levels of Aesthetic Experience in Music" by Prem Lata Sharma, In *Indian Music Journal*, April 1964, pp. 19–21.

8

The Body as an Instrument

A Theoretical Choice Made by Śārṅgadeva

Mukund Lath

I wish to discuss a notable section right in the beginning of Śārṅgadeva's *Saṅgīta-Ratnākara* concerning the question of *nādotpatti* – the process by which sound is produced in the human body. Śārṅgadeva's aim, evidently, was not only to explain *nādotpatti*, the production of sound in general through the human frame, but to picturize *svarotpatti*, the more specific process, by which musical tones arise in the body. It is in this context that Śārṅgadeva makes use of the notion of *mahābhūtas*.

Śārṅgadeva's handling of his material is worthy of attention. He had three different theoretical pictures of the process before him, all three of which were available to him from widely different disciplines and approaches to the human body. He outlines all three of them and quite visibly makes a choice from among them, picking out the one most appropriate for his purpose as a *saṅgīta-śāstrī*. His understanding of the human body, as it emerges from the standpoint he opts for, is to treat the human body as an instrument which the soul – or rather the embodied soul, the *jīvātman* uses for its own creative purpose of making music.

Interesting as the view Śārṅgadeva accepts as an answer to the question of *nādotpatti* is, what I find even more interesting is to observe him making a choice between available alternatives. In this, curiously, his approach is not discursive. He does not argue for the propriety of the choice he makes, treating, as he should have, the alternatives he rejects as *pūrvapakṣas* which must be dismissed through reason. The intellectual tradition of the *śāstras* such as *alaṅkāra* in which he was obviously trained, not to speak of the *darśanas*, do indeed follow an articulate argumentative path for arriving at conclusions. And yet Śārṅgadeva does make a choice, a choice which, among all the alternative theories he had at hand, fits most suitably with his picture of music-making as an activity of a free agent, a creative *vāggeyakāra*. In the theory he finally accepts, the process of *nādotpatti* emerges as a causal, physical process which a person desirous of singing can freely use.

Curiously, it also appears that Śārṅgadeva was being pulled in two different directions. He seems, on the one hand, to be selecting an appropriate scheme from among those he had before him, but at the same time one also feels that he wants to present the different schemes as forming a large coherent whole into which the exiguous process of the production of tones in singing fits as a part. Noteworthy is also the fact that the two schemes he 'rejects' and which he takes up in some detail, clearly contain elements he could have used or adapted in order to formulate a process suitable for his purpose. Such a procedure would, indeed, have given him a theoretically more well-rounded whole. But he does not take up this course. The process he actually ends up by adopting does not mesh well with the rest and is, surprisingly in comparison, also sketched quite cursorily.

Fortunately, Dr Prem Lata Sharma's paper has provided us with many details as to what Śārṅgadeva actually says.[1] One could also refer to the English translation of the *Saṅgīta-Ratnākara* by R.K. Shringy and Prem Lata Sharma (Vol.I, *adhyāya* 1, *prakaraṇas* 2 and 3).[2] This will allow us to be reasonably brief and save us from lengthy textual references. Although I find that I must reproduce some details for my own critical reflections on the text.

The two 'larger' schemes which Śārṅgadeva gives us are outlined in a single chapter which he terms *piṇḍotpatti*, 'the birth of the body'. This chapter is in a significant sense the first in the text: it follows a preamble containing a list of contents. *Piṇḍotpatti* deals not only with the birth of the body as the name suggests but also its structure. Of the two distinct schemes it contains, the first is a picture sketched in some detail of bodily processes as mapped in the discipline of medicine available to Śārṅgadeva, the Āyurveda. Śārṅgadeva gives us quite a detailed picture which he had in fact studied in much greater detail, even writing an independent book on the subject to which he refers us for further information. The book, which he had, interestingly, named, *Adhyātmaviveka* – 'Distinguishing the Self' – is no longer extant.[3] Śārṅgadeva was, as he tells us, also a practising doctor.

In the picture of the 'self' – clearly, in this context, the body as an embodied self – visualized here, the human frame is conceived as a psychosomatic entity, a whole, a 'person', which combines entities and properties that may be distinguished as material, organic and conscious or mental. Processes which are inner or psychic, whether of thought, emotion or resolve, are made part of the 'body'. They are conceived as emanating from a much larger cosmic scheme founded on the idea of a single 'spiritual' stuff which manifests itself in entities both physical as well as psychic. *Jīvas*, individual souls, emerge like sparks from a fire out of the ultimate spiritual reality, *brahma*. Shrouded by *avidyā* and propelled by *karma*, they assume physical form, doing so again and again, till they attain *brahma*-hood and *mokṣa*.

This is not an unfamiliar picture in the tradition of Indian ideas about creation. It also lies at the basis of the picture that Śārṅgadeva draws for us of the human body as a 'person'. What is important for our purpose here is a glimpse into the actual mapping of the human body that the picture envisages.

Right from the moment the *jīva* enters the womb to be born a human person, it begins to be formed as an extremely complex psycho-physical entity. The properties it acquires as an embodied 'person' have been analysed into six different *bhāvas* – 'states of being': which includes a collection of such different things as organs, properties, functions, propensities and entities. These *bhāvas* are shaped by six distinct sources or causes: mother, father, *rasa, ātmā, sattva* and *sātmya.* It will be useful to have before us some idea of what they give rise to, even though this might mean covering grounds which Dr Prem Lata Sharma has already covered.

Important is the fact that each *bhāva* is in itself a complex mosaic of plural characteristics within a single entity, containing a mixed bag of elements which can separately be classed as physical or material or organic. The logic behind the mix is not easy to perceive. Let us have a look. The *bhāva*, which is said to be 'born of the mother' (*mātṛja*), contains entities which are said to share a common quality: that of 'softness' or 'delicacy' (*mṛdu*): these are mainly organic entities such as blood, fat, the navel, the heart, etc. But the heart is not only a physical organ, it is, as we shall see, also the seat of consciousness. *Bhāvas* born of the father have, on the contrary, the property of being 'hard'; they consist of veins, arteries, body-hair, beard, teeth as well as semen. Veins and arteries play a vital role in the functioning of the body, as envisaged in this scheme – or they would in any scheme – being instrumental not only in aiding organic functions, but also as carriers of the stuff of consciousness. *Rasa*, as the word suggests, stands for fluids which nourish the body and make it grow (*śarīropacaya*), but it is also responsible for a sense of satisfaction (*tṛpti*), absence of greed (*alolupatva*) and a continuing strength of resolution (*utsāha*: a word which in this context is perhaps suggestive not of a property of the will but a general sense of optimism and 'pep' arising out of sheer good health). In any case, what we have is plainly a motley of very different things carrying the single label *rasa*. *Ātmā*, as can perhaps be expected, consists of somewhat more clearly distinguishable features associated with consciousness. Like the *Nyāya ātmā* it contains pleasure, pain, desire, effort and memory (*bhāvanā*: the word being evidently used in the *Naiyāyika* sense) as well as knowledge. But this *bhāva*, too, unlike the *ātmā* accepted in *Nyāya*, is not an unmixed one. *Ātmā* is also responsible for the sense-organs – the *indriyas* – and the age to which a body survives (*āyu*). The *indriyas* meant here are both the *jñānendriyas*, the senses through which one knows: the senses of sight, hearing, touch and the like and the *karmendriyas* or the 'senses' of action, the motor organs. These are: the organs of speech, the hands, the feet, the anus and the reproductive organs. There are also two internal organs, two *antaḥkaraṇas*, associated with *ātmā* as part of it. These are *manas* and *buddhi*. Pleasure and pain are the functions of *manas*, while the functions of *buddhi* are, expectedly memory and conceiving (*vikalpa*); but, curiously with another, somewhat odd mixture of categories, also fear (*bhīti*).

Manas and *buddhi* are clearly important for our reflections here. But we are bound to ask some questions about them before we can picture their role in a process such as *nādotpatti*. How, to begin with, are they related to desire and effort? Are desire and effort included under *vikalpa*, noted as function of *buddhi*? – Śārṅgadeva makes no indication of such a sort and it is difficult to see how this could be so: *saṅkalpa* is plainly quite different from *vikalpa*. If supposing we were to think of desire and effort as in some sense 'disembodied' parts – it is indeed difficult to think of them as purely physical – even then the question of how they are related to the other *bhāvas* in order to function through them and perform voluntary activities such as singing will somehow have to be woven into the picture. Perhaps a cogent connection can be made between desire and effort and voluntary activity through the *indriyas*. This is an idea which not only seems fitting on its own but looks plausible in Śārṅgadeva's scheme. Of the *indriyas* Śārṅgadeva speaks of two contrary views. Some regarded them as physical (*bhautika*) but others considered them to be non-material or 'spiritual' (*brahmayoni*). Indeed, they do seem to share properties which are both conscious as well as material. They could be made to form a bridge between the body and more 'disembodied' entities like desire and effort. But there is nothing in Śārṅgadeva that might lead us to think that he envisaged any such connection. He does, however, speak of the heart, dscribed as a lotus-shaped physical organ, as the seat of consciousness. This, too, we shall see has possibilities which could have lead to a cogent picture of *nādotpatti* but Śārṅgadeva does not follow the lead.

Sattva is another *antaḥkaraṇa* with three different 'aspects' or 'modes of operation' which are, in this case, conceived in terms of the three Sāṃkhyān *guṇas*: *sattva, rajas* and *tamas*. These are in their distinct capacities responsible for inner properties such as faith (*āstikya*), altruistic propensities (*śukladharmāḥ*), lust, anger, sleep, laziness etc. It is difficult to see why *sattva* was needed as a distinct *bhāva* and could not be subsumed under *manas* and *buddhi*. And again we do not know where to place this *bhāva* as a 'part' of the body and relate its functioning with the body as a whole. A doctor would have to ask this question if he were to administer to the body in order to treat a malaise relating to this *bhāva*. Or is it simply a theoretical notion unrelated to the functioning of the body and included merely for the sake of completing the picture of 'man'. In which case why call it a *bhāva* if it is not really related to the other *bhāvas* in any interconnected and organically meaningful sense?

Sātmya is an even stranger entity. It cannot be said to be an organ. But neither is it described as another *antaḥkaraṇa*, though perhaps it could have been classed as such since it is certainly not a material thing. It is said to be the source of good health, clarity in the functioning of the *indriyas* and absence of laziness. It is difficult to see why its functions could not be included under *sattva* or another *bhāva*.

The body, being made up of the five *mahābhūtas*, imbibes properties from them, too. These again are a mixed bag. *Ākāśa* imparts to it sound, the power of hearing (*śrotra*), hollowness (*suṣiratā*), and interestingly, a distinct identity in space (*vaiviktya*). But it also imparts a conscious property: subtlety of understanding. *Agni* is responsible for the eyes, form and colour, the quality of 'ripeness' or 'maturity', the state of being 'cooked' (*pāka*); it is not clear whether the *pāka* spoken of here is a quality of organic entities or also of entities such as *manas* and *buddhi*. *Agni* also causes bile as well as the property of making manifest (*prakāśatā*) – a property which is patently a property of consciousness – as well as heat, sharpness and energy. It is also the source of other inner qualities: bravery, anger and intelligence. *Vāyu* or wind is responsible for the awareness of touch and the *karmendriya* of touch. Besides, it is also responsible for the various movements of the body. Ten modifications of *vāyu* (*vāyuvikṛtayaḥ*) reside within the human frame and are responsible for various bodily movements and functions. These are the well-known *prāṇa*, *apāna, samāna, udāna* and *vyāna*, which are the five major *vāyus*. There are five others with a more minor role. The ten *vāyus* help in carrying out various functions with and within the body, functions both voluntary and involuntary. *Apāna*, for example, expels urine and excreta. *Vyāna* is stationed at the eyes, the ears, the nose as well as the ankles and the waist. Its role is not quite clear from Śārṅgadeva's account. Perhaps it helps other *vāyus* in carrying out functions such as smelling, hearing, batting of the eyes (for which one of the five minor *vāyus* is said to be responsible), functions which, like the function of the *indriyas* have in some sense both the aspects of being intentional and unintentional. But its functions in the ankles and the waist, whatever they are, are in no way within our control. *Samāna* performs functions which are purely organic and involuntary. Moving all over the body through *nāḍīs* or arteries numbering 72000, it distributes all over the body the juices resulting from food and drink.

The chief of the *vāyus* is *prāṇa*. From its station below the navel, it moves to the navel, the nose and the heart. It is responsible for breathing in and out, coughing and emitting sound.

A question to my mind arises as to why the *mahābhūtas* were needed in addition to the six *bhāvas* which together presumably form a complete picture. How are *mahābhūtas* related to the *bhāvas*? They might be said to constitute the purely material elements which make up the body. But then we have seen that they are not quite material in nature, being as complex as the *bhāvas*. This makes it even more difficult to understand why they could not have been included in the *bhāvas*.

And yet despite questions that might arise, the *piṇḍotpatti* presents us with a fascinating picture which is not merely conceptual in content but clearly takes detailed observations into account. We cannot but be impressed by it and its complexities which display the object needing a doctor's attention as not only a body but also a soul. But, to come back to our present purpose, how is *piṇḍotpatti* relevantly tied up with the process of *nādotpatti*. Śārṅgadeva himself does not try to do this. For him it is only a *general* picture of the structure of the body as a whole. For the more specific processes of *nādotpatti* and *svarotpatti* he paints a separate picture. One would have expected him to have shown how these specific processes are related to the general structure of the body as a whole but Śārṅgadeva does not make such a connection. This is puzzling, since it is not difficult to see that he could have done this with slight additions and modifications in the structure of the body as understood in the *piṇḍotpatti* picture. We have spoken earlier of a possible move he could have made. There was, as far as one can see, another potent possibility in the notion of the heart. The heart is plainly described as both an organ as well as the seat of consciousness. It is further described as forming the centre of important arteries (*mūlaśirā*) which are carriers of force or energy (*ojas*). Many of these arteries are indeed channels of communication between the heart and various organs being responsible for functions such as smelling. Two of these, connected to the tongue, are said to have a role in the act of speech. There are also other arteries, called *dhamanīs*, which emanate from the navel as the centre, like spokes from the nave of a wheel. Some of these are connected to the heart from where they move into different directions creating channels through which awareness of sound, form and colour, taste and smell are conveyed. Two such arteries are responsible for the making of sound and speech (*bhāṣaṇa*, *ghoṣa*).

The picture obviously has elements which could have been suitably moulded to construct a model for explaining the process of *nādotpatti*, if not *svarotpatti*, which would have needed further modifications in the picture to accommodate an organ that could produce different tones – such as an artery with appropriately placed holes which could function like a flute. Why did Śārṅgadeva not do so? As we said earlier, Śārṅgadeva is not articulate on this point. For him the picture of *piṇḍotpatti* seems to form a kind of larger basis which can serve as the ground for understanding the more specific process of *nādotpatti* and *svarotpatti*. But he makes no effort actually to tie up the picture presented in *piṇḍotpatti* with *nādotpatti* and *svarotpatti* in any significant manner.

What held him back? What kept him from remodelling the *piṇḍotpatti* picture in order to envisage *nādotpatti* and *svarotpatti* within it or at least tying it up in a relevant sense with it, since without this, *piṇḍotpatti*, fascinating as the picture it presents is, yet remains an attractive but only loosely attached appendage to the rest of the text, constituting a major *doṣa* in the *śāstra*. Śārṅgadeva is silent. But, perhaps, we can speculate concerning his possible reasons.

There are, I think two major reasons why Śārṅgadeva did not tamper with the *piṇḍotpatti* picture in order to modify it any way. One seems to be the fact that he considered the picture as complete and fixed and so unchangeable in principle. No doubt, to begin with, the science of medicine had strong elements of an empirical science, needing observation and critical examination (*parīkṣā*) by its practitioners. It also, evidently, allowed for a plurality in its interpretations of the human body as a person. The two pictures we have concerning this matter from Caraka and Suśruta, both ancient and foundational authors, are divergent in important ways: The Caraka picture is more *Nyāya*-like while the Suśruta picture leans much more obviously and significantly on *Sāṃkhya*. The two distinct views regarding *indriyas*, which Śārṅgadeva speaks of, one believing them to be material and the other putting them in the category of the conscious also points at an important difference in Caraka and Suśruta. Suśruta calls them *bhautika* while Caraka takes them as distinctive of beings that are *cetana* – living and conscious.[4] Yet despite disagreements between them, and their acceptance of theoretical plurality in practice, Caraka and Suśruta agree in considering their science as revelatory and unchangeable. Changes and new insights were no doubt incorporated within the *śāstra* during its long history, but, paradoxically, the myth of unchangeability was carefully maintained. Significant intellectual opinion in the days of Śārṅgadeva seems to have regarded Āyurveda as no less than a revelation, considering it a transcendental and not an empirical science. This may be confirmed from the strongly expressed views of the famous and influential philosopher, Vācaspati Miśra (9th century, Śārṅgadeva wrote in the 13th). The Śāstra of Āyurveda, says Vācaspati, like the Vedic *mantra* is authored by God himself; its truth is evident from the success of its operation, but it is not a *śāstra* that could be conceived as being created by the exercise of merely human observation or reason; neither is it a *śāstra*, which can be thought of as the result of a growth of knowledge in a śāstric tradition where subsequent works build up on what had preceded.[5] By Śārṅgadeva's time the science, then, seems to have acquired a kind of sacrosanct nature, resisting modification. In this it was different from *Saṅgīta-śāstra* which allowed for changes both in theory and practice – *lakṣa* and *lakṣaṇa*. The category of the *deśī* as opposed to the 'given' and 'fixed' *mārgī* is one evidence of it: new musical forms could be freely created. And that such a development actually took place can be seen from the long list of *adhunāprasiddha rāgas* – 'modern' as opposed to 'traditional' forms – that Śārṅgadeva notes and describes. Kallinātha, commenting on Śārṅgadeva not much after him, explicitly states that a description of these *rāgas* required basic changes in the theoretical structure of the *śāstra* – its *lakṣaṇas* – in order to mesh with the new material – the changing *lakṣya*.[6]

The second reason why Śārṅgadeva did not remodel the given picture he had for his purposes seems to be connected with the purpose behind the picture. The body in the Āyurveda model, however conscious and incorporating volition as an important element in it was yet seen as an object to be acted upon, a network of causally linked entities that could be administered to and were thus passive. It was not a model designed to reveal the workings of human agency and the role played by the body in it.

The second picture he gives us is also included in the *piṇḍotpatti* chapter. It does seem to be drawn with the role of an agent in view, but the agency it has in mind is a kind of *yogic*, 'spiritual' agency and not the ordinary volition used in acts such as singing. The picture is a *kuṇḍalinī* map of the body, a map familiar enough from popular writings on *yoga*. The body is believed to have a number of 'centres' – *cakras* – through which the yogic energy called *kuṇḍalinī* passes on its path to the highest centre at the apex of the head where immortality resides. The home of the *kuṇḍalinī* is at the base of the spinal column in the lower-most *cakra*. Awakened through *yoga*, the *kuṇḍalinī* begins to flow upwards through a *nāḍī* called *suṣumnā*, which is one of a vast network of *nāḍīs*. As it reaches a new, higher *cakra*, pictured as a lotus with a certain number of petals, it can avail itself of the 'fruits' of that *cakra*, which lie as 'powers' on the petals of the *cakras*. The sixteen-petalled *cakra* at the throat is the home of Sarasvatī, where the music of the *sāma* resides. The seven *svaras*, the musical tones also reside there. One who can move his *kuṇḍalinī* to that *cakra* can be a musician, as Śārṅgadeva says.[7] If the *kuṇḍalinī* can be made to reach up to the highest *cakra*, then one can, as is to be expected, achieve a very superior proficiency in music.[8]

Clearly this picture focuses the role of the agent. But the agent here is a spiritual *sādhaka*, not a musician. The picture is not designed to explain the ordinary, everyday act of singing. And so, Śārṅgadeva gives us a third picture, moving now to a new chapter for the purpose. This is the final picture he gives us, the one he seems to silently favour and after which he moves on to other things. This picture, where the body is envisioned as an instrument, does have elements, in Śārṅgadeva's description, which seem to tie it to the *kuṇḍalinī* picture also but the cementing is done half-heartedly and does not really succeed. The description begins with a well-known *śloka* which is worth a look. Let me quote:

> *ātmā vivakṣamāṇo'yaṃ manaḥ prerayate manaḥ* |
> *dehasthaṃ vahnimāhanti sa prerayati mārutam* ||
> *Saṅgīta-Ratnākara*, 1.3.3.
>
> The *ātmā* desirous of saying something impels the *manas* which in turn strikes at the fire contained in the body. The fire then propels the air.

We notice that Śārṅgadeva says: *ātmā vivakṣamāṇo'yam* – "The soul desirous of saying something . . ." when he should – and easily could – have said, *ātmā jigāsamāno'yam*: "The soul desirous of singing . . .".[9] The reason for Śārṅgadeva's not quite appropriate phrase is not difficult to see. He has borrowed it from an older theorist who had used it in describing a process for the production of speech, rather than song. The *Pāṇinīya Śikṣā* begins its description of the process of how speech arises in the body with the words:

> *ātmā buddhyā sametyārthānmano yuṅkte vivakṣayā* |
> *manaḥ kāyāgnimāhanti sa prerayati mārutam* ||
> *Pāṇinīya Śikṣā*, 6
>
> Wishing to speak, the *ātmā* gets together with meanings through the *buddhi* and harnesses the *manas* for the purpose. The *manas* strikes the fire in the body which in turn propels the air.

Here obviously lies the source of Śārṅgadeva's own *śloka*. The date of the *Śikṣā* is not certain but it is certainly many centuries older than Śārṅgadeva. It was an important text for any one who learnt Sanskrit grammar and every educated person had to do so. Or, perhaps, Śārṅgadeva had before him another text parallel to this *Śikṣā*, since the doctrine it espouses was ancient knowledge born in the traditions of Vedic learning and the transmission of the spoken Vedic vocables. We also find a step missing in Śarṅgadeva's account. *Buddhi* has no role there. The reason is apparent. The function of *buddhi* in the *Śikṣā* account is to pick out the right words for what the *ātmā* wants to say. But singing is not speaking and so this function is not needed. But then what replaces *buddhi*? Or does *ātmā* pick out the tones directly without a go-between which it needs for *vivakṣā*? But if so the *ātmā*, in this conception must be significantly different from that of the *Śikṣā* picture. Where lies the difference? Śārṅgadeva provides no answers. He did not reflect on the matter. And yet, a borrower as he was, Śārṅgadeva could not help retaining the word *vivakṣā*.

There are also other modifications in Śārṅgadeva as we can see in the details of the process of *svara*-production as he describes it. These are, however, modifications not made by him – he seems to have been too tradition-bound in this matter for that – but accepted by him from older *Saṅgīta-śāstras*.

The *Śikṣā* account of the process of speech production describes it in some detail. Low and high pitches arise as the fire-heated air moves to different regions of the human frame, the chest, the throat and the head. Different syllables are produced in the cavity of the mouth on the basis of *svara* (pitch), *kāla* (time taken in utterance), *sthāna* (chest, throat and head where different registers of a gradually higher pitch are produced) and *prayatna* (the nature of the effort). Further details of these categories and the distinct roles in the production of different syllables are also noted with care by the *Śikṣā*; but we need not enter into these. It is an impressive account based on careful observation.

Śārṅgadeva's account of *svara*-production somewhat parallels this account, though its basis is imagination rather than observation. He speaks of a harp-like *vīṇā* placed within the human frame. This was an old idea. The ancients called this *vīṇā* the *śārīra-vīṇā*, the 'body-harp', to distinguish it from the normal harp made of wood. It was the body-harp which was said to produce the musical tones in singing. The body-harp account of the production of tones shares the concept of *sthāna* with the *Śikṣā*. As in the *Śikṣā* scheme, different *sthānas* produce different octaves. The *Śikṣā* scheme also spoke of the seven *svaras*, but *svaras* there are only meant as general areas of pitches used in producing the different Vedic accents (*Pāṇinīya Śikṣā*, 12). They are not distinct tones for musical rather than verbal expressions. In singing these distinct tones are produced by different 'strings' of the body-harp. These 'strings' are *nāḍīs* stretched across the various *sthānas* with a gradually decreasing length so that the higher the position of the *nāḍī*, the higher its pitch. Each *sthāna* has twenty-two such *nāḍīs* which account for not only the seven *svaras* but also the *śrutis*, the shades of minute tonal distinctions that are audible to the human ear and can enter musical expression. The heated air as it moves over these strings causes them to sound.

This was a picture which Śārṅgadeva had inherited from older musicologists. He intended, apparently, to place it in the larger theoretical perspective of the two other pictures that he draws for us. But the connection, as we can see, between the harp picture and *piṇḍotpatti* cannot be established in any meaningful sense and any connection that we might think of – such as in the notion of the *nāḍī* – remains, to say the least, very shadowy. The body-harp can hardly be said to fit as a part of the larger *piṇḍotpatti* picture. Neither does Śārṅgadeva attempt to connect the two.

He does, however, attempt to connect the harp picture with the *yogic* mapping of the *kuṇḍalinī*. He speaks of five *sthānas* including two others besides the three already mentioned. These two extra *sthānas*, his own additions, produce sounds which are *atisūkṣma* – very subtle – and *sūkṣma* – subtle – and are connected with the *brahma-granthi* and the *nābhi*, two yogic centres. But these subtle sounds, Śārṅgadeva adds, lie outside the range of musical sounds: they are not related to the *vyavahāra* – the actual practice – of the art. They are not accorded *nāḍīs* of any kind which could manifest them. Their role lies purely in the realm of theory. The idea seems to be to connect the musical sounds needed in *vyavahāra*, the so-called *āhata* or 'struck' sounds which we can actually hear and produce for the ordinary purposes of speaking and singing with the transcendental – *pāramārthika* – *anāhata* or 'unstruck' sound of the *yogīs*. *Anāhata nāda* forms part of the *kuṇḍalinī* picture.[10] The two extra *sthānas* where Śārṅgadeva locates his subtle sounds were obviously suggested to him by the *kuṇḍalinī* map. Śārṅgadeva himself tells us that the *anāhata* sound is of no real use to him as a musicologist. He says, since it is devoid of all 'colour' and cannot please men, therefore, I shall speak only of *āhata* sounds, which when produced in the form of the *śrutis* produce song.[11] Yet he did feel obliged somehow to create a cogent joint between the harp picture and the *kuṇḍalinī* and did not mind bending it to his own ends. One wonders what made him feel freer with the *kuṇḍalinī* picture than with the *Āyurveda* one.

The notions of *sūkṣma* and *atisūkṣma* are for Śārṅgadeva stages that connect the *anāhata* with the audible *āhata* sounds. These notions are however empty of any real content in his scheme. The bridge he builds between the yogic and the musical picture of sound production has no real descriptive function and is not spoken of later in his *śāstra*.

Another thing before I close. The concept of the body-harp, interesting as it is, is yet somewhat incomplete in comparison with the *Śikṣā* picture of the production of speech. The *Śikṣā* picture goes into the details of how every distinct syllable is produced, noting the exact placement of the tongue in the cavity of the mouth and the kind of distinct effort required. In the harp picture different tones are produced when the air arising from the navel strikes different *nāḍīs*. But where is the means by which it is ensured that a particular chosen string is struck when required and not just any of them? Where, in other words are the 'fingers' evidently needed to play upon this harp?

Notes

1. See her paper entitled, "The treatment of Mahābhūtas in Saṅgīta-Śāstra: With Special Reference to Yoga and Āyurveda".
2. *Saṅgīta-Ratnākara* of Śārṅgadeva, Text and English Translation, Vol.1 by R.K. Shriṅgy and Prem Lata Sharma, Munshiram Manoharlal Publishers Pvt. Ltd., New Delhi.
3. *Saṅgīta-Ratnākara*, 1.2.118: *iti pratyaṅgasaṅkṣepo vistarastviha tattvataḥ* | *asmadviracite'dhyātmaviveke vīkṣyataṃ budhaiḥ* ||
   The book is not available if we are to believe the New Catalogus Catalogorum, which only refers to the work without the reporting of any manuscript of it.
4. *Suśruta, Śārīrasthāna*, 1.10: *bhautikāni cendriyāṇyāyurvede varṇyante tathendriyārthāḥ. Caraka, Sūtrasthāna*, 1.48: *sendriyaṃ cetanasthānaṃ nirindriyam acetanam.*
5. See Vācaspati's *ṭīkā* on the Vyāsa-bhāṣya on Patañjali's *Yoga-Sūtra, samādhi-pāda, sūtra* 24. Vyāsa says that the *yoga* as a *śāstra* was composed by a transcendental supreme being (*prakṛṣṭa sattva*). Commenting, Vācaspati adds the *śāstra* of *Āyurveda* to the list of such divinely-composed *śāstras* with the words: *ayamabhisandhiḥ: mantrāyurvedeṣu tāvadīśvarapraṇīteṣu pravṛttisāmarthyādarthāvyabhicāraviniścayātprāmāṇyaṃ siddham* | *na cauṣadhibhedānāṃ tatsaṃyogaviśeṣāṇāṃ ca mantrāṇāṃ ca tattadvarṇāva-poddhāreṇa sahasreṇāpi puruṣāyuṣairlaukikapramāṇavyavahārī śaktaḥ kartum-anvayavyatirekau* | *na cāgamādanvayavyatirekau tābhyāṃ cāgamastatsantāna-yoranāditvāditi pratipādayituṃ yuktam* ||
6. *Saṅgīta-Ratnākara*, 2.2.161–194. Note Kallinātha: *idānīmadhunāprasiddha-rāgāṅgādīnāṃ lakṣye pratītānāṃ lakṣaṇavirodhānāṃ virodhaparihārārtham-udyamaḥ kriyate.*
   He proceeds to give us a formidable list of *virodhas.*
7. *Saṅgīta-Ratnākara*, 1.2.141: *Viśuddheraṣṭamādīni dalānyaṣṭau śritāni tu* | *dadyurgītādisaṃsiddhim* . . . . ||
8. *Ibid.*, 1.2.143: *brahmarandhrasthito jīvaḥ sudhayā sampluto yadā* | *tuṣṭo gītādikāryāṇi saprakarṣāṇi kārayet* ||

9. An interesting discussion had taken place on this expression and scholars wondered if Sanskrit has an independent word for, 'the desire to sing'. I am thankful to Dr Prem Lata Sharma for drawing my attention to the word *jigāsa* which, she points, has been used by Abhinavagupta.

10. *Saṅgīta-Ratnākara*, 1.2.162–165.

11. *Ibid.*, 1.2.166–167.

9

Lines of Fire, Lines of Water The Elements in Śilpaśāstra

Bettina Bäumer

In more than one culture the artistic creation is likened to the creation of the universe, and the artist to the creator. This is all the more true in the context of sacred art, where the artist becomes an instrument of the cosmic creator and is identified with him (Viśvakarman, Prajāpati, etc.).[1] But the physical and metaphysical creation, which is the prerogative of the creator, is in this "transformation of nature in art"[2] transferred to a symbolical creation, where all the elements are present. The question is, how does this symbolical transference and identification happen, what are its means and what is the expression and end-product of such a process?

A symbol always partakes in the nature of the symbolized, without exhausting it. But the symbol has its own power, derived from the symbolized, and it acquires an inherent quality which remains valid and effective even outside its original context. Unlike a conventional sign, a symbol has a certain universality.

This is all the more true in the case of the fundamental elements constituting the universe, which have a universal importance in all spheres of life and creativity, whether acknowledged or unconsciously assumed. It is clear that no artistic creation can take place without the involvement of the five fundamental elements, in one way or another. These are some basic assumptions which underly the texts dealing with the creation of the temple and of images, the *Śilpaśāstras*. Many of these assumptions are so much understood by the living tradition in which these texts have grown, that more often than not they did not even find it necessary to express or explain these ideas. The cosmogony and cosmology of the *Vedas, Purāṇas* and *Āgamas* formed the general background and fertile soil on which the arts could grow.

This is the reason why the *Śilpa* texts, when they speak of these connections, are extremely brief. They could rely on the living cosmology. This is no longer true today, when the intellectual and artistic activities have been alienated, if not divorced, from a cosmology which has supported the life and thought of traditional people.

Some of the *Śilpaśāstras* dealing with temple-architecture and image-making, dating from different periods and different regions of India, have thrown some light on the symbolic relationship between the cosmic elements and the creation of art. Though sometimes extremely brief, these texts contain important hints which can be developed and applied. Historical and stylistic questions do not have much importance in the context of our present inquiry. But generally the texts referred to date at least from the ninth century up to the early seventeenth century. This range only indicates a time-span, which could be extended in both directions, as long as a certain traditional cosmology was valid and accepted. Instead of following a historical sequence, we will follow a thematic and symbolical development, starting from simple geometrical components and ending with the temple-structure.

1. The first and simplest element given to the artist – he may be a painter, sculptor or architect – is the line. It is only from the point and the line that two-dimensional and three-dimensional forms can be created. So far I have only found one *Śilpa* text which is astonishingly conscious of the importance and symbolism of the line (*rekhā*), that is the *Vāstusūtra Upaniṣad* (*VSU*).[3] The artist is called the one "who has the knowledge of circle and line". (*Sūtra*, I.4)

What is developed here is a complex and yet clear symbolism of the fundamental lines constituting a diagram (*pañjara*) which serves as a compositional framework for an image or panel. The line is here called "the support of the composition (*rekhānyāsasyādhāraḥ*), it is like a flow. It corresponds to the elements (*adhibhūta*) and to the divinities (*adhidaiva*)." (I.8) The first line to be drawn on the stone surface is a circle which represents the universe (*viśva*) and fullness (*pūrṇa*, II.6–7), and whose centre point (*bindu* or *marman*) is its life-breath and firm support. Then the artists "divide the circle by the line, just as the creators by their action divide the world." (II.9) Creation has to do with differentiation, otherwise it remains an unordered chaos (*salila* in the *Veda*), and the lines serve to differentiate the undivided totality. But they are not neutral geometrical entities, they have a symbolical value expressing their dynamic nature.

Straight lines are like rays of light (*tejas*, II.9), moving in all directions. Again, each direction has its own inherent quality, which is identified with one of the elements, according to their quality. The reason is as the text says: "As in the creation of the world arise the five great elements, similarly with the circle as support the artists conceive and dispose the features of beings and elements (on the panel)." (II.10)

The two central lines are the vertical, called *agnirekhā*, fire-line, and the horizontal, called *aprekhā*, water-line. The nature of fire consists in rising upward vertically, and the nature water in creating a horizontal surface, or flowing as in a great river. (II.21) The diagonal lines have the nature of wind, expressing movement and dynamism, and even aggressiveness.[4] The element earth is represented by a square or rhombus (*karṇikakṣetra*) inscribed inside the circle symbolizing the universe. The element *ākāśa* is obviously invisible and all-pervading, and hence not represented by a particular line or form. It is rather within *ākāśa* that all these forms emerge.

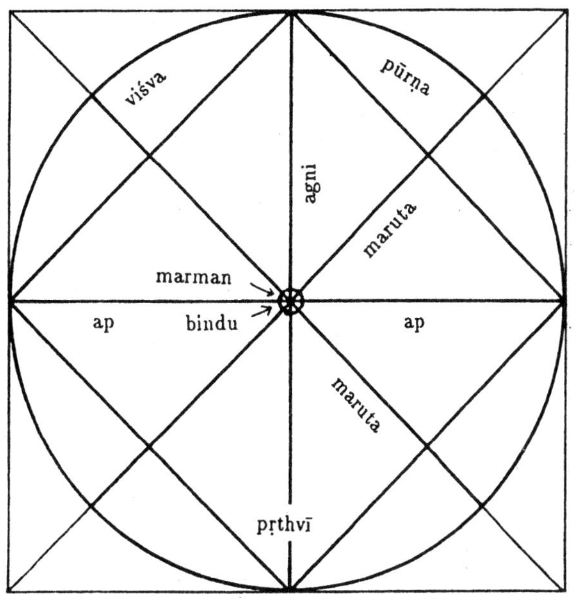

As in the cosmic creation, the elements are not isolated, but are in constant interaction. The *Vāstusūtra Upaniṣad* in its laconic way describes two of these interactions: One is the contact of water and wind, represented by the horizontal and diagonal lines: "As from the contact of water and wind, foam arises, again in the foam bubbles arise, thus when the square is joined with the diagonals that relief-field becomes active." (II.12) The diagonal line without contrast to the horizontal does not manifest its dynamism, just as wind alone remains invisible, unless it comes in touch with another element, such as water, creating waves etc., and of course fire (not mentioned in the text), making the flame move in other directions than its natural uprising verticality. The basis for it all is the earth – the rhombus which is divided into four continents by the cross of the central vertical and horizontal.

The two most opposite and mutually exclusive elements are fire and water, whose complementarity has played an important role in Vedic cosmology and ritual, and in Āgamic-Tāntric ritual and *Yoga* (in the form of the pair *agni-soma*). We cannot enter here into this rich symbolism which could almost serve as a *leitmotif* for the continuity of Vedic and Āgamic cosmology and spirituality. The dynamism of creation is only possible when these two elements meet, and the integration of *Yoga* equally.

Not only the vertical and horizontal lines represent fire and water, but also their geometrical extensions: the triangle with its apex above is fire, the triangle with apex below is water. The combination and intimate union of both is the hexagram, an essential element of all *maṇḍalas* and *yantras.*

> When both (the fire and water-triangle) are conjoined arises the state of union. Those who realize this become perfected. This is the state of awakening. By the joining of Fire and Water (man) becomes divine, which the priests know as Supreme Delight (*maha-cchandas, chandas* also meaning metre). (II.16)

In the words of Alice Boner: "On the cosmic plane Fire and Water stand at opposite ends. They are eternally conflicting, irreconcilable mutually destructive elements. And yet it is precisely the union of these opposites which makes man transcend the limitations of earthly life."[5]

To complete the whole symbolism of the fundamental diagram (see figure), the central point (*bindu* or *marman*) is called "the life-breath of the earth" (*rasāyāḥ prāṇaḥ*, II.14). As in the symbolism of the lines identified with the elements, this also indicates that the diagram, and of course the image which is carved on its basis, is enlivened from within, that it is not dead matter but a living entity. As the cosmos consisting of a combination of the five elements is enlivened by the breath-of-life (*prāṇa*), so is the image-panel which represents the divine beings. It is thus clear that there is a correspondence and symbolical parallelism between cosmos and image, as well as cosmos and abstract diagram.

The *Vāstusūtra Upaniṣad* then relates the qualities gained from the elemental lines to the mood or expression (*bhāva*) of the represented image. The text is too short here to be fully developed, but the basic ideas can be used in the interpretation of images. The general result of the combination of these lines with the images is this: "By a harmonious form a meditative mood is induced." (*Sūtra*, II.22) To give only two straight-forward examples: The image of Viṣṇu Śeṣaśāyī is based on the horizontal water-line, and it represents the world-ocean with the serpent Ananta in ondulating forms, and Viṣṇu reclining on Ananta. The whole stress on horizontality gives an impression of the watery element with a movement like the one described as the waves created by the contact with wind.

On the other hand, any image of Viṣṇu Trivikrama or of another deity engaged in a fight against demons, has a stress on the diagonals and contains the whole energetic dynamism of the wind-element.[6] We need not elaborate this application here, but it is necessary to mention it, to show the connection between cosmic elements and their symbolism, abstract lines and two-dimensional forms, and the image or panel. One *Sūtra* sums up the relationship between the lines and image:

> When the limbs in the panel adhere to the lines they become harmonious.
> Comm.: On vertical lines erect limbs, on horizontal lines restful and quiet limbs, on diagonal lines limbs showing movement. Setting them in this way the images attract the mind. (IV.28)

In the context of the parts of the composition of a panel, the *Vāstusūtra Upaniṣad* again goes back to the creation:

> All these gods and the five great elements earth, wind, ether, water and fire have been created by Prajāpati. According to the knowledge of these elements the respective qualities of the forms embodying the sentiment (*bhāvarūpa*) are shown. (VI.21)

The attendant divinities or *Śaktis* have the nature of the elements, like Varuṇa's flowing *Śakti* represents Water, Viṣṇu's *Śakti* of enduring is the earth, etc. "Sacrificial, cosmic and human elements have to be combined in order to achieve the object of sacred art: bringing man in harmony with the cosmos and with the gods and thus making him attain his goal, which is ultimately *mokṣa*, liberation."[7]

The cosmic elements, though not all the five *mahābhūtas*, also play a role in the making of a standing image, where parts of its body are equated with certain elements. Here the feet are called the "earth-part" (*pārthivāṅga*, IV.19) and the divinity governing the same part in the *Yūpa* is *bhūmidevatā*, obviously because it is this part by which the *Yūpa* and the image are firmly established on the earth (cf. IV.13). The top-part or head is assigned to Savitṛ, and it is called the light-part (*jyotiraṅga*, IV.14). This description appears to be simple, but it contains the whole symbolism expressed in *Sūtra*, IV.17: "The Puruṣa (Man) is like the pillar (of the universe)." The upright form of the *Yūpa*, of the standing man and of the erect figure connects, so to say, earth and heaven, heaviness and solidity with light and open space (*ākāśa* as the sphere of light).

2. Besides the process of image-making with its constitutive lines and diagrams, it is the temple itself which is identified with the cosmos. Like the

Ṛgvedic *Puruṣa*, the temple is the cosmos with all its elements and it also transcends it.[8] M.A. Dhaky, in his article "Prāsāda as Cosmos", quotes two texts, one from the *Agni Purāṇa*, and the other from the *Vāstuśāstra* of Viśvakarman. Both texts assign different parts of the temple to various deities and cosmic elements, in a ritual context. The *Agni Purāṇa* conceives the whole temple which is pervaded by Śiva to consist of all the *tattvas*, and considering it as a microcosm (*brahmāṇḍakam*, V.20), it places the five elements in the wall-portion, "acting as they do as the latter's physical wrappings."[9] Here only the general conception is visible but not a detailed identification of elements of the temple with elements of the cosmos.

In the case of the *Vāstuśāstra* of Viśvakarman, the most obvious identification is the placement of the earth-element in the *khuraka* (the lowest moulding of the *vedibandha*). The next moulding is *kumbhaka* and it is made to be pervaded by *sṛṣṭi* here, it must be connected with the water-element, because of the very shape of *kumbhaka*, a water-pot. Leaving aside other parts which are connected with various deities, the text says: "Let Mountains descend in the pillars and the Sky pervade the *karoṭaka* (i.e., the central ceiling of the *maṇḍapa* hall)."[10] Dhaky comments on this: "The wish to make Meru descend in the wall's *jaṅghā* and again for Mountains to dwell in the hall-columns is prompted for lending firmness to the wall for bearing the enormous weight of the superincumbent *śikhara* spire in the first case and of the pyramidal roof in the second. Since the *vitāna* (ceiling), as one beholds it from within the hall, is the metaphorical sky of the hall, the Sky (*ākāśa*) is bidden to pervade the ceiling." (*art. cit.*, p. 218–19). We find thus the two ends of the five *mahābhūtas* in their logical position, *pṛthivī* at the base and *ākāśa* as the inner space of the vault representing the vault of the sky.

I have quoted this material presented by Prof. Dhaky in order to show how the same general conception of the temple as cosmos is pervasive in space and time: from western to eastern India, and through a span of six or seven centuries.

An unpublished *Śilpa* text from Orissa, the *Śilparatnakośa* (which is dated 1620 A.D.), gives a more complete symbolical identification of elements of the cosmos with elements of the temple.[11]

First of all the ascending order of the temple follows the three *guṇas: tamas* is related with the heaviness of the earth-part below, *rajas* with its multiplicity of forms and figures in the middle, and *sattva* which is light and lightness at the top (cf. V.7). The base-mouldings of Orissan temples consist of five mouldings and they are hence called *pañcakarma*. In the identification of the temple with the *puruṣa* or human form, these are compared to the five toes of the foot.

In the cosmic conception of the temple *pañcakarma* is identified with the five elements.

> 84. The *khura* (i.e., the hoof-shaped lowest part of the base) is the great earth, according to the element earth *tattva.*
>
> As the world is created from the five elements, thus the temple is conceived.
>
> 85. Above that is the part of the *kumbha*, of equal height of the *khura.* The *kumbha* represents the element water, and it always bestows auspiciousness.

These two parts correspond to the description in the *Vāstuśāstra* of Viśvakarman. The third part of the *pañcakarma* is a band, *paṭṭa*, which is equated with the fire element. (V.92) There is no symbolical similarity between the two, but the simple development of the sequence of elements. The fourth moulding is a sharp edge, "*kaṇi*, which should be shown as if blown by the wind (*vāyu*)". (V.94) As we have seen in the symbolism of the lines of the *pañjara*, the only way of showing the dynamism of wind in a static form or structure is the use of the oblique line. The *kaṇi* is formed by two oblique lines and it projects out, this is the only symbolic connection with the wind element.

Obviously the top-most part of the *pañcakarma*, the decorated *vasanta paṭṭa*, is the symbol of the element *ākāśa.* (V.101) Here again there is not much of a symbolical similarity between *vasanta* and *ākāśa*, except that it is the highest of the five elements. The point of similarity lies in the total conception: As the five elements form the basis of creation, so the *pañcakarma* is the base of the temple. The proliferation of vegetal forms above the *pañcakarma*, on the wall-part, is explained keeping this conception in mind:

> 111–112. Many types of creepers should be made on the *latājāṅgha.*
> Just as in the beginning trees (and plants) were created out of the five elements,
> thus on the *śikhara jāṅgha* creepers and trees are pleasing.

The symbolism is clear: Out of the primordial simplicity of the five elements the forms of nature and the rich superstructure of the *śikhara* grow. Without the basis of the five elements neither natural nor artistic growth would be possible, nor spiritual fulfilment which is the ultimate aim of image-making and temple architecture.

Even the few hints given by the *Śilpaśāstras* are enough to reveal a whole symbolic interconnectedness between cosmos, man and the Divine.

Artistic creation, just like cosmic creation, means ordering an otherwise chaotic material. The original chaos, in India as well as in other cultures, has always been understood in terms of the undifferentiated waters. It has long been recognized that the lotus petals surrounding the plinth of temples and even houses signify the emergence of the temple from the primeval ocean, the solid and ordered structure resting on the cosmic chaos. Here many cosmogonic myths could be interpreted in relation to the creation of art by means of the elements: the myth of *samudramanthana*, and the theriomorphic *avatāras* of Viṣṇu. By way of example we may liken the artist to Varāha *Avatāra*: He dives deep in the chaotic mass of the primeval waters to resurrect *bhūmi*, the Earth described as a beautiful goddess. It is She who provides a solid ground and a structured wholeness. What is expressed in the language of myth finds a symbolical expression in the grammar of form, in the lines, geometrical shapes and in the temple structure. In every case the cosmic elements are the ground and building blocks of the creation of art.

Notes

1. Cf. Bettina Bäumer, "The Divine Artist", In: *The Indian Theosophist*, Jaideva Singh Felicitation Number; 1985, Vol. 82.
2. Cf. the book by A.K. Coomaraswamy with this title.
3. *Vāstusūtra Upaniṣad, The Essence of Form in Sacred Art*, ed. and transl. by Alice Boner, S.R. Sarma and Bettina Bäumer, Delhi (Motilal Banarsidass), 1982 (reprint 1986).
4. In the *Atharvaveda* wind or breath is said to move transversely: *prāṇena tiryaṅ prāṇati*, X.8.19.
5. Introduction to *VSU*, p. 14.
6. See Alice Boner's analyses in: *Principles of Composition in Hindu Sculpture, Cave Temple Period*, Delhi (Motilal Banarsidass) 1990.
7. A. Boner, *Introduction to VSU*, p. 12.
8. Cf. M.A. Dhaky, 'Prāsāda as Cosmos', In: *The Adyar Library Bulletin*, Vol. XXXV. Parts 3–4, 1971, pp. 211–26.
9. Dhaky, *art. cit.*, p. 220.
10. *stambheṣu parvatāḥ proktā ākāśaśca karoṭake*, V.10.
11. *Śilparatnakośa. A Glossary of Orissan Temple Architecture*, ed. and transl. by Bettina Bäumer and Rajendra Prasad Das, Delhi (IGNCA and Motilal Banarsidass), 1994.

10

The Unity and Gravity of an Elemental Architecture

Michael W. Meister

India's *Pañca-Mahābhūtas* have been given an order different from the Western system of four Elements – Earth, Air, Fire, and Water.[1] First, in India, comes Water and Earth; then Fire and Air; and finally Ether, the latter particularly important for the Indian-held sense of an eternal reality lying behind what we make or experience (Plates 10.1, 10.2).

Indian ritual begins with earth and fire. In the fire-pit or on the stone altar, all the Elements are combined, with ritual potency and for cosmic effect. The temple also roots itself in water, placing among its wall's base-mouldings (*vedibandha*) a fruiting, flowering, water-pot that represents India's water-oriented cosmogony. This fertile vase (*kalaśa*; Plate 10.5) acts both as the source and as a ritual lustration for the sacred mountain – which is the temple – acting both as the house for a divinity and as a 'crossing' intended for the transformation of mankind.

The temple, by the intention of its architects, is poised between the Elements: always placed near Water; built of and on the Earth; it is itself the home of Fire. Its tower is the embodiment of Air; and its apex – or rather the space above it – of Ether (Plate 10.4). "Let the earth reside in the [moulding's] *khuraka* hoof" says one fragment of an architectural text translated by M.A. Dhaky; and let the cosmos be distributed throughout the structure.[2]

The mouldings that support and bind the temple (both *pīṭha* and *vedibandha*) have at their root the petals of the lotus.[3] This, in India, is always the supernal support for deity, seen as the plant that spans the Earth, Water, and Air, and opens itself – that is its calix, the potent seed-pod – toward Ether and eternity (Plates 10.1, 10.4). Among these mouldings, elephant courses suggest the rain clouds hovering, like Indra's elephant, between the earth and sky (Plate 10.10). Above is the temple-mountain – Śiva's mansion – which, like the Himalayas themselves, hovers above the monsoon's water-laden clouds (Plate 10.6).

Through the centre of the temple's tower, a cosmic pillar is made to ascend, clasped by the pod of the tower itself (Plates 10.4, 10.6). Is this tower, called the 'sheath' (*veṇukośa*) of the temple, meant also as a ritual tool for clasping the Ether? Does it hold the cosmos, as if by a ritual instrument, in order to make it material?[4]

The walls of the temple are themselves a 'cage' (*pañjara*) forming a pillared enclosure giving a body to Air (Plate 10.4). The *Agni-Purāṇa* states that "the five Elements – Water, Light, Air, Sky, [and Earth]" – act "as the wrappings", in the temple's wall-frieze (*jaṅghā*), for the microcosm (*brahmāṇḍaka*) guarded within.[5]

Embodied up the corners of the curvature of the shrine and used as its crowning member, ribbed stones called *āmalakas* – the myrobalan fruit (Plates 10.7, 10.8) – ascend, supported by their own pillared *kūṭa* cages (Plates 10.4, 10.6). They grow upwards and proliferate, as if toward their final realization at the pinnacle. It is this seed – placed beyond Ether, not in Air – that may one day flower at the tower's top.

Like the flagpole bearer who carries the temple's standard upward, each worshipper is said to ascend the temple's invisible axis from materiality toward the transcendent eternal.[6] The spaces within the temple, both the flat surface of the hall and the womb-chamber of the sanctum, are meant to be the Earth-altar of human sacrifice.[7] The sky-ceiling is both the cage/body and the Air within, much like the whale-bone cathedral in Melville's *Moby Dick*.[8]

At the temple's top, flags are used to signal the wind; and the seed-*āmala* again signals space in its endless, unrealized, potential. It is, indeed, the temple as Cosmos – as Dhaky's early article had put it – the temple as Cosmic Man.[9]

Four personified figures of the *Mahābhūtas* were placed on the corners of the upper *vedi*-platform of the famous Shore temple at Mahabalipuram, near Madras, in the seventh century; but the full range of 'Elementals' – the particulate fragments or atoms of reality – are infinite in number and at times associated with Śiva's host of spirits (*pramathas*).[10]

The architects of the Śiva temple at Amrol in Central India, built early in the eighth century, have placed such *bhūta*-goblins, in part representing Elements, in corner niches on the wall (Plates 10.12, 10.14). These take the place of a familiar set of deities that act as "guardians of the Quarters", the Dikpālas.[11] One of these goblins, placed on the southeast (Plate 10.14), is radiant with Pramoda's fire and by its very location has been compared directly to the Vedic fire-deity, Agni, on the adjacent *kapilī*-wall.[12]

The architect of this temple has placed images of Agni and Īśāna on the south and north *kapilī* entry-walls, clasping the worshipper's approach (*mārga*). He has done so, perhaps to represent the purifying ritual of Fire along with the goal of transcendent Ether. Yama is shown among the goblins on the southwest corner (Plate 10.14).

The temple has, in its overall ornament, a cosmic geography. It places on its doorway both the personifications of the two most sacred rivers of India, the Gaṅgā and Yamunā, and representations of Himalayan sages (Plate 10.11). The walls of the Gupta period Śiva temple at Nachna in the fifth century were rusticated to look like the foothills of the cosmic mountain.[13] Its doorway's ornament suggests the world's cage of illusion; its sanctum, the fertile womb of the cosmos (Plate 10.9). At the doorjamb-bases, Gaṅgā and Yamunā are meant to mark an Āryan earthscape, and at the door's top are placed earth-spirits (*yakṣīs*) sheltered under flowering trees (Plates 10.9, 10.11).

If the Elements of Water, Earth, and Space can be seen as the fertile forge for the growth of actual lotus and *āmala* plants in Nature, to temple architects, the flame of temple ritual generated growth toward transformation of the worshipper that could be represented, both ornamentally and iconically, by vines and other foliage encircling the temple in their many furling coils (Plates 10.3-6, 10.9, 10.11).[14]

Figures of the eight Guardians of the Directions of Space (Dikpālas) are placed on the corners of most temples (Plate 10.13). They both measure space, as its guardians, and provide one further manifestation of the *Mahābhūtas* as they 'wrap' the wall of the temple – in the *Vāstuśāstra's* description – around the microcosm within.[15] Varuṇa appears on the West on a crocodile, associated with Water, as is the *Mahābhūta Pramukha.* Agni is placed on the South, like Pramoda, encircled by an aureole of Fire (Plate 10.14). Vāyu, the wind-god, on the North like Durmukha, carries a fluttering flag or is wrapped by a billowing scarf filled by Air (Plate 10.13). The war-god Indra, on the East (like Amoda), can be taken as an embodiment of Matter; and Śiva as Īśāna some texts associate with Ether.

We should not be too literal, however, in our attempt to 'read' monuments made within a worldview that sees in each particular, the whole and in each proliferation of a thing, everything. The basal square form of the Universe, for example, is implicit in each of the temple's increasing and encircling offsets (Plate 10.6).[16] It is God's unfolding that creates the *Bhūtas*; and they are always a part, if only one part, of God's ritual unfolding.[17] They are indeed his physical wrappings and the substances from which each of his multiple particles is made. But whether in medicine or cuisine, philosophy or architecture, these material parts are only a clothing for the microcosm. They cannot define its essence, nor more than transmute us back to its ceaseless centre.

Notes

1. In presenting this paper at the Indira Gandhi National Centre for the Arts Pañca-Mahābhūta Seminar, I preferred to call it "A Meditation on the Temple and the Elements". I later presented it also at the School of Architecture, University of California, San Diego, for a workshop on "Creating Environments: Nature, Space, and Form". There I began first by referring "to India's many village-squares, in which people often have planted a central tree and placed an earth platform below for the village's residents to gather, sheltered under its spreading branches. In such villages – with their shifting lanes and public spaces – and in the cool courtyards of her village houses is India's real universe and the source for many of her ideas about cosmic order and form."
2. M.A. Dhaky, "Prāsāda as Cosmos", In *The Adyar Library Bulletin* 35 (1971), pp. 211–26.
3. Michael W. Meister, "Maṇḍala and Practice in Nāgara Architecture in North India", In *Journal of the American Oriental Society* 99 (1979), pp. 204–19.
4. Michael W. Meister, "On the Development of a Morphology for a Symbolic Architecture: India", In *Res: Anthropology and Aesthetics* 12 (1986), pp. 33–50.
5. Dhaky, "Prāsāda as Cosmos", p. 200.
6. See Ananda K. Coomaraswamy, "*Svayamātṛṇṇā: Janua Coeli", Zalmoxis* 2 (1939), pp. 3–51.
7. Michael W. Meister, "Symbology and Architectural Practice in India", In Emily Lyle, (ed.), *Sacred Architecture in the Traditions of India, China, Judaism and Islam*, Edinburgh: Edinburgh University Press, 1992, pp. 5–24; *idem.*, "Maṇḍala and Practice".
8. Herman Melville, *Moby Dick; or, the Whale,* New York: Harper, 1851, Chapter 102, "A Bower in the Arsacides".
9. Dhaky, "Prāsāda as Cosmos." See also Stella Kramrisch, "The Temple as Puruṣa", In *Studies in Indian Temple Architecture,* ed. by Pramod Chandra, New Delhi: American Institute of Indian Studies, 1975, pp. 40–46.
10. M. A. Dhaky, "Bhūtas and Bhūtanāyakas: Elementals and Their Captains", In *Discourses on Śiva, Proceedings of a Symposium on the Nature of Religious Imagery*, ed. by Michael W. Meister, Philadelphia: University of Pennsylvania Press, 1984, pp. 240–56. Some scholars, however, have questioned such an interrelationship between Vedic and Purāṇic figures.
11. Michael W. Meister, "Āma, Amrol, and Jainism in Gwalior Fort", In *Journal of the Oriental Institute*, Baroda, 22 (1972), pp. 354–58; *Encyclopaedia of Indian Temple Architecture*, Vol. I, Part 2, *North India: Period of Early Maturity*, ed. by Michael W. Meister and M.A. Dhaky, Delhi: Oxford University Press, 1991, pp. 12–15. Of the normal set of Dikpālas, only Yama appears on

the west corner of the south wall with Agni and Īśāna placed on the *kapilī* walls flanking the doorway.

12. *Encyclopaedia of Indian Temple Architecture,* II.2, Plate 11.
13. Joanna G. Williams, *The Art of Gupta India: Empire and Province*, Princeton: Princeton University Press, 1983; *Encyclopaedia of Indian Temple Architecture*, Vol. II, Part 1, *Foundations of North Indian Style*, ed. by Michael W. Meister, M.A. Dhaky, and Krishna Deva, Delhi: Oxford University Press, 1988, pp. 39–40 & Plates 52–59.
14. For garden-*paṇḍāls* grown over with foliage as ornament see Michael W. Meister, "Construction and Conception: *Maṇḍapikā* Shrines of Central India", In *East and West*, New series 26 (1976), pp. 409–18.
15. Dhaky, "Prāsāda as Cosmos".
16. Michael W. Meister, "Reading Monuments and Seeing Texts", In *Śāstric Traditions in Indian Arts,* ed. by Anna Libera Dallapiccola, Stuttgart: Franz Steiner Verlag, 1989, 2 Vols., I. pp. 167–73, II. pp. 94–108 and plates.
17. See also Michael W. Meister, "Fragments From a Divine Cosmology: Unfolding Forms on India's Temple Walls", In Vishakha N. Desai and Darielle Mason, (eds.), *Gods, Guardians, and Lovers, Temple Sculptures from North India A.D. 700–1200*, Ahmedabad: Mapin Publishing, 1993, pp. 94–115.

11

Concept of Space in the Vāstu Tradition
My Experiences

V. Ganapati Sthapati

In this paper of mine, I have poured out many a concept of the traditional Science of Vāstu of Indian origin. These concepts, I was able to identify, internalize, experience and implement in actual practice. To have access to these *vaijñānic* concepts, I actually retraced my steps from Technology to Science. I have been working on this subject for years, as there is no technology without science. Added to this, the wisdom and knowledge of the tradition came to me as heritage. My father and forefathers, were all *Vāstuśilpīs* of very high repute. My teaching and working in the Government College of Architecture and Sculpture, Mamallapuram, as Principal, for about three decades gave me many insights into the Science and Technology of the *Vāstuvidyā*.

My deep involvement in creative works both in the religious and secular fields enriched my knowledge and experience yielding large dividends. This is with respect to temple sculptures of religious nature and secular sculptures of literary and ethical value, coupled with new spatial concepts, new forms and motifs. I have also successfully attempted to create spaces for two different belief systems under one common roof without detriment to their respective *pūjā* modalities – evolved and continued over the centuries.

Further, my deep involvement in the design and execution of huge sized secular buildings for certain universities in Tamil Nadu as also Indianization of certain modern buildings in conjunction with contemporary architects have helped me to understand the problems of contemporary architecture in India in respect of spatial concepts and aesthetics preferred by modern society. In all those interactions and connected attempts, I was able to prove also the fitness of indigenous technology and the traditional *śilpī's* command over the handling of modern materials.

Another project that came in my way was that of a documentary report on Housing Architecture, sponsored by the National Housing Bank, New Delhi. This gave me an opportunity of going deep into the principles of Building Architecture and to re-interpret them in a way that would be intelligible and inspiring to the comtemporary minds, since they have been in search of a tradition suited to the indigenous culture and changed circumstances. In this research project, I had to work with a contemporary architect and got my interpretations internalized so as to present them in modern English in a way that would attract the contemporary minds, particularly to the basics. The impact of this work is going to be very great. Foreign scholars are already very much ahead of Indians in this respect.

My contacts with overseas architects particularly of UK and USA provided me ample opportunities to impress upon them the traditional principles of design. These interactions enboldened me to march on the chosen path with added pace and hope. The universal nature of the traditional space-theory and its applicability in the design of secular and religious buildings, in today's context, have been well appreciated and responded by them. They have also closely observed the day-to-day artistic activities of the team of *śilpīs*, put on work in those foreign countries. They were amazed to see young *śilpīs* working with simple tools and doing impressive works. They appreciated the validity of the indigenous technology.

My discovery is, that they appreciate the orderliness of the horizontal and vertical modulated forms as well as commend the spatial aesthetics and its order being analogous to the musical forms. In other words they were able to recognize a musical order and harmony in the spaces that go into the fabrication of building parts. Added to this, they were amazed to hear me saying that every building in the tradition is designed into an organic form, filled with vibrant and orderly live-spaces.

In spite of all these, I see that there is still a vast area to be covered. The subject is as vast as the Space. I have shown only a *paramāṇu*. Experiments are going on under the roof of one Vāstu Vedic Research Foundation. I am confident that this brief essay would be an eye-opener to many who doubt the independent and spiritual nature of the *Vāstuśilpa* traditions and the efficacy of Temple-worship and Temple-culture anchored in these principles. I have shown elsewhere that the temple building is the form of God, rather than a home of God. Further, a section of the contemporary architects that I have come into contact with, is able to appreciate the timelessness of the *Vāstuvijñāna* and I hope that they would, with confidence, recreate the building tradition, putting into their built up spaces the spiritual vibrations and make the occupants respond to them and live in harmony with the environment created inside their homes as much as they enjoy outside. Such a life in harmony with nature affords both spiritual and physical well-being.

House buildings can also be designed to suit individual nature and taste taking into calculation the occupant's birth star. The wave-lengths of individuals are taken here as the basic unit of measure and various parts of the building designed. This is another point that the contemporary architects look at with amazement. Added to this the age of the houses can also be determined, not the physical aspects of longevity but in respect of the spiritual vibrations that would continue to exist in them. The house building is considered as a living organism as already stated.

The ancient authority for the Science and Technology of *Vāstu* is Mayan of Indian origin. He was born to a father and mother with flesh and blood. He is not a mythological person as our *Purāṇas* and *Itihāsas* exhibit him. The repeated occurrence of his name in such ancient literature speaks much of his remote antiquity. He was the *vijñānī* of Bhārat having specialized in *kāla jñānam*. His name is found linked to the authorship of *Sūrya Siddhānta* (vide three opening verses). My request to the scholars at this hour is, that few of our Indian scholars should take up a serious research into his identity and personality. Over and above the points related to this originator, I would like to invite the pointed attention of scholars to a fact that there are a number of sculptors whose names have been recorded in the inscriptions but not exposed by the archaeologists for public interest, in a separate volume with photographs of their creations. Foreign scholars are already ahead of us, in their inquiry into Mayan's whereabouts, his culture and civilization. We can do at least a local search for restoring the identity of our own men.

As one practising in the hoary tradition of *Vāstuśilpa*, with a lineage of over one thousand years as a backdrop, I would like to say, that for the so-called Mayan civilization of Mexico and for such other civilizations of the remote past, the Indian Mayan of *Vāstu* tradition looks like the author. I am able to perceive this, and recognize this, in those monuments spread all over the world, as a shepherd capable of identifying the owner of the individual sheep of which his flock is composed. That sense of recognition and basic knowledge I am blessed with, in view of years of exposure and involvement. But I know that this is the area of historians and anthropologists. Concurrently I feel that the time has come to identify him and explore his contribution to Indian as well as world culture and civilization. The shutters have to be unlocked and lifted. Banging on the door has already started.

To me the Science of *Vāstu* looks very basic and fundamental as also incredibly old, besides the spiritual culture of Bhārat looking anchored in this science and technology of *Vāstu*.

The science behind the *vāstupuruṣamaṇḍala* that signifies the universal rhythm of the Space and the emanation of universal objects therefrom, in musical phrases, is the key to the culture of India as a whole. Mayan is the author of this discovery.

To this Mayan I offer my respects and homage.

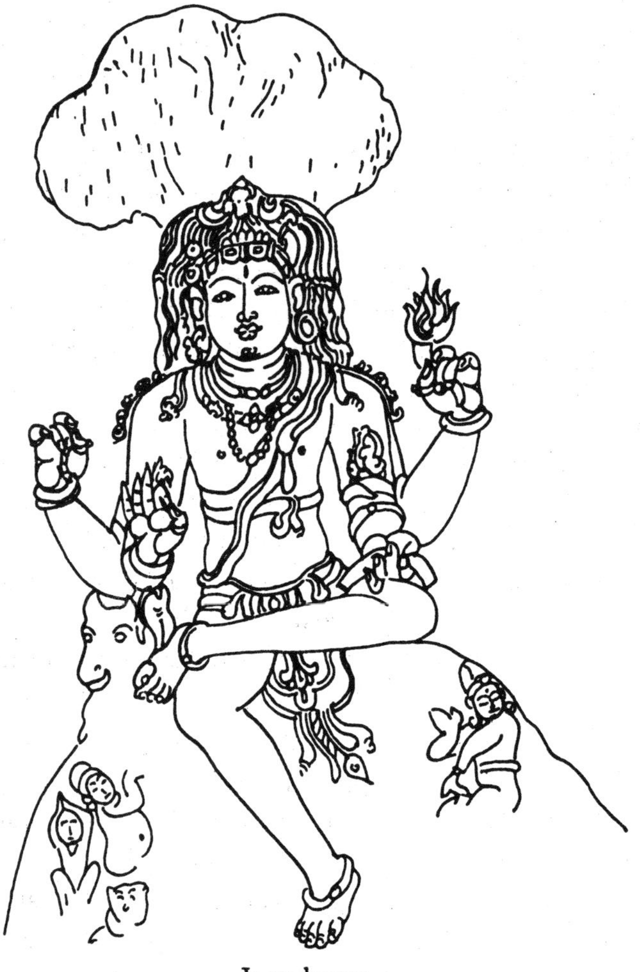

Jagadguru

The quintessence of *Vāstuvidyā*

Space is *ākāśa*, the primal element. There are two such spaces, the inner space and the outer space. This space exists in all animate objects. Nothing in this universe is inanimate. That which within the individual space also happens in the universal space. They experience, vibrate and take form.

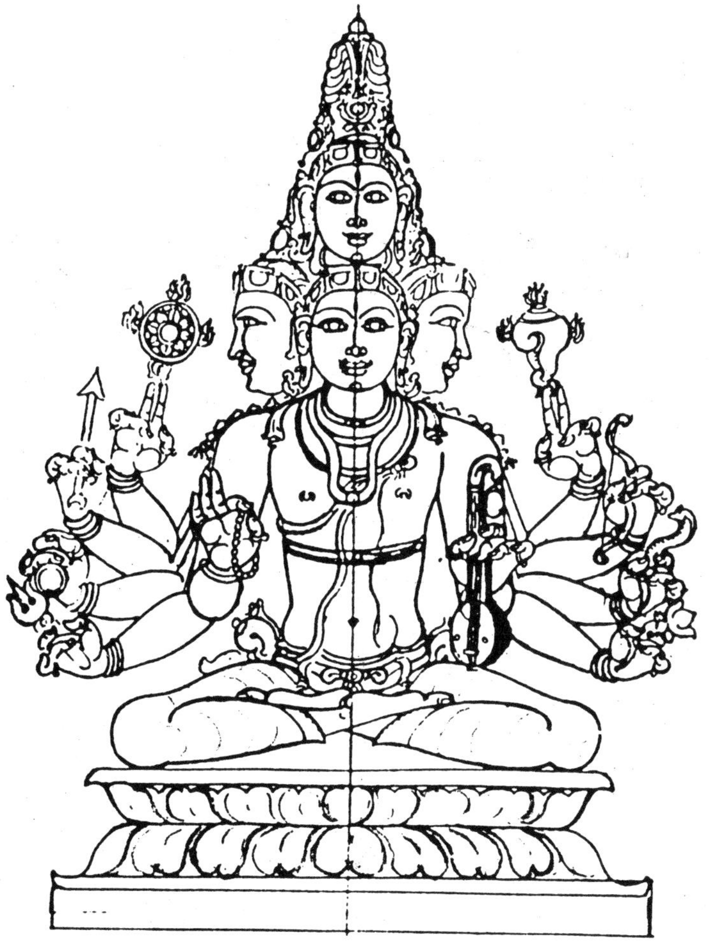

Viśva-Brahman

Vastu and *Vāstu*

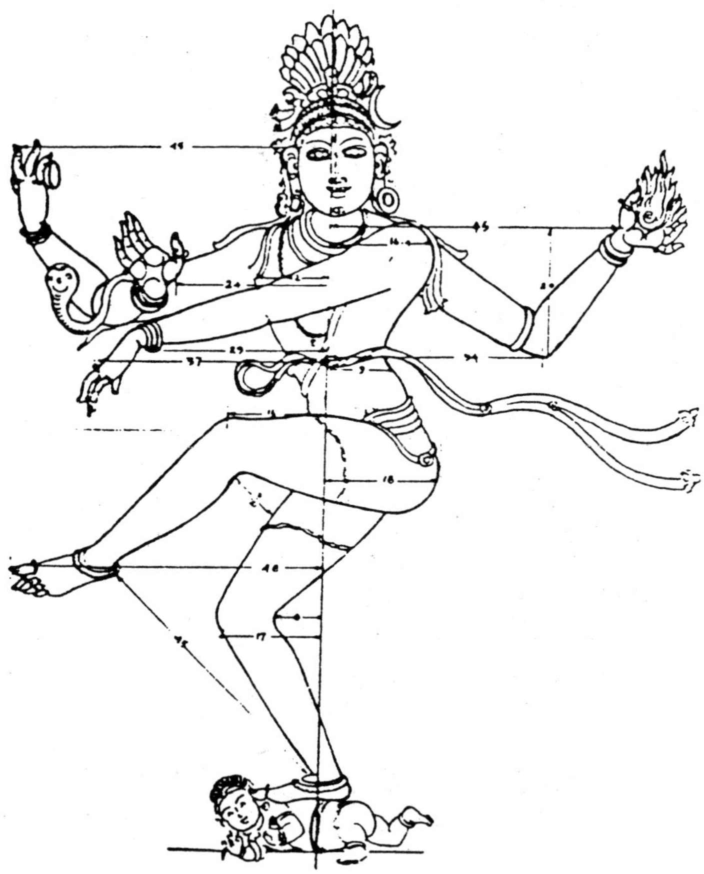

Vastupuruṣa

Vastu is the Energy. Vastu is the Unmanifest. Vastu is the Substance of all substances. Vastu is the *Puruṣa* – the "Vāstu-Brahman".

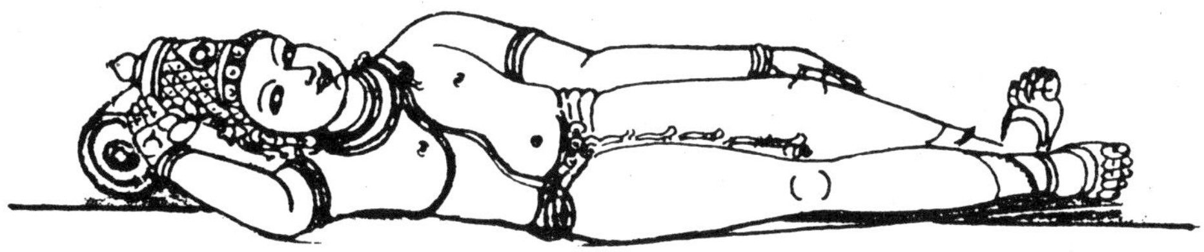

Vāstupuruṣa

Vāstu is the Energy manifest – Vāstu is substantial – Vāstu is the micro space. Vāstu is the macro space. Indwelling Energy is *Vāstupuruṣa* – the "*Vāstu-Brahman*".

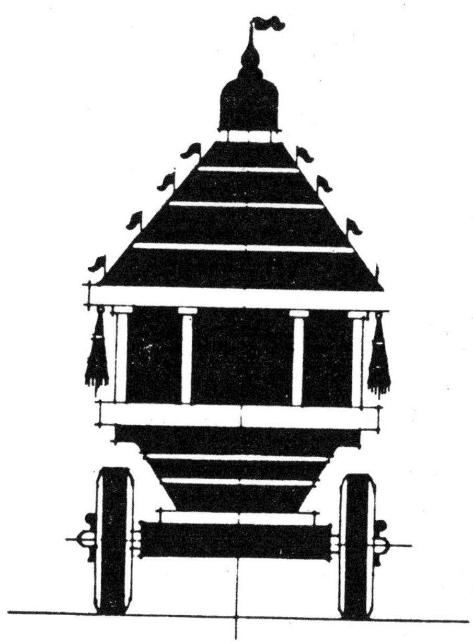

Vāstupuruṣa

Time and Space

Space is the substance of all substances, the Ultimate substance. It is a space filled with minutest particles called *paramāṇu*. Every *paramāṇu* is a minute space possessing Energy. It is square in form basically and cubical three-dimensionally. It is absolute or abstraction of all visual and aural phenomena of the universe or the ultimate form. The space is luminous, as the particles are always emitting light. This is called foetus or germ, the basic material for the emergence of subtle forms in the micro as well as macro spaces. This material is called *vastu*, and it is Eternal. This is the live material which has metamorphosed itself into the manifest world. All the objects of the universe are therefore 'Space–turned spatial forms'. This is just like the gold turned into gold ornaments.

Space, whether of the individual or the universal, possesses a unique quality of experiencing. It is hyper sensitive, besides being super potential. This is capable of giving form to its experience. For the experience to take form, the space goes into self-spin. It vibrates. This effortive force of the Space is called *Kāla*, thc Λbsolute Time. *Kāla* literally means that which emerges from within. This happens to be the intrinsic property of space. This is contained in all animate objects of Nature. What is actually experienced by the Space is vibrated into a form within. This is just like the vibrations of the stringed instrument turning into sound forms. The Space is sensitive enough to order these vibrations into rhythms and to evolve itself into the desired forms – rhythmically structured and aesthetically alluring. This is its unique quality.

In art, *Kāla* becomes *Tāla*. In the physical world *Kāla* measure is produced by the dancer by beating her foot (*tāla* or *pāda*) on the ground. The same is produced by the musician by his hands (*kara tāla*). *Tāla* is rhythm. The dancer produces bodily forms by dancing to this Time-scale. The musician signs his song to the same Time-measure. Time produces musical forms. Poetical compositions are also governed by Time-measure called *Mātrākāla* or *Akṣarakāla*.

These rhythms, in abstraction, are discovered to be rhythmic numbers. They are the spatial measures for the *śilpī* to shape his experiences into the forms desired. They are spatial forms produced by the time-scale. ***Time and space are therefore equated in the Vāstu science, a discovery of the Indian genius***. Mayan, the celebrated authority on the *Vāstu-śilpa* tradition is the discoverer.

Through this unique grammar of the *Tālam*, the *śilpī* creates and his own feelings take form. He feels transformed into the gross forms that he has created. Seeing himself in the forms, he experiences inestimable joy. He looks upon them as *Ātmajans* – his own sons and daughters in flesh and blood.

Time is stilled in such visual creations of the *śilpī*. They do not suffer distortion, deterioration or decay as the objects of nature do undergo. They become therefore timeless objects signifying the attribute of Brahman. What is amazing and to be remembered in this context is, that they are the forms (geometrical patterns) of the Spirit, reproduced in its own Time-Scale. They are the *pratimās* (replicas) of the subtle forms experienced at heart. Further, the verbal forms that we produce by mouth are all spatial forms, of course, but the force of vibrational Time dissolves them into the cosmic space, as soon as they shoot forth from within. So the dictum, "Absolute Time creates life".

> *kālaḥ sṛjati bhūtāni kālaḥ saṃharati prajāḥ* |
> *sarve kālasya vaśagāḥ sa kālo'sya vaśe sthitāḥ* ||
>
> *MBh*, III.57.1.
>
> Time is the creator, sustainer and destroyer.

What the *śilpī* has created outside according to the *Tālapramāṇa* can be designated as *Kalpita Ātman*. The *śilpī* is *jīvātman*, the microcosm. The macrocosm is the *paramātman*. The common vibrational measures that they possess, provide a link among the three. Indian traditional art causes this wonder. By virtue of this unique *Kāla*-measure they resonate with each other as two *vīṇās* set to the same pitch (vibration) resonate and lose their individual identities. This is an advaitic state of experience. This is *Ātma Saṃyogam*. This is pure love. This is divine love. This is *Bhakti* – a scientific interpretation! This is spiritual experience leading into the world of peace and bliss. This is liberation from earthly involvements. This elevates us to the realm of divinity, the *Ākāśa*. This is the ultimate goal of Life.

12

Ecology and Indian Myth

Kapila Vatsyayan

In October 1977 an Inter-governmental Conference on Environmental Education was held in Tbilisi, Georgia, USSR. The declaration began with the following words:

> In the last few decades man has, through his power to transform his environment, wrought accelerated changes in the balance of nature. The result is frequent exposure of living species to dangers which may prove irreversible.[1]

It was a significant coincidence that the Conference should have been held in Georgia, USSR, because by some accounts, major Indo-Āryan migrations of Man took place from this region to the sub-continent of India. It was Man + men from these regions who settled in India and who ultimately gave India the most complete holistic perspective of the Universe. The cosmology, the science and philosophy, in short the total worldview, has been sustained by this civilization through millennia. The Man-Nature relationship was at the core of this vision enunciated repeatedly at all dimensions – biological, physical, psychical, philosophical, metaphysical and spiritual. All life was interrelated and inter-woven: the process of transmutation and cyclic degeneration and regeneration of life was a perennial postulate.

We have come a long, long way since then. Despite the traditional holistic view embedded in each and every discipline, articulated through sacred incantations and systematised as ritual for constant reminder of the need to sustain and foster the ecological balances of nature, we stand at the threshold of disaster in a manner never before faced by Man, who as the Tbilisi declaration states, has "used his power to transform his environment". We may even substitute the word 'transform' with words like 'conquer', 'destroy', 'desecrate', 'plunder', so as to bring home the fact that a single factor of Man who can be distinguished from all living matter through his distinctive power to reflect, to articulate and be wise, has been the very instrument of these ecological imbalances – imbalances which threaten the very existence of Man. As one eminent scientist-philosopher put it in the context of India: "Even more than population explosion, the imbalances in the environment and ecology is the greatest threat to the continent. We may be able to control the first, but the process of devastation we have begun in the second may bring final doom."

The question to be asked is what are the diverse components of the disturbance, the ecological imbalances and what methodologies and strategies were adopted in the past to sustain these balances. Can we, even at this state, learn any lessons from the past for equipping ourselves to face the human predicaments today?

Let us begin by enumerating the principal components of the environment most polluted, species most threatened and how each disturbs the ecological balance. Thereafter, we can return to the worldview of the historical past, the myth, ritual and art of this country or for that matter, practically all cultures, pre-renaissance. The worldview is mercifully sustained by so-called primitive societies, be it in India, Africa, Australia or America. At the philosophic speculative level, the living continuities can be seen only in India.

So today, this moment where four-fifths of humanity lives (i.e., India and Asia), what is threatened? What are we polluting, destroying, thus bringing forebodings of the annihilation of Man on earth? What is the quality of life we can hope for?

First and foremost is water, the basic sustaining principle – clean water or to use a traditional phrase 'pure or unpolluted (*śuddha*) water' – is becoming scarce. Water systems are increasingly over-exploited and polluted. Any Indian is familiar with the daily rituals which serve as reminders of the concept of pure and, therefore, holy water. No daily, monthly, annual ceremony is complete without ritual purification with water. At birth, marriage, death, this concept is articulated and yet we have polluted these waters of life.

Next, the pollution of the earth – Mother Earth, floating free ball beneath the most gleaming membrane of bright blue sky. And what have we done to it? Arid lands have increased, soil which was venerated has been eroded and infertility, sand and salt have taken over. It is estimated that in this part of the world, a million hectares are being desertified each year. Desecration of the bowels of the earth through excessive quarrying is common. Man's power has asserted its most destructive tendencies and the collective greed of Man has hollowed the still centre of life. *Pṛthivī*, the eternal mother, has been polluted and desecrated.

Related to the pollution of water and earth is the massive unprecedented deforestation. The Indian sub-continent has been progressively deforested: the soil's ability to absorb and hold water has diminished. Severe floods have occurred more frequently and deforestation has affected most adversely the eco-system of the Himalayas where our major river systems – the Indus, the Ganges and the Brahmaputra – originate. Each day we learn of the increase in wastelands and the consequent effect upon rural life, be they the forests of Bastar or the hills of the Himalayan range. In the language of Indian myth, this is the rape of the tree and river goddess, the *Vṛkṣikās*, and the destruction of the gods of the woods, the *Vanadevatā*. No wonder the Chipko Movement and Protect the Silent Valley is a cry of anguish. Most of all, the present destruction is a dangerous play with the mythical centre – *Sumeru*, the world axis, the Himalayas.

The disturbance in water, earth, vegetation, river and mountain ecology systems has naturally threatened all manner of life – aquatic, terrestrial and celestial. Mythically, *Śeṣanāga* upholds the earth, the Gaṅgā rides the crocodile, Yamunā the tortoise and each is threatened. Boars and elephants upheld the earth; they too are dying. So who upholds the earth now? The birds of heaven, the Swan, the Garuḍa and others who carried the gods are vanishing. So who sustains the moral and cosmic order? There can only be chaos.

And worst of all, there is the pollution of the holy space – the air, *Vāyu*, and the sky which permeates and envelopes all life. The tragedy of Bhopal is too close for comment, but equally demonic are the *āsuric* chimneys of black *tāmasic* forces which pollute the 'lungs' of life. Acid rains are common elsewhere and man looks in vain for the purity of the water to flow from the rain-filled clouds. Destruction is writ large on the balmy skies, once azure blue, today smoke grey.

Finally, we have polluted holy sound, the primeval *Nāda*, through the chaos of our life. Noise pollution makes Man deaf to the inner voices of his wisdom.

And so Man aspires higher and higher, beyond the pollution of his making, to that one source which sustains all and is yet beyond his reach, namely, the Sun – *Āditya* – the giver of light in the sky and fire on earth – *Agni* – the source of energy which appears unpollutable unlike the fuel of his making. This energy, physically and metaphysically, is Man's only ray of hope for the continuance of life.

The brief description given above can be multiplied a hundredfold to underline the disastrous effects of wind and land erosion, the infertility of soil, disturbance of bio-ecology of aquatic, terrestrial and celestial life, and to speak of the pollution of the *Suṣumnā nāḍī*, the central artery of the Indo-Gangetic plains – the Gaṅgā.

But perhaps these illustrative examples will suffice to convince us that stated differently or stated in the traditional language understood by the literate and illiterate of this country, Man has disturbed the cosmic order, the rhythm of the movement of the earth, water, fire, ether and *Agni* (*Sūrya*), i.e., the five elements, where interaction, inter-connection and inter-weaving was the rule rather than the exception. The sustenance of the ecological balance was Man's first and last duty for only then the moral order of the world, *Ṛta* as also *Dharma* in their fundamental connotation, could be or would be sustained. The emphasis was both on the notion of purity and non-pollution as also on ecological balance. Any assertion of greed or power disturbed the balance, and this is the story of all those who are called *Asuras* in mythical terms. Restraint in the use of power was the central message.

My limited purpose here is to revive the collective psychical memory of this heritage, to draw attention to the myths, art and ritual, science, religion and philosophy in India, the strategies through which this holistic worldview of ecological balance was articulated.

Cutting across historical developments, philosophic debates, scientific controversies, religious sects and cults, the one principle which underlies and provides unity as also continuity of vision and perception is the assertion that Man is only one among all living matter; in short, the notion of the *Jīva*. Man's life depends upon and is conditioned by all that surrounds him and sustains him, namely, inanimate, mineral and animate, aquatic, vegetative, animal and gaseous life. It is, therefore, Man's duty constantly to remind himself – in individual and collective life – of the environment and the ecology. Such veneration is no animistic primitive fear; it is wisdom contained in the language of myth and symbol. Their efficacy lies in their capacity of multiple interpretation at the biological function, societal, philosophic and religious levels. The pivot around which Indian myth moves, not unlike that of other parts of ancient world, is ecological balance.

Developments in Indian science specially mathematics, chemistry, biology, owe their systems to this holistic worldview of ecological balance. The philosophic systems, whether from the polarity of the realist Caraka or the Sāṃkhya assert it, the language of Indian myth and art manifest it in an unparalleled lucidity of narrative statement and depth of thought, meaning and a clarity of message which has a validity here and now.

Although we can discuss separately the five principal components of the environment or what in traditional language are called the five basic elements of water, earth, air, space and fire, which comprise the microcosm of the biological Man as also the macrocosm of the universe, it must be remembered that no single element is autonomous. It is in their ecological interaction that they assume significance.

Let us begin with primary elements. First, the water that sustains life, the first principle of fertility and of life whether of ocean or river or clouds or sky. The archaeological evidence of Mohenjodaro, Harappa, Lothal and the recent excavations of Gaṅgā valley leave no doubt about the fundamental ritual importance accorded to water and its fecundity. The *Vedas* devote many hymns to waters. Mythically, Varuṇa is the god of the waters; he is considered the great superintendent of the cosmic moral order (*Ṛta*); he is the guardian of the West. In a hymn dedicated to Varuṇa in the *Atharva Veda* (IV.16), it is said:

> This earth is King Varuṇa's as also this great far-flung sky: the two seas are his belly (appetite); at the same time he is hidden in this little water. Even we who may cross the sky will not escape King Varuṇa; from heaven his spies are patrolling this earth with a thousand eyes; they scan through the earth. King Varuṇa sees all that is between heaven and earth and that which is beyond (them).

Perhaps there is no need to decode the myth. In saying that Varuṇa's sphere is the earth and heaven and in the waters, the Vedic poet is referring to an eternally known natural phenomenon of the primeval waters rising as vapour (as spies) in the sky only to descend again to Earth. Understandably, the emblem of Varuṇa is 'fish', his vehicle the crocodile, the wind is his breath (as *Dikpāla Vāyu* or wind is the guardian of the North West). He spans boundless paths for the sun and ensures that the rivers fall into the ocean. He knows the paths of ships on the ocean and the flight of birds in the sky. He punishes those who transgress his laws.

Indeed, in the Indian worldview, as also of other ancient civilizations and cultures, life on earth emerges from the eternal waters that hold the potency of fire: the two together transform into forms of world, mineral, plant, animal and divine. From the primeval waters emerge stones in the shapes of ovoid pebbles and spheres with ammonites going back to millions of years. Many a devout Indian is familiar with *bāṇaliṅgas* and *śālagrāmas* which are sought and collected for worship. Perhaps the modern Indian has not paused to ponder over the significance of the myth of the Varuṇa, the vigilant superintendent and the symbolic ecological significance of the *bāṇaliṅgam* and *śālagrāma*. Stated differently, they articulate an intuitive scientific comprehension or wisdom through a conceptual parallel in imaginative form. While on the surface, myth has a dreamlike structure, its meaning and value lies in its pointing at natural phenomenon. As has been pointed out, Indian science and philosophy and thus its symbols develop on the postulate of the perpetual movement of creation, degeneration and regeneration of the cosmos. This is quite distinct from an evolutionary model. Time and existence are conceived of as systems of interconnected cycles, not in linear terms starting from one specific divine act of creation. Resultantly, Indian cosmology tends to be circular or what was the fluid within is the ocean.

It is obvious that intuitively, without perhaps empirical verification and analysis, this is an ecological statement through metaphor of the greatest significance. The *bāṇaliṅga* form the Narmadā, i.e., waters and the *śālagrāmas*, i.e., the ammonite fossils coming from the mountains, are the concrete symbols of the creation from the waters and solar energy. The radial lines and a projecting centre of the *śālagrāmas* point at the latter. Equally widespread is the myth of their personifying the horizontally floating golden egg, i.e., Viṣṇu himself lying upon an undulating serpent which represents the inexhaustible primordial ocean of *pralaya*. The symbolic significance of these simple stones reflects a sensitive comprehension of ecology, specially when it is further said that fire rises from the waters or the sun from the ocean. In sum, the waters and these stones are a meditative help leading to a comprehension of continuous evolution and devolution process of all time and existence.

The myths of waters take innumerable other forms relating to the ocean (*Sāgara*), the rivers and the nymphs of the skies. Indian literature is replete with their names – Sarasvatī, Gaṅgā, Yamunā, Urvaśī or Menakā. Indian folklore sanctifies these. All these deities are members of the vast water cosmogony so vital and central to Indian thought. Little wonder that from the simplest tribal to the most sophisticated the Indian venerates water in some form or the other. Rituals of purity of waters are known to all parts of India. The Indian is familiar with the common (but little understood today) custom of a full pitcher greeting guests and being kept at the entrance of the house. Has he reflected over what cosmic significance this may hold?

From Varuṇa, let us turn our attention to the great river systems of India, i.e., Indus, Gaṅgā and Brahmaputra. Countless myths have been woven around the eco-systems of these rivers – sensitive, meaningful stories narrate imaginatively the ecological movements. As an example, from the vast storehouse of these myths, we chose the most familiar one which has sustained Indian life and one most polluted. Our anxiety for its physical purity is obvious in the establishment of the Gaṅgā Authority. But let us see how she dominates Indian myth and cosmogony from earliest times. Jawaharlal Nehru had called her a symbol of India's age-long culture and civilization, ever changing, ever flowing, and yet ever the same Gaṅgā. The late Indira Gandhi did not consider it strange that the "Gaṅgā should have such an extraordinary hold on the imagination of the peoples of India. For millennia, she has watered and nurtured an entire civilization, and become a symbol of eternity – a theme of art, myth, legend and literature. The moods of rivers are fascinating to watch but even more so are the faith and reverence they evoke in the heart of millions."

And what is the myth of the creation of this great river Gaṅgā and how has she captured the imagination?

Gaṅgā like the *śālagrāmas* and the floating egg on the serpent of undifferentiated waters continues to be related to serpents, crocodiles, and aquatic life. In Indian myth and iconography, she often assumes a mermaid form protected by a hood of snakes.

If Varuṇa has spies in heaven, Gaṅgā descends from heaven. She is the holy water in the *Kamaṇḍala* of Brahmā which purified the world; she descends from the heavens from the foot of Viṣṇu as *Trivikrama* when he traversed the three orders of space, nether, terrestrial and celestial, with his three steps, but most important she is the drop of water from the celestial heavens which fills the ocean (*Sāgara*). The descent of the Gaṅgā from the heavens evolves through centuries in the form of an elaborate, ecologically charged myth.

Several versions of the myth are found in the *Rāmāyaṇa*, *Mahābhārata* and the several *Purāṇas*, while details of names of saints and heroes differ in many cases and sometimes become localised. Central to the myth is the connection of the ocean and the sky and the channellization of river systems through human effort. In traditional language, it is the story of the King of Oceans, *Sāgara*; the Milky Way of the sky, Gaṅgā; the saint Agastya; the *tapas* or austerities of Bhagīratha, the Man; and the forests of the locks of Śiva.

In one version, Agastya who in some ways is related to solar energy, once swallowed the entire ocean. Although he meant well as he wanted to expose the demons hiding in the sea, it had the effect of depriving the earth and all beings of the necessary life-sustaining water. This made it necessary for the celestial river, a kind of Milky Way, to descend from the sky.

Now it fell to the share of another human, the pious Bhagīratha to undertake great austerities so as to bring the heavenly Gaṅgā to earth. He was sorely in need of water to appease and gratify the ashes and souls of his deceased forefathers who had perished in a similar natural catastrophe of drought. Leaving the administration of his kingdom to his ministers, he left for a place in South India called Gokarṇa (Cow's ear). With unflinching determination and perseverance, he practised austerities, *tapas*, through discipline and commitment. Eventually, Brahmā was pleased and promised to grant him a wish. Bhagīratha asked the god to let Gaṅgā descend to earth. Brahmā agreed but drew attention to the necessity of soliciting Śiva's help and grace. He feared that if the mighty river of heaven with her torrential waters were to descend directly, it may cleave the earth and shatter it. Someone would have to break the fall by receiving the gigantic cataract on his head. This only Śiva could do. Bhagīratha once again continued his austerities until the god was appeased. He stood on one leg with his arms uplifted (*ūrdhvabāhu*); he practised the penance of the five fires (*pañcatapas*) and finally Śiva appeared and acquiesced. The head of the great god took the first full impact of Gaṅgā's torrential flow. The matted hair of the *jaṭās* plied high, delayed the cascading current which then in meandering through the labyrinths of the forest of his *jaṭās* lost its force, was tamed and channellized. Its water descended gently to the Himalayas and then, majestically, to the Indian plains, and thus the earth and its creatures were rejuvenated, for she was the life-giving boon.

The ecological message of the myth is as clear as the physical reality of the course of the Gaṅgā; with its origin in the Himalayas whether mythically Kailasa or actually Gomukha or Gaṅgotrī, the Vasundharā falls into the rich Deodar forests through which it meanders, the several streams into which it breaks before reaching Haridvāra (literally the entrance to Hara Śiva). What is sanctified in the myth is both the ecological process as also the power of austere discipline to uphold the moral and ecological order and not to destroy it. Man, if he so wills, can accumulate an immense reservoir of physical and psychical energy through concentration and discipline. *Tapas* is the power, armour or commitment that becomes a high power electric charge, which in a flash can cut through and melt all resistance. Today, Man's *tapas* lies in keeping the great river pure and clean at the source and through all its meandering journey through the forests, plains, fields, villages and cities, it is again received by the ocean, *Sāgara*. The celestial skies are the pilgrim centres of Kailāsa, Gomukha or Gaṅgotrī which must be nurtured, the locks of Śiva are the Himalayan forests which must tame the river so as to avoid wrathful floods and landslides and the *tapas* of Man is the exercise of his selective discriminating power for using water for hydro-electric energy. The ecological connection of the North and the South and their inter-connected systems is reflected by Bhagīratha's undertaking his austerities in Gokarṇa in the South.

The myth is elaborated in many ways in all regions of India and throughout Indian history. It assumes paramount significance on account of the present state of pollution. The work of scientists, programmes of afforestation, rural and urban sewage systems have only to reach out for support and reinforcement in Indian art. Indeed, Indian architecture, sculpture and painting is the most effective, aesthetically pleasing, symbolically loaded message totally contemporary and valid statement of the ecology and concern – if only it could be utilised. To use an inelegant phrase, the great temples of India, ranging from Badrīnātha, to Gaṅgaikoṇḍacholapuram to the countless figures of Gaṅgā riding a crocodile, surrounded by aquatic life sustaining life are the natural hoardings of mass media only if we had eyes to see and a mind to comprehend, and ears to hear the incantation of thousands to Gaṅgā as *sukhadā* and *mokṣadā*. Countless images and *mantras* lie all over India in every nook and corner from Assam to Rajasthan and Gujarat, Kashmir to Kanyākumārī. Are they hollow and ineffective? Can new meaning and significance not be given?

Surpassing in stature, beauty and ecological significance is the monumental dramatic relief of all time in Mamallapuram. It represents the celebrated myth of the descent of the Gaṅgā in a manner which leaves an indelible impression. On a huge wall of rock rising vertically towards the clear blue skies of South India, a cosmic tableaux in relief is enacted on a space of twenty-seven meters length, nine in height. It is teaming with hosts of serpents, plants, animals, men, women, *Apsaras* and *Gandharvas*, all converging towards a natural cleft in the middle of the composition. The decisive moment of the effectiveness of Bhagīratha's *tapas* no doubt dramatically captured, but what is more, the series of events or ecological phases are all depicted in one setting. The celestial stream rushed down metaphorically through a cistern above the great rock. Today we imagine this stream. A giant serpent king (*Nāgarāja*) is covered by the torrent, moves upward in undulating movements, i.e., all aquatic life rejoices at her descent. To the right of the saint are large aquatic birds, large geese. All manner of life flocks together – reptiles, animals, birds, gods and goddesses. Here are elephants, families of perching monkeys, deers, lions, *Apsaras* and *Gandharvas* – all watch the miracle. In a superb animated sculptural style, this is the true celebration and consecration of life, asserting, reaffirming the basic kinship of all living creatures. All is sustained by one life source, one life giving energy; this is universal eternal play of matter and energy. The waters of the dried *Sāgara* descend from heaven to purify all.

One could go on *ad infinitum* not only about the myth and this serpent relief, but about the innumerable masterly examples of Gaṅgā and of Śiva, as Gaṅgādhara and Gaṅgā, as woman descending through the dance movement called *Gaṅgāvataraṇa*.

But from the Gaṅgā water, we must move to the first vegetative and aquatic life principle. The lotus and the snake in botanical and zoological terms are born of the waters. In mythical terms, the lotus emerges from the primeval waters, whether river or pond. It is the most important of vegetative forms born of water, connected to the mythical centre of the earth through its stem, and always above the water; its leaf the symbol of untainted purity, its flower blossoming with fragrance. Physically, the lotus is a typical ecological statement of the processes of nature. Symbolically, it assumes the greatest importance in Indian myth, art and ritual. The metaphor of the lotus leaf, the lotus flower and stem permeates Indian literature in practically all languages. If the motif of the lotus was excluded from Indian *mantra, tantra, yantra*, poetry, prose, music, dance, sculpture, monumental as the free standing pillars with inverted lotus, or relief as the magnificent panels in Sanchi, or Indian painting, the Indian heritage would be impoverished beyond recognition.

The lotus is a comparatively late entrant into Indian myth, but once it finds a place, Hindu, Jain, Buddhist art, thought and myth consider it indispensable. In all cases, whether as seat (*āsana*) or as emblem or epithet, it denotes fecundity, abundance, well-being. Logically, lotus becomes goddess and is personified as *Śrī* and *Lakṣmī*. She is praised as lotus-born (*padmasambhavā*), standing on a lotus (*padmasthitā*), lotus coloured (*padmavarṇā*), lotus-thighed (*padma-ūru*), lotus-eyed (*padmākṣī*), abounding in lotuses (*padminī*), decked with lotus garlands (*padmamālinī*), and a thousand other names. We are familiar with *Bodhisattva Padmapāṇi*, the female *Prajñā* as counterpart, *Pāramitā* who sits on a lotus and holds a lotus. Underlying this preoccupation with lotus as symbol, is the sheer physical reality of the lotus: ultimately the lotus and its petals are the multiplicity of form. Its centre corresponds to the centre of the universe, the navel of the earth, all is held together by the stem and the eternal waters. Tāntric physiology regards the nervous system as a series of lotuses, and the sacred geometry of lotus is called the *Śrīyantra*.

The life of the waters is intrinsically related to that of other species, the first creations of nature, namely the reptiles. Just as the lotus connects earth, water and air, so also the reptiles represent that moment of transition. All ancient religions have given a special significance to the snake. The coiled and intertwined snake represents a moment in the undifferentiated condition of creation on which human life rests. The snake is the symbol of this interconnection – swift, silent, limbless and deadly. The sign of transition is vital to man, who must be assured that this world is a cohesive unity: he cannot exist either in chaos or isolation. Thus, Viṣṇu at the moment before the creation of the universe, is depicted lying in a yogic sleep upon the serpent *Ananta* (Endless) with its multiple cobra heads forming a canopy. Man and reptile as man and water and vegetation are inter-related and inter-dependent.

The countless myths relating to snakes again pervade the Indian psyche in all regions, all levels of society giving rise to major cults which have great ecological significance. Its detailed unfolding could fill volumes. In art, *Nāgas* and *Nāginīs* abound in Hindu, Buddhist and Jaina art. In a beautiful relief of the Śuṅga period (Pauni, Maharashtra), beneath the *Bodhi* tree, the multi-headed cobra, King Muchilinda, rises up to protect the seated Buddha. Eastern India defies the snake goddess as Manasā. Bādāmī caves have the coiled serpent as the eternal movement of cyclic time on the ceiling and the coiled *Nāga* from the Cālukyan period is a perfect geometric statement of the lotus – *Nāga*, water and earth.

The snakes and reptiles in a dramatic moment of biological mutation acquire wings and become birds. They are inter-related antagonist and yet complementary. Intuitively, the Indian sees this ecological connection and Indian myth provides many examples of reptiles changing to birds or reptiles and birds seemingly antagonistic to each other being vehicles of gods. Thus, Viṣṇu lies on the *Ananta Śeṣanāga* and he rides the Garuḍa. The animals follow suit, and the entire range of evolution, from the hare to the lion, from the rodent to the primate, is vividly represented. They crowd the outer walls and lower lintels of Indian *Stūpas* and temples by the hundred, sometimes in processional rows, in pairs, or yet again in conjunction with trees, floral motifs, and as conjoined images of fantasy. Occasionally they are aquatic, as in the mythical crocodile (*makara*) who is the vehicle of Gaṅgā; at other times, they are of the earth or the desert, as are the elephants and lions; while others are monkeys who befriend man.

Amongst the creations of fantasy are the mythical lion or tiger, the *śārdūla*; more fearsome is the *vyāla*, the vicious beast. These mythic animals appear either in isolation or in conjunction with dwarfs and women on temple walls, guarding sanctuaries. There are also the many-winged animals called *suparṇas*. Each animal acquires its own symbolism, and by the fourth century they develop into a systematised pantheon closely related to the world of humans and celestials. Most Indian sculpture is structured to comprehend the world of aquatic plant, animal and human life. Each is an aspect of the other; superficially they appear as decoration, yet at a deeper level, the aquatic, vegetative, and animal elements represent aspects of the human psyche. Metamorphosis and transmutation is logical and traditional. This rich abundance of nature, its manifold creations and organic coherence, logically culminates in the universal fertility theme known to all ancient religions.

But we must pass on to the next most important element of environment which has provided the world with vast oceans of myth. Earth is known to all civilizations and cultures as the great Mother Goddess. Predating the *Vedas* are the figures of Mother Earth Goddess in the form of ring stones. The *Vedas* dedicate many hymns to *Pṛthivī*, the *Bhūmisūkta* being one of the greatest hymns. She is invoked as born of the waters of the ocean. Surrounded by space, she is the creator, the sustainer. In the *Atharva Veda* there is a prayer which draws attention once again to ecological balances and how the earth, like Varuṇa, is the upholder of the moral order. Like the river goddess, she represents fecundity. Truth and moral order sustain her. She is the mistress of past and future, giver of the wide and wildlife world of human life. She has high heights, stretches on level ground, reaches to the sea, bears herbs of manifold potency, on whom food and crops grow and animals roam whom Indra from the sky fertilises, and that earth is invoked as Mother. Man says "I am the son of the earth, the rains are my father, let him, the Lord of the rain, fill the Earth for us. O Earth, protect us, purify us. Let people milk her with amity. O Earth, give us sweet words. The snowy mountain heights and thy forests, O Earth, shall be kind to us and we to them."

What could be a more lucid ecological statement of the intrinsic relationship of water, earth, air, sky and sun, and Man. As in the case of water, the emphasis is on purification-purity, i.e., non-pollution.

Her fertility is symbolized through the image of the brimming vase, the bowl of plenty. Foliage and the lotus emerge from the bowl: the waters below the life-giving forces of regeneration and energy of sun blossoms as the vegetation is the sap of life (the *rasa*). Water, earth, plant, animal, human and the divine come together in images of the goddess *Pṛthivī*, also identified as *Devī*.

Pṛthivī, the Mother Earth, sustains plant life in all its multitudinous variety. Volumes could be written on the veneration of plants, forests and herbs in India. The tree is sacred to one and all. In the Himalayas, the *Deodāra* is considered the abode of the gods; one may cut a tree only at his own peril; when they were felled, it was with due ceremony. Plural planting was the norm. The *Sāl* is equally venerated in Uttar Pradesh, Bihar and Madhya Pradesh. The forests of *Deodāra* and *Sāl*, the flowering *Aśoka*, the *Kadamba*, the *Rudrākṣa*, the *Pārijāta*, the *Campaka* are all sacred. So also are *Palāśa* and *Amalatāsa* and *Ketakī*. The *Aśvattha*, Banyan, *Neem*, coconut, palm and bamboo are ecologically important, mythically central; herbs of all varieties, the *Tulasī*, the *Kesar* and grass, *Dūrvāghās* to *Mūñja* are venerated.

Have we paused to question why the Indian psyche paid this attention to trees, herbs, plants, and related them to characters, divine, human, seasons, moods, *rasas, bhāvas*? It is these life-giving plants and trees where the gods dwell who have been vital and crucial for maintenance of ecological balances whom we have desecrated and destroyed. Myths evolved around each and everyone of these trees and plants. *Aśvattha* was central, so also was *Bilva*, the mango, the *Sāl*, the coconut and the bamboo. If one was the tree of life, the other was of the upturned tree of Upaniṣadic thought. The *Sāl* is not only central and vital to the ecological cycle of the forests of Bihar and Bastar providing vast communities with the famous Karma festival, but it is the *Sāl* tree whom *Māyā* embraced as the Buddha was born. The significance of the coconut tree is botanical, functional, nutritional and mythical in ritual terms, and this is too well-known to need recounting.

In Udayagiri the myth of *Pṛthivī* is carved in stone. This time the Varāha, the bear in mundane terms, the wild pig, the scavanger of the terrestrial space, rescues her from the deluge. Viṣṇu Varāha rises from the waters where cosmic upheavals have taken place. In the relief the gigantic Varāha rises from the waters, seen as incised wavy patterns, unruffled and effortlessly lifts *Pṛthivī*, the mother goddess with garland and lotus stalk. His monumental body, the strong legs, the posture of *ālīḍha* are in contrast with the delicacy and kindness with which he lifts *Pṛthivī*. A total cosmic drama is enacted in monumental proportions in stone as in Mamallapuram where the *joviga* the myth is recreated in plastic form of all proportions.

The Udayagiri relief is another powerful statement of ecological balance where the waters, the *Nāgas*, the animals and human are inter-connected. The Varāha deity represents the primeval organic relationship of animal and humans – so necessary for conserving the life energy of our planet.

The tree-woman relationship dominates Indian myth. The most functionally meaningful and inspirer of countless myths and the richest treasure of Indian sculptural motif is the *Vṛkṣikā*, also called by other names – *Yakṣī, Surasundarī* and many others. They stand against trees, embrace them and thus become an aspect of the tree articulating the interpretation of the plant and the human. The tree is dependent upon the woman for its fertility as is the woman on the tree.

These *Vṛkṣikās* or *Yakṣīs* are the creatures of the water, earth, plant and human. No wonder in point of time the original river goddesses – principally Gaṅgā, Yamunā and Sarasvatī – submerge into each other. *Yakṣīs* along with Gaṅgā, Yamunā and Sarasvatī standing on their respective aquatic vehicles, the crocodile, tortoise and swan, are guardians of sanctuaries and prepare the devotee for the inner journey.

Fergusson considers them as the pictorial representation of the primitive faiths of the casteless *Dāsas* (slaves) who inhabited northern India before the advent of the Āryans. Vogel studies them as part of the *Nāga* or serpent cult.

Vincent Smith speaks of them as fertility goddesses, and Coomaraswamy wrote one of his earliest books on them and their male counterparts the *Yakṣas*. They are seen in Indian art from the earliest Mauryan remains (second century B.C.) to the medieval sculpture and painting. They are mentioned in classical Sanskrit literature and Kālidāsa centres the plot of one play, *Mālavikāgnimitra*, around the ceremony of the woman and the tree (the *Aśoka dohada* motif). The myth in all its diversity of manifestation is an excellent example of a purely functional aspect of life being transmitted into myth. The *Aśoka* tree is known for its medicinal value in curing certain feminine diseases. Its bark and flower is used in indigenous medicine even today. The tree is essential for the natural health and regularity of women's biological system. The myth inverts the functions and transforms it into the woman's embrace being essential for the flowering of *Aśoka* tree: thus the word *Aśoka dohada* or the generic work *Śālabhañjikā* (she who leans on the tree). In some parts of India, there continues still a periodic ritual where women embrace the tree and partake of its bark or flower.

The myth then enters literature, architecture and sculpture and becomes a dominant artistic motif. Viewers of Indian art will easily recall the outstanding example of the motif in Sanchi where she performs a purely architectural function as a diagonal bracket and is the symbol of the fullness of vegetation and life. She appears repeatedly in Indian art of all ages and regions as brackets or ceiling figures, isolated reliefs in conjunction with trees, plants and animals. The medieval temples of Khajuraho, Bhuvaneswara, the temples of Mount Abu and Ranakapura are crowded with these figures on the outer walls and as pillar or ceiling figures. While she is tree and plant, she is also the celestial beauty (the *Surasundarī*) and the dancer. In plastic form she is invariably in the attitude of dance and often holds musical instruments symbolising the sound of music and harmony. She is in close proximity with animals or occasionally rides them. Nameless, she is the epitomy of the inherent harmony of plant, animal and human life. She is the ecological balance between the natural and the human. The *Yakṣī* is another manifestation of the goddess of the forest, the *Araṇyānī* of the *Vedas*. The poet invokes her:

Goddess of wild and forest who
Seemest to vanish from sight
The goddess never slays unless
Some murderous enemy approaches.
Now have I praised the Forest Queen,
Sweet scented redolent of balm

The mother of all sylvan things,
Who tells not but hath stores of food.

(*Ṛ V*, X.146)

Water, earth, tree provide the basis of three distinct types of goddesses and women in myth and art. The sky although the father is the atmosphere which sustains other goddesses. Predominant amongst the goddesses of the atmosphere is Dawn (*Uṣas*) and her companion the night (*Rātri*). A famous hymn of the *Ṛgveda* invokes Dawn; she is described as a dancer who appears on the stage and unveils herself. She is the provider of light and life. The verse runs:

Oh Uṣas, nobly born
Bestow thou on us vast and glorious riches
Preserve us, evermore ye gods with blessings

(*Ṛ V*, VI.78.6)

and again

The fire well kindled
Sings aloud to greet her
And with their hymns
The priests are chanting welcome
Uṣas approaches in her splendour, driving
All evil darkness far away, the goddess.

A complementary theme is that of *Rātri*, the night. The night too is invoked as a goddess, a *Devī*, who is the daughter of the heavens above, who pervades the worlds, who protects all beings and gives them shelter. Later this night is explained as coming forth from the *Māyā* (creative power) of Brahman. She is then called *Bhuvaneśvarī* (the sovereign power over the worlds). The poets invoke her as follows:

With all her eyes the goddess Night
Looks forth approaching many a spot.
She hath put all her glories on Immortal,
She hath filled the waste,
The goddess hath filled height and depth.
She conquers darkness with her light.
The goddess as she comes,
Has put her sister Dawn in her place.

(*Ṛ V*, X.127.3–8)

The Dawn and the Morning are seen in their dual divinity. The two goddesses endlessly follow similar paths but they never cross nor is there any rivalry between them. They are indeed the divine mothers of the celestial order (*Ṛta*).

Water, earth, tree and plant maintain the spatial balance of the cosmos, the night and dawn are the keepers of celestial temporal order and each is the goddess, mother, wife, woman or girl. They are essential for the celestial or terrestrial order, the *Ṛta* – a central concept of Indian cosmology and philosophic thought. Any disturbance in the order needs penance, ritual or sacrifice.

But the earth and water, the sky and the nether-world must have a centre, and hub around it which the wheel moves spatially and temporally. This mythical centre is the Mount *Meru* or *Mandara* known by different names in other cosmologies.

In physical geographical terms, it is the peak of the Himalayas, the Kailāsa and the Triśūl, the ranges of Kedār and Badrī. They represent the central axis. The symbol of a mountain, tree or a column situated at the centre of the world is widely distributed in all ancient cosmologies, specially the Orient. Corresponding to the *Sumeru* of Indian mythology, is the concept of Haraberazait of the Iranians, Norse the Himingbjo of Mound of the Lands in the Mesopotamian tradition, Mount Tabor and Gerizim of the Palestinian tradition and Golgotha of the Christian tradition. In India, the Kailāsa and the Himalayas are the final journey of man's ascension; all aspire to this goal of reaching the heights and moving inward. Ecologically important, psychically and metaphorically the mountains, their height and their being equated to the centre of the cosmos naturally led to other correspondences, first the cosmic tree, then the straight column, the *yūpa* of the *yajña* and ultimately the building of temples, *stūpas* and even *masjids* in India, as a human endeavour, recall the experience of the Himalayas, specially the Kailāsa.

Kailāsa and Mānasarovara are important pilgrimage places, consecrated and revered. Men made Kailāsa of Ellora, Kanchipuram and innumerable other temples concretised through rock, stone and brick the mighty all pervasive myths of the mountain Kailāsa. Again in the myth, importance is attached to the mountain merging from the egg-shaped cosmos. The slopes of this mountain are propelled by a multitude of life, creation of the water, the vegetation of the earth, forests and fields, the animals, deers, monkeys and lions, the human gnomes, dwarfs and the flying celestials. The reality and the myth is recreated in architecture, for the summit of temples and *stūpas*, Amarāvatī (the eternal or immortal city). Early Buddhist *stūpas*, Bharhut, Sanchi and Amarāvatī are an architectural statement of the myth. Indian temples, throughout the length and breadth of India relive the physical journey to Kailāsa through the ritual circumbambulation of the temple and the pilgrimage from the outer to the inner. The metaphor is logically worked out for the *Śikhara* of temples rising from the hypothetical navel, the *garbhagṛha*, the centre to the summit.

Whether Amarnāth in Kashmir or Badrīnāth or Kailāsa, the Himalayas are the abode of the gods, particularly Śiva. He dominates the mountains as does Viṣṇu the waters and earth. The two, along with Brahmā, are the creator, sustainer and destroyer of the universe. The mythology relating to the Himalayas is naturally intrinsically connected with the Gaṅgā and of course that other symbol of purity, virginity, austerity – Umā, Pārvatī, Devī. Although Śiva appears in the *Vedas* only as Rudra and Śatarudriya, the *Purāṇas*, specially *Śiva Purāṇa*, are full of descriptions, myths and stories full of ecological significance and meaning. In this case also, Śiva as the Lord of the Himalayas is everything and anything in the universe. He is the Lord of animals, *Paśupati*, and the Lord of place, *Vāstoṣpati*. Significantly, among his progeny, one belongs to the animal kingdom, Gaṇeśa, and the other to water and fire. Kārttikeya Somaskanda rides a peacock. Viṣṇu lies on the snake. Śiva rides the mighty bull, his friend and companion, in effect an aspect of his nature which he must transcend. Each of these myths moves concurrently on an ecological, biophysical and psychical plane. Each in the iconographical form is a complete ecological statement and yet none can be conceived without the other. So Śiva is incomplete in art without *Śakti*, Viṣṇu without Lakṣmī, and the two are complete in the fusion of the conjoined image Hari-Hara.

The dance of Śiva is another perfect iconographical statement of ecology. What are his emblems? *Agni* and deer. What are his locks? They are the forests. Whom does he hide within himself? Gaṅgā (water). What adorns his hair? The sun and the moon. What are his garlands? The snakes. What does he wear? The tiger skin. And what he brings to this world is the cosmic rhythm of his *ḍamaru* in the incessant process of cyclic creation, degeneration and regeneration and finally of enlightenment, of knowledge and wisdom by trampling upon the dwarf, demon of darkness, ignorance and finally he blesses with the gesture of beatitude of life. And his energy is *Śakti*. Without her, he is incomplete. She herself, the daughter of the Himalayas, must undergo penance and austerities. The emphasis here is like in the case of Bhagīratha on discipline and austerity, purity and concentration.

Before we finally reach that ultimate source of energy, the Sun, we have to pause to look briefly at two other elements: one *Vāyu* (air), and other *Ākāśa* (space). We can only mention the other deities of the skies – the *Aśvinīs* and the *Maruts*.

Many beautiful hymns are dedicated to *Vāyu*, the pure air. Mythical *Vāyu* in the Vedic pantheon, is associated with *Indra*; he rides the same chariot with him, indeed *Indra* and *Vāyu* are often identified with each other. We know that Indra is the most powerful god of the skies and free spaces. Logically, just as Viṣṇu and Śiva are inter-connected and finally conjoined as *Śiva-Śakti, Agni, Vāyu* and *Sūrya* constitute a distinct group. The place of *Agni* is on earth, of *Vāyu* (air) or Indra in space and of *Sūrya* in heaven. *Vāyu* is the guardian of the north-western region, and thus in close proximity to *Varuṇa*. Its indispensability is obvious: *Vāyu* is limitless, effortlessly it crosses boundaries of land and sea, earth and water. Invisibly, it pervades all that lives, and without it all would die; it pervades all space, crossing the ocean and continents and is higher than the reach of fire, the flight paths of migrating birds or clouds. It is the force which protects ships across the seas or down the rivers, which moves the water and the forests, which kindles and nurtures fire, drives it forward and brings rain clouds.

Finally, air is that pure breath of life (*prāṇa*) through the control of which man attains a state of consciousness which is at one with the *empyrean*. Like the holy waters of the Gaṅgā, it is also giver of *mokṣa*, release and emancipation. Hymns and myths of such intensity could not have been created by those who feared the elements; they were created by those who were intuitively aware of the necessity to keep the environment pure and clean within men and without. The *Vāyu Purāṇa* elaborates upon the myth here. *Vāyu* is like *Varuṇa* and *Pṛthivī* is the upholder of the cosmic moral order, *Ṛta* and *Dharma*.

Myths relating to the skies and space are innumerable. The most powerful amongst these is about Indra. He is the most important war god. He is naturally connected with rainfall and hence thunder storms and wields the thunderbolt. The consciousness of the life-giving function of clouds and thunder, its relation with water and fire is also common everyday knowledge too often taken for granted without noting its significance. The companions of *Indra* are the twin gods *Aśvin* and *Maruts*.

And finally to that source of energy, fire, belonging to the nether, terrestrial and celestial worlds. We had already noted the connection between water and fire in the context of the myth of *Varuṇa*. At the terrestrial level, *Agni* is venerated as the sacrificial fire of the *Yajña*. The three ritual fires of the *Yajña* represent the domestic, terrestrial and celestial fires. The altars are made in the shape of a semicircle, circle and square. This symbolically states the interconnection of three orders of energy. We may not try to find modern equivalents of bio-mass, bio-spheres and solar energy, but the parallels are not far to seek. Innumerable epithets suggest the many forms of *Agni*.

And finally to that great ball of fire, the Sun, to whom all aspire and which is our one ray of hope.

Like water, earth, mountain and forests, the Sun also dominates all mythologies of the ancient world.

From the pygmies of Congo to the Pharoahs of Egypt, from the Incas of Mexico and Peru to the fire-worshippers of ancient Iran the Sun has been a symbol of moral light. He is again *Ṛta*. He takes different shapes, names and forms in different cultures and civilizations recognised as Ahura Mazda, Shamash, Helios and of course Apollo. In India, he is Sūrya, Āditya. He is the first principle of the non-manifest into the manifest. Vedic rituals consecrate through the chanting of *mantras* for this light and life-giving energy. In the ritual or domestic routine of tribal and rural societies, *Agni* and *Sūrya* are central. Myths relating to Sun, Āditya, abound. Son of Aditi, who had eight sons, but approached the gods with seven having cast away the eighth Mārtaṇḍa (the Sun). Myth and ritual of Sūrya, from the daily *Sūrya namaskāra* to the metaphysical significance of the Sun representing the process of self-awareness, has been consecrated like the Gaṅgā, Pṛthivī, Himalaya in architectural edifices and sculptural statements of the deepest significance.

Temples are dedicated to Sūrya in all parts of India: Mārtaṇḍa in Kashmir, Modhera in Gujarat, Koṇārka in the East. Sūrya is personified as the charioteer riding the seven horses, and images of the finest quality, again made ecologically valid plastic statements of the myth, are found in all parts and in all ages.

Like the Descent of Gaṅgā panel at Mamallapuram, the monument of supreme beauty, juxtaposed with the first principle of the mighty ocean, the open skies shrouded by vegetation and glowing with energy is Koṇārka, the Sun Temple. Will we maintain its purity physically, i.e., of the environs of Koṇārka, the cultural heritage, significance of the myth, by asking, pleading for light and life?

The energy of the Sun, the relationship of Sun, Earth, vegetation and water gives rise to a whole aesthetics in India where the changing seasons, the *Bāramāsa*, the *nāyakas*, the *rāgas* and *rāgiṇīs* are all myths of ecology. Another chapter of ecology is unfolded in Indian aesthetics. We must end this article with a prayer of peace and well-being:

> Pure and peaceful be earth,
> peaceful ether, peaceful heaven,
> peaceful water, peaceful herbs, peaceful trees,
> may all gods and environs be pure and peaceful;

> may there be purity, non-pollution and peace
> through these invocations.

So the lessons are obvious. Non-pollution, discipline, restraint, awareness of inter-dependability and inter-relatedness is taught to us through custom, daily routine, myth and ritual, but we don't learn. We should learn before it is too late.

Note

1. UNESCO, UNEP Inter-Governmental Conference on Environmental Education, Tbilisi, USSR, 14–26 October, 1977. Final Report, Paris, UNESCO, 1978, p. 67.

13

The Cosmic Elements in India
An Agenda of Questions

Ashok R. Kelkar

Not being an Indologist and not knowing Sanskrit I am at best a curious layman full of questions. I decided that I could play a limited but useful role in this preparatory seminar by asking questions and looking not only for answers but also for evidence in the texts and other artifacts of the Great Traditions and the Little Traditions that would have a bearing on the answers.

Instead of cluttering the presentation with question marks, I have a numbered series of propositions to offer, each with an implied question: Isn't that so? The propositions are grouped according to certain perspectives against which the cosmic elements have been viewed. 'India' here stands for ancient and medieval south Asia. The Islamic Tradition has been left out – though not completely.

The Perspective of Cosmology

Any cosmology worth the name presupposes a certain philosophy of reality in relation to a certain philosophy of understanding. There are two alternate ways of relating these two with two concomitant styles of philosophizing.

1-A. There cannot be a philosophy of reality distinct from a philosophy of understanding. Indeed the former flows from the latter. In philosophizing it pays to be sceptical, reductionist, and parsimonious. In India this style of philosophizing was called the philosophy of search (*ānvīkṣikī*).

1-B. Of course there can be a philosophy of reality distinct from a philosophy of understanding. Indeed the latter flows from the former. In philosophizing it pays to be boldly speculative, phenomenological, and integrationist. In India this style of philosophizing was called the philosophy of vision (*darśana*).

Indian cosmology started by asking what the Prime Cause (*ādi-kāraṇa*) (not reducible to others) of the universe is. The two styles correspondingly offered two different answers.

2-A. The world (*viśva*) is a universe. The universe comes from atoms (*aṇu, pīlu*).

2-B. The world is a universe. The universe comes from a single principle or Urgrund.

The second answer has been variously elaborated.

2-B.1. Vedic tradition: This was the principle of growth (*brahman*).

2-B.2. Āgamic tradition: This was the principle of energy (*śakti*).

2-B.3. Synthetic traditions:

2-B.3-a. This was the principle of conjunction of the male and the female.

2-B.3-a-1. The constant male and the variable female stand in a joyful union (*mithuna*).

2-B.3-a-2. The many potent yet passive males (*puruṣas*) make it possible for the one active yet latent female (*prakṛti*) to become more specific-and-manifest (*vyakta*). At a certain point the male loses interest in watching (being *sākṣin*) and become free from involvement; and the female loses interest in becoming more specific-and-manifest and desists from it.

2-B.3-b. This was the principle of delegation, the constant 'growth' delegating variable 'energy' to –

2-B.3-b-1. The male power (*īśvara*)

2-B.3-b-2. The female power (*śakti*)

Indian cosmology continued with the question as to what the universe was made of or reducible to –

3-A.1. The Universe was reducible to certain running (or binding) threads (*guṇa*, namely the thread of essences (*sattvaguṇa*), the thread of activity (*rajoguṇa*), and the thread of inertia (*tamoguṇa*).

3-A.2. The universe was reducible to certain sensible quanta (*tanmātra*), namely, sound (*śabda*), touch (*sparśa*), visible form (*rūpa*), taste (*rasa*), smell (*gandha*).

3-B. The universal power has created and controlled certain material beings (*bhūta*), namely, earth (*pṛthivī*), water (*ap*), fire (*agni*) and wind (*vāyu*).

In the synthetic tradition the last two answers were married together after adding a fifth member to the second list.

3-C.1. The universe is made of five grossly accessible elements (*sthūla-bhūta, mahā-bhūta*), namely, earth, water, fire, wind, ether (*ākāśa*), and five subtly accessible elements (*sūkṣma-bhūta, ādi-bhūta*), namely, smell, taste, visible form, touch and sound that correspond to them.

In the synthetic tradition (3-A.1), the first of the three answers was also accommodated.

3-C.2. The animating energy in the universe may be either manifest (*vyakta*) and uneven (*viṣama*) or unmanifest (*avyakta*) and even (*sama*). When the thread of essence is operative energy tends to go from the unmanifest to the manifest state (*avasthā*), when the thread of activity is operative, energy tends to stay manifest, when the thread of inertia is operative; and energy tends to go from the manifest to the unmanifest.

Note: (3-C.2) read with (3-A.1) makes one feel tempted to find an analogy between the three threads and, correspondingly, information, energy and matter of modern physics as its three variable primes.

The Perspective of Human History of Ideas

There is an interesting parallel between Greek and Indian cosmology. Was there an Indo-European cosmology? The European order of the first four elements is variable.

4. The Indo-European cosmology: The Universe is made of four elements:
   earth (hot and wet to Greeks, heavy and dense to Indians)
   water (cold and wet to Greeks, cold and soft to Indians)
   fire (hot and dry to Greeks, hot to Indians)
   air (cold and dry to Greeks, light to Indians)

Note: Medieval Europe added ether as the fifth element (*quinta essentia*) on the authority of Plato, who spoke of the fifth non-limited element. Ancient India added ether as the fifth neutral element.

The parallel extends to their account of the microcosm of the human person. The Greeks spoke of the four elements:

blood
phlegm: the cool temper
choler (yellow bile): the hot temper
melancholia (black bile)

The wind (of the respiratory and alimentary canals) was never added to this list but often considered to be a major variable. The Indians spoke of the three elements (*dhātu*) corresponding to the middle three of the five cosmic elements.

phlegm (*kapha*): water: the system of fluids
choler (*pitta*): fire: the system of heating
wind (*vāta*): air: the system of impulses

The first two are also called: coldness (*śaitya*), hotness (*uṣṇatā*). (Incidentally, the Arabs came up with a synthetic list: wind, bile, phlegm, blood.)

5. The Indo-European cosmology: The human person (the body-mind complex) is governed by three elements.
   water: phlegm
   fire: yellow bile
   air

Note: The Greeks split the fluid system into blood and phlegm, split the heating system into yellow hot bile and black cold bile, and left out air. The Indians recognized two manifestations of bile: hot bile and cold bile.

The earth was recognized as the inert substratum of the human body by the Indians and the Semitics. The respiratory wind (*prāṇa, anima, spiritus*) was recognized as the animating principle of the human body by the Indians, the Greeks, and the Semitics.

Speech (*śabda, logos*) was recognized by all the three as the animating principle of the universe; the Indians linked it with sound (*śabda, nāda*); the Greeks linked it with musical sound.

It will perhaps be worthwhile to compare these with the classical Chinese system of elements. (The expression *wu hsing* is probably better translated as 'five virtues or forces'.) They are usually enumerated as follows:

chin (metal, which accepts form by melting and moulding)
mu (wood, which accepts form by cutting and carving)
shui (water, which soaks and descends)

huo (fire, which blazes and ascends)
thu (earth, which accepts seeds and allows reaping)

It is interesting that air and ether are missing and that metal and wood are present.

The Perspective of the Theory of Art

The animating principle of the universe was also identified with water – *jīvana* means both. The powerful image of the monsoon cloud burst on the sun-parched earth, which then turns green, may be at the back of this. Consider also the coupling of the earth (*pṛthivī*) and the sky (*dyaus*). (Vedic *dyaus-pitṛ-* is cognate with *Zeus* and *Jupiter*.)

Another powerful image is that of vital sap (*rasa*) rising in the growing plant. The criss-cross semantic links can be shown thus:

6. *rasa*
   (1) juice
   (2) taste
   (1a) (metaphor from 1) animating principle
   (2a) (metonymy from 2) enjoyment

Note: The historical link, if any, between (1) and (2) is obscure. But the identity of sound between (1a) and (2a) has been exploited twice. That both (1a) and (2a) are relevant for the theory of art is argued in A. Sankaran, 'Some Theories of *rasa* and *dhvani*', Madras 1926, reprinted New Delhi 1973, chapter 1.

7-A. *rasa*
   (1a) animating principle of the universe
   (2a) enjoyment from contemplating this

Note: *Taittirīya-Upaniṣad* "*raso vai saḥ* | *rasaṃ hyevāyaṃ labdhvānandī-bhavati* |"

7-B. *rasa*
   (1a) animating principle of a work of art
   (2a) enjoyment from contemplating this

Note: The parallel between 7-A and 7-B was noticed by Jagannātha.

The sense (1a) of *rasa* has also been exploited in Āyurvedic Pharmacology. There is an interesting parallel between that and the theory of *rasa* as the animating principle of a work of art.

8-A. Āyurvedic Pharmacology:
   (1) material cause (*kāryin, upādāna*): herbal substance
   (2) efficient cause (*kāraṇa*): the active principle (*vīrya*)
   (3) animating energy: animating principle of medicinal cure (*rasa*)

Note: See Suśruta cited S.N. Dasgupta, *History of Indian Philosophy*, pp. 361–62, note.

8-B. Theory of the reception of dramatic art
   (1) material cause, story content of the text (*kāvyārtha*)
   (2) efficient cause, the various *bhāvas* in the work
   (3) animating energy, animating principle of art – reception and enjoyment (*rasa*)

Note: The parallel between 8-A and 8-B was pointed out by D.K. Bedekar (*Alocanā*, Delhi, April-July, 1952; reprinted, January-March, 1990).

The Perspective of the Practice of Art

The cosmic elements can appear in the experiential content of literary art and figurative plastic art. In European and Chinese art the elements appear as powerful presences animating the scene –

earth as mountains, vast expanse of land
water as sea, flowing water, rain, snow
fire as destructive fire, hearth fire
wind as storm

and thus often powerfully affecting the human lives on the scene: giving a turn to events, sympathizing with the emotional upheavals, and so forth.

In the practice (and the theory attendant on it) of the classical Tamil poetry of the Interior (*akam* – essentially love poetry), five phases of love (*uri*) are associated with five kinds of landscape. Thus, anxiety and separation in love is associated with –

the *neytal* flower, the plants *atumpu, punnai*
seashore
night fall
any season
seagull, crocodile, shark
wells, sea
selling fish and salt
fisherfolk

9. There are three literary traditions in India:

9-A. *ārṣa* poetics (Vedic hymns and the two major epics)

9-B. *saṃskṛta* poetics (Classical Sanskrit literature and theatre and poetry modelled on this)

9-C. *prākṛta* poetics (Classical Tamil literature of love, war, and *bhakti*, Buddhist literature in Pali and Sanskrit, Prakrit and Sanskrit poetry with a Little Tradition base such as *Gāhāsattasai* or *Gītagovinda, Bṛhatkathā* and other narrative cycles like *Kathāsaritsāgara*, and *bhakti* poetry).

10. The Cosmic elements play on the whole a supportive rather than a dramatic role in these three traditions, although there are important variations.

Indian figurative plastic art is very much man-centred.

11. The cosmic elements play a minor supportive role in Indian figurative plastic art.

In Indian architecture, the temple is conceived either in the image of Man or in the image of the sacred Mountain. Earth, water, air, and light play important constitutive roles in Indian architecture.

In Indian arts of performance (*saṅgīta*, comprising singing, instrument-playing, and dancing), the cosmic elements play at best the role of a model for the technical organization of the medium.

It is hoped that the various hypotheses proposed will bear examination, and induce a fruitful reconsideration of received accounts of the subject-matter.

14

Mahābhūta in Determining Cultural Ecology

Bryan Mulvihill

"Aesthetics determines Cultural Ecology"[1]

In most ancient or 'traditional' societies a deep respect for the elemental forces in which human beings found themselves immersed is evident from the cultural histories, rites and artifacts that have been passed down to us here in the late twentieth century.

Native Americans held all of nature as sacred, a transmitter of knowledge, their cultural rites fostered a sensitive respect for the elements in nature. As one of the world's oldest surviving traditional societies, North American indigenous peoples consider themselves as part of the environment in which they live rather than as superior agents put on earth with divine right to conquer and control.

The oriental cultures of the Asian Northeast, developed a spiritual interdependence with the elemental forces through the philosophy of Dao which emphasized harmony in opposites and the constant transformation of the solid and moving forces. Early European societies expressed their relationships to the elements through the gnostic cults predating the Christian era, with alchemical fascinations which continued to express themselves up to the present time in images of androgyne, uniting of opposite forces, and through sympathetic magic rituals.

Perhaps no other society has developed the human interdependence with nature to such a refined and elaborate degree than the cultures of the Indian sub-continent where the relationship with the elemental forces is portrayed on every level of human and cultural expression through the vision as held in the tradition of the *Mahābhūtas*.

Now at this time, in the history of humankind, all the cultures of the planet are faced with the same dangerous dilemma of a serious disregard for the natural order of the elements upon which existence is dependent. The very bases of the traditional five elemental forces, the *Mahābhūtāni*, have been undermined. The rapid degradation of the natural environment have been irrevocably disturbed with mass scale deforestation, desertification, chemical and nuclear pollution. The worlds, oceans and rivers are increasingly poisoned.

Global warming, with encroaching drought, is threatening large areas of habitable lands. The windswept affects of pollution and radiation spreading from one corner of the planet are affecting all others while the very ether itself is being radically rearranged as is becoming evident in the ozone holes. At the same time large oxygen producing areas are dangerously being deforested.

It has become essential to collectively develop a respectful understanding for the world in which we find ourselves. To do this we can learn much from the ancient societies who had developed cultural attitudes and practices which were in relative harmony with the elemental forces of both nature and human nature.

Perhaps it is equally the first time in history that the various cultures have access to each other's traditions and histories to be able to develop a healthy respect through understanding, if not an interdependent transcultural foundation for a harmonious relationship with the earth and its beings. Still today the greatest danger to human survival is human-kind itself. Without checking human greed and intolerance no amount of environmentally friendly actions will ensure a future for the family of man. In this light cultural sensitivity, with understanding, play the most essential role in transforming and maintaining a harmonious relationship with our physical, social and spiritual environment. The culture of a people is itself the most fundamental environment, "Aesthetics determines cultural ecology".

Indian cultures have in the past developed refined, comprehensive, relationships to the elemental forces which can provide valuable insight for developing a modern 'cultural ecology' that is in harmony with the forces of nature along with the physical and physiological needs of the human community. An appreciation of the nature of the elements, as transmitted in the conception of the *Mahābhūtas*, has in the past been diverse and effective over long periods of history of the sub-continent's dynasties, spiritual traditions and diverse communities in harmonizing man's relationship with the environment in which he found himself. The Indian sub-continent flourished, supporting the world largest populations and diversity of culture in a co-existent balance with nature. It was not until the full effects of the British Raj and massive industrialization that the attitude towards the effects on the natural environment became self-centred.

The detailed analyses of this history and practice in light of contemporary social, ecological and human needs reveals many dimensions that provide ample evidence of the depth and complexity that is required in a functional cultural vision successfully to integrate human and environmental harmony. In the space of this short commentary the writer will briefly try to indicate but a few of the many possibilities for detailed application in this research. As the dimension of the current global interdependent ecological disintegration is equally vast and complex, the need for such study, and all the more, effective practice, is paramount.

The cultural dissemination of the philosophic, spiritual and attitudinal perspectives necessary to effect a holistic relationship between all aspects of "being-qua-existenz"[2] has continuously proven the most effective way of unifying the maximum segment of any society with nature. This is essential for the well-being of all aspects of a human environment. Political systems, that function on a fifty-one per cent of the popular demand, which is the current practice of parliamentary representation, or rule economic productivity or military force, often with far less than even half the voting population's support, have proven woefully ineffective in providing a functional human ecological balance. The very fact that culture is currently regarded by most governments, world banks, and international development agencies as an additional frill or luxury of a society rather than an integral necessity is itself one of the primary misconceptions hindering both local communications and the global instigation necessary to maintain a humane ecological balance. One is reminded of Mahatma Gandhi's terse statement "The earth provides enough to satisfy every man's needs, but not for anybody's greed".[3] To provide adequately for all and curb the greed of even a few requires at least a ninety per cent participation in the shared resolve which only a creatively functioning cultural unity can provide, no matter what political, social and religious system is in practice.

During the intense period of interdisciplinary philosophic, spiritual and cultural development, from the fifth to eighth centuries A.D., as was afforded by the establishment of large Buddhist universities, such as Nālandā Mahāvihāra, the five elemental forces were iconographically presented in their configurational complexity as a *maṇḍala*. *Maṇḍala* means a concentration of energy or a circle, *la* means to take up and hold. The experience of being in the phenomenal world of elemental forces has meaning, being itself as the ground. Therefore, the energy of the forces is the ground or foundation of meaningfulness. The *maṇḍala* of the *Mahābhūtas* expresses the meaningfulness of being as experienced and expressed through the elemental forces. *Ma* also means beautiful and *la* beautified. Rendered literally, this term refers to a total sphere, globular and wholly encircled. The centre is the primordial awareness of being itself surrounded by a circle of elemental forces. Thus being is enhanced, beautified by the awareness of understanding and appreciation of the nature of the elements. Being is equally dependent upon, and an expression of, the elements. Both together form the whole, as expressed by the image of the five directional *maṇḍala* principal, with four cardinal points arranged around being, either expressing the cognitive awareness of being. If this central awareness is solidified into an egological projection of a self, in control of the elements, the whole process is affected. The elements become tainted by the independent self-centred projection, becoming poisonous conflicting emotions, ignorance, attachment, greed and envy. By transforming the centre from an ego-centred perception into an interdependent relaticnship configuration, the poisons are purified into experienced creativity of a harmonious interaction of forces.

The perception of the phenomenal world made up of the *Mahābhūtas* initiates the possibility for the development of a thematically directed consciousness within which the thematizing perception assumes the dominant role and becomes, in a certain sense, a centre around which all other cognitive operations are arranged. Whether such imaging is directed toward the external, internal, or arcane features of this being conscious, it occurs in an undivided wholeness whose complexity is included in the five elements of the five directional *maṇḍala* of the *Mahābhūtas* the whole ensemble constituting the amazing unity and continuity of what we call a conscious individual.. The divisiveness between the phenomenal world and its perception, as organized with respect to the experiencing individual, are united in a configurational whole which allows the individual to function in a holistic frame of mind, both being part of the whole and individually responsible for its manifestation.

In comparison with European philosophic traditions Socratic notions made up the world of separate identifiable substances, which become the building blocks of 'reality', linguistically termed nouns. Human beings also assuming the position of a noun with a separate identity, against all experiential evidence to the contrary, created the heterogeneous relationship to nature which increasingly is the source of the disintegration of both the natural and social environments. In the *Mahābhūta* perception of all phenomena, men, women, and their thematic ideation, are part of the holistic process which is entirely interdependent. Each aspect affects the whole. The external world of elements is dependent upon the physical properties, the perception of an experiencing individual, and the social cultural context which all must be in harmonious balance with the elements to sustain effective interdependence.

Briefly, if we take the organizational structure of the *Mahābhūta maṇḍala* as a model for developing an ecologically sound cultural system, we must consider it in all its complexity including the (a) external, (b) internal, and (c) arcane or primordial features of being conscious to assure an undivided wholeness whose complexity we can outline as follows. The four directions are quaternary of (a) externally earthy solid, watery cohesion, fiery combustion and stormy motility, (b) what is internally the perceptible, feeling, ideation, and actualizing, and (c) what is arcanely dullness, arrogance, addiction, and envy, all temporally abiding as cognitive fields constituting the four directions. The triad of irritation, horizon, and thematically directed consciousness constitute the centre, because it abides as reflective perception which is inherent as the nature of the human mind, and that which put in front of the mind reflects, known in Buddhist *Vajrayāna* terminology as mirror-like pristine cognition. All of these form configurations surpassing the imagination, actually abiding externally as the five elemental forces which can be referred to as the five femininities and internally as the five psychophysical groupings which are then the five masculinities, and arcanely as the five poisons which when transformed are the five pristine cognitions.

The human relationship to the five elements is not a simple, nor straightforward, as outlined very briefly here in this simplistic overview of the *Mahābhūta maṇḍala*. However even the most elementary examination of these principles reveals deep insights into the complexity of the relationship.

Indeed if we consider the primordial poisons or misconceptions, arising out of ignoring the subtleties of human interdependence with the phenomenal world and, the underlying mental states of irritation giving rise to closing down of one's protective ignoring awareness, the effects of one's actions result in the environment. For example the earth element when perceived as that which goes on, no matter what you do to it, exemplifies the attitude of dullness. Dullness operates internally to ignore or close off that which is perceptible. The transformation by turning this earthy attitude of dullness is achieved by a vibrant paying attention, which notices the constant affects and interdependent changes with every interaction with the phenomenal world. The earth is not a solid unresponsive lump but a vibrant relationship of elements.

The globally embedded arrogance, which makes possible the overt delusion, inflation of ego operations, that man is independent of nature, is represented by the water element, internally constituted as feelings and, externally, watery cohesion, which allows multinational and personal greed to become the *modus operandi* without noticing the consequences. The fire element represents addiction, which becomes a craving for and attachment to that which has been singled out, and obsessive inordinate possessiveness reinforced by ego operations internally constituted as ideation and, externally, fiery combustion. The air element expresses an embedded envy which is a reluctance to accept how things are developing into the urge to meddle, internally as actualizing of innate tendencies and, externally, stormy motility. The above reads like our current state of world affairs and gives a working picture of the causes and effects of the ecological disaster we are collectively faced with. The process of becoming attuned to the *maṇḍala* of the five elemental forces is in itself a way to begin to transform the negative aspects into positive or functional cooperative interdependences.

The *Mahābhūta maṇḍala* is not based on ideas of imagination but the actual physics and psychophysical nature of human interaction which is embodied in physical structure. A transformation always indicates first an awareness of the actual situation to be transformed. The very fact that we now talk about the global environment, which during the last two centuries of global industrialization we have somehow managed to ignore in the blind view of 'progress', shows how far the world's cultural systems have gone astray. We can no longer point the finger at one group or in one direction for in the globally interdependent ecology there is no east or west, nor south or north. The industrialization and human addiction to greed has become a world-wide phenomena. What we can, and must do, if we are to survive as a species, is develop a culture based on an awareness of the actual nature of our physical and psycho-physical situation. A deep study into the *maṇḍala* principles contained in the *Mahābhūta* will provide profound insights to this all-pervasive nature of things as they are.

However, study alone is only the beginning. To be effective we need to bring the awareness and sensitivity of these basic underlying principles to the forefront of the human community which will require a dynamic and energetic re-looking at the process and necessity of a cultural ecology. To begin this enormous task it will require national and international network of the cultural communities getting to know one another and collectively exploring the ecological imbalances and finding effective ways to transform the human relationship to our mother earth. India with its enormous human potential and deep historical understanding, as amply displayed in the *Mahābhūta* vision, will have to play a leading role in this process.

Notes

1. A quote from the Miss General Idea File, Morris/Trasov Archives, Image Bank Directory, Vancouver, 1965.
2. A term adopted by Herbert V. Guenther, in '*Matrix of Mystery*', Shambhala, Boulder & London, 1984. In brief this term encapsules the entirety of living existenz as defined by Guenther, "By its very nature Being, in its totality, tends to structure itself in and as the unifying continuity which most decisively determines the uniquely experiential character of being human. The unifying continuity which determines experience as such as we can call existenz". Being-

qua-existenz indicates that this continuity is always suffused by the highly energized process of Being.

3. As quote on Lino cut of 'Bapuji, 12.4.1930' by Nandlal Bose. Gandhi Book House, Rajghat Colony, New Delhi.

List of Contributors

P.P. Apte
1999 Sadashiv Peth, Madiwale Colony
Tilak Road
Pune–411030

Bettina Bäumer
B-1/159, Assi
Varanasi–221005

H.N. Chakravarty
B-1/159, Assi
Varanasi–221005

S.S. Janaki
11, VI Main Road
Raja Annamalaipuram
Madras–600028

Ashok R. Kelkar
7, Dhananjaya 759/83
Off Bhandarkar Road
Pune–411004

Mukund Lath
A-37/38 Vishwamitra Marg
Shyam Nagar, Ajmer Road
Jaipur–302019

Bryan Mulvihill
OPERA,
4001, Berri, #399
Montreal, Qc, H2L 4H2
Canada

S.P. Sabarathinam
167/17, IV Avenue
Jawahar Colony, Anna Nagar
Madras–600040

Prem Lata Sharma
'Amnaya'
209/1 Nand Nagar, Karaundi
Varanasi–221005

V. Ganapati Sthapati B-5, Geethalaya
3rd Seaward Road
Valmiki Nagar, Tiruvanmiyur
Madras–600041

K.D. Tripathi Deptt. of Āgama and Dharmaśāstra
Faculty of Oriental Learning,
Banaras Hindu University
Varanasi–221005

Radhavallabh Tripathi Deptt. of Sanskrit
Doctor Harisingh Gour Vishvavidyalaya
Sagar–470003 (M.P.)

Michael Meister Deptt. of the History of Art
University of Pennsylvania
3440 Market Street, Suite 560
Philadelphia, PA 19104
USA

Kapila Vatsyayan Indira Gandhi National Centre for the Arts
Janpath
New Delhi–110001

Index

PLATES

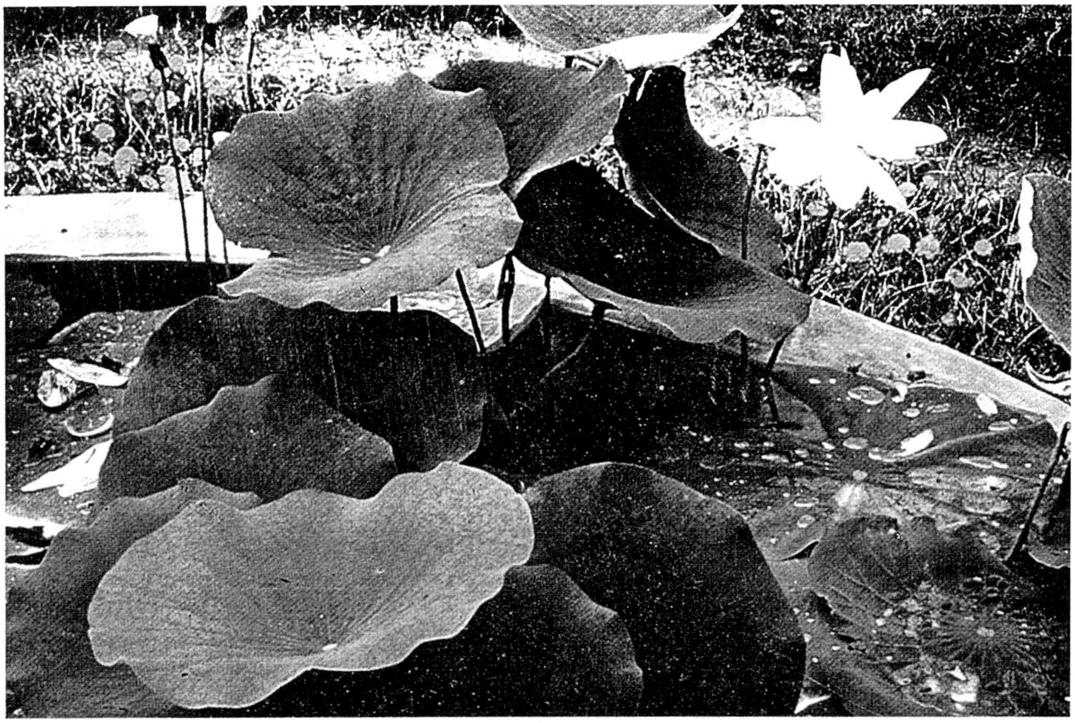

Plate 10.1. Benares, Uttar Pradesh. Lotus pond

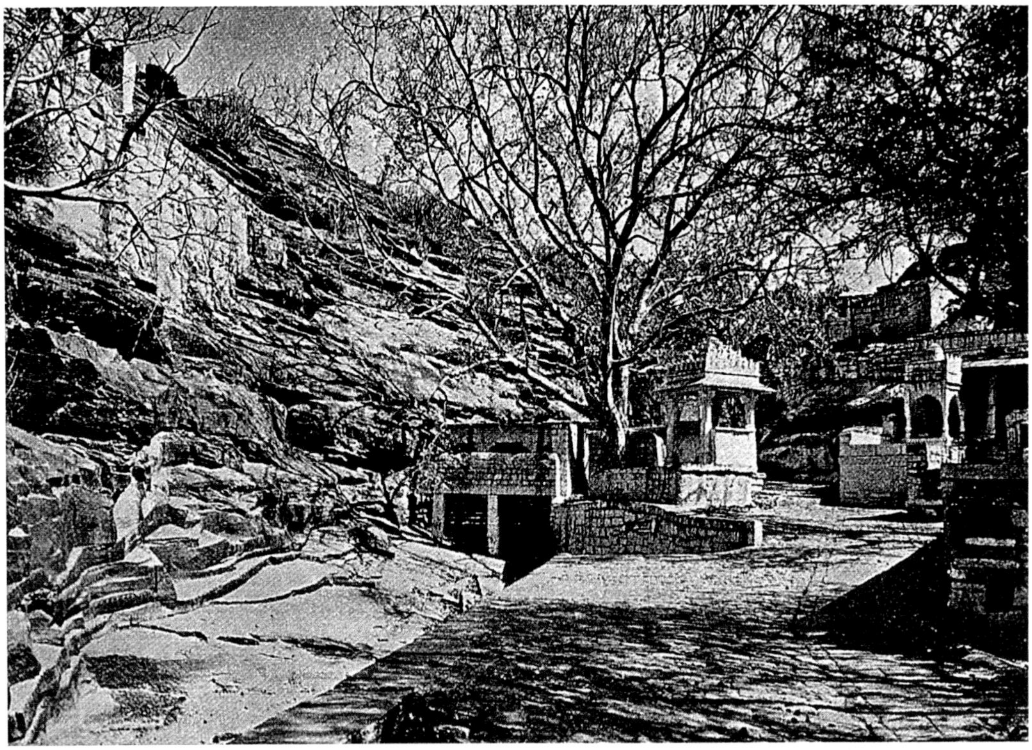

Plate 10.2. Arna, Rajasthan. Natural *tīrtha*

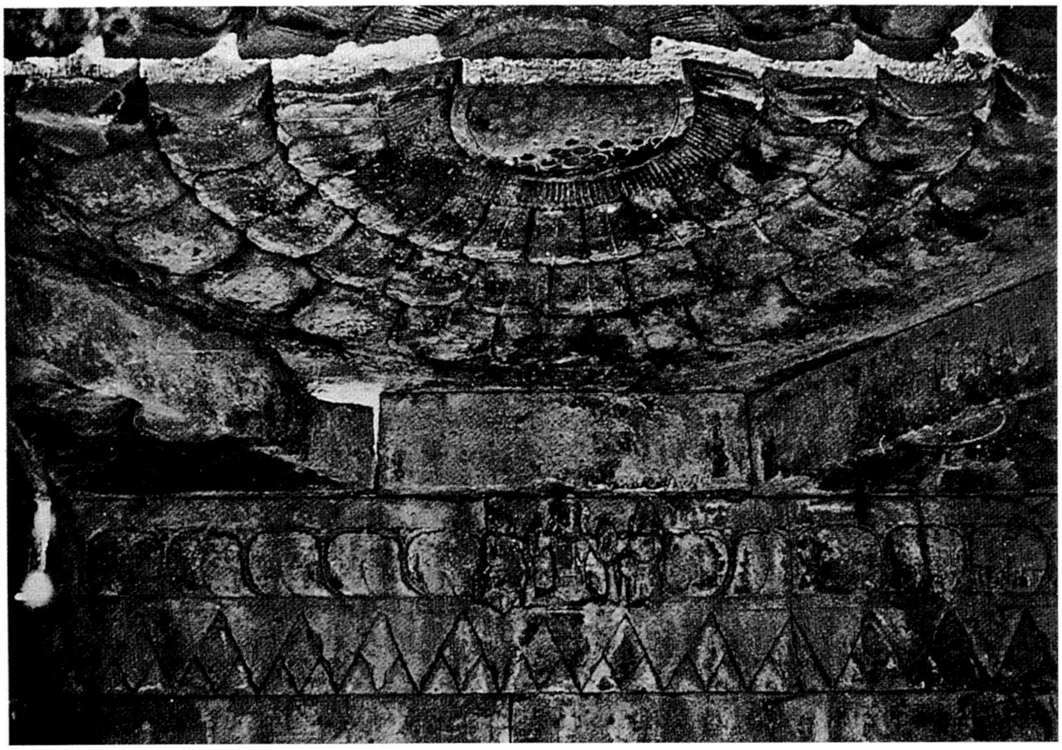

Plate 10.3. Khidarpura, Rajasthan. Śiva Temple, *ca.* AD 825-50. Lotus ceiling in sanctum

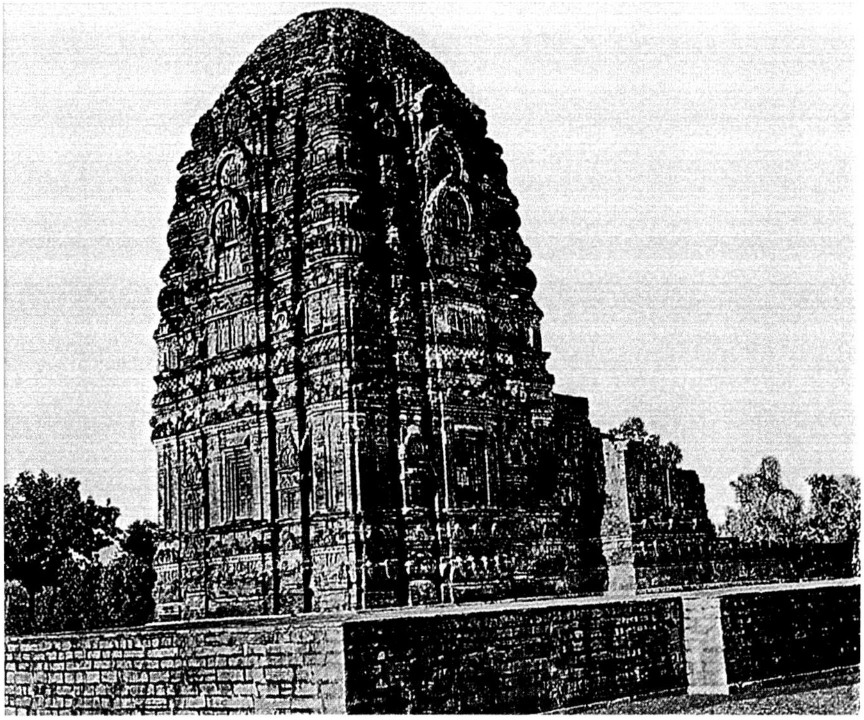

Plate 10.4. (b) Sirpur, Madhya Pradesh. Lakṣmaṇa Temple, *ca*. AD 600-25, from southeast

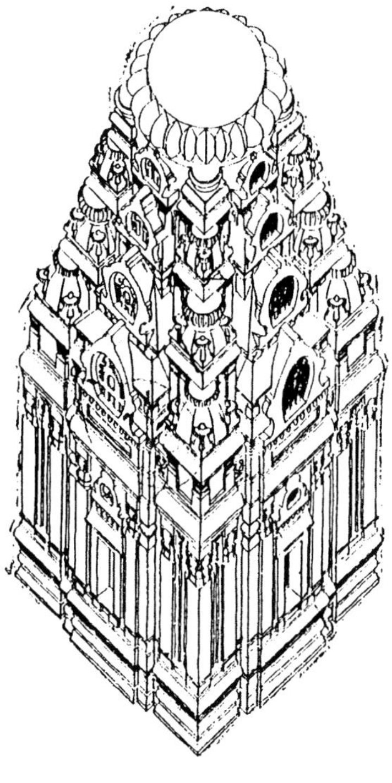

Plate 10.4. (a) Rajim, Madhya Pradesh. Rājīvalocana Temple, *ca*. AD 600

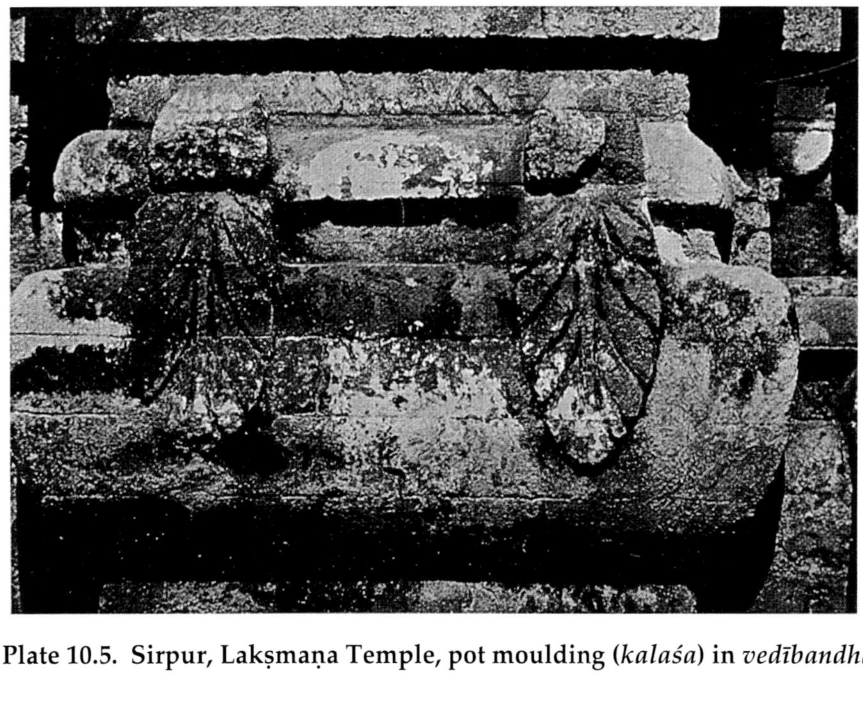

Plate 10.5. Sirpur, Lakṣmaṇa Temple, pot moulding (*kalaśa*) in *vedībandha*

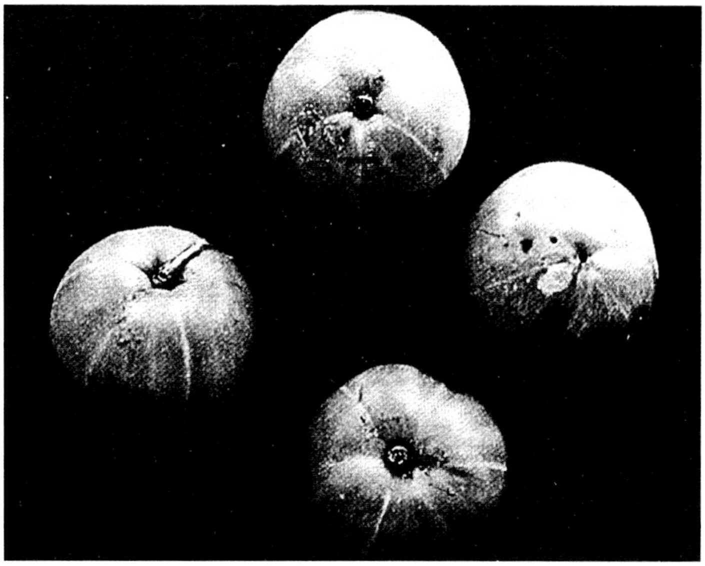

Plate 10.7. *Āmalā*-fruits

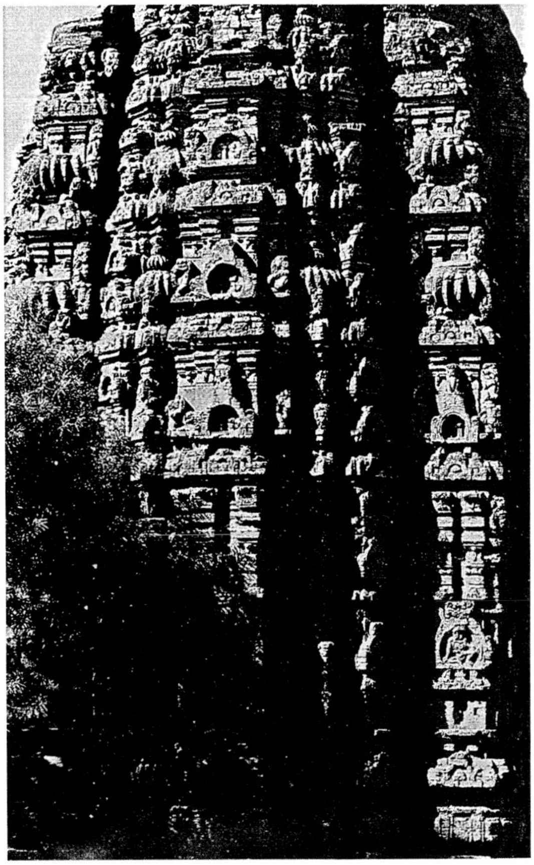

Plate 10.6. Palari, Madhya Pradesh.
Siddheśvara Mahādeva Temple
ca. AD 675-700, from east

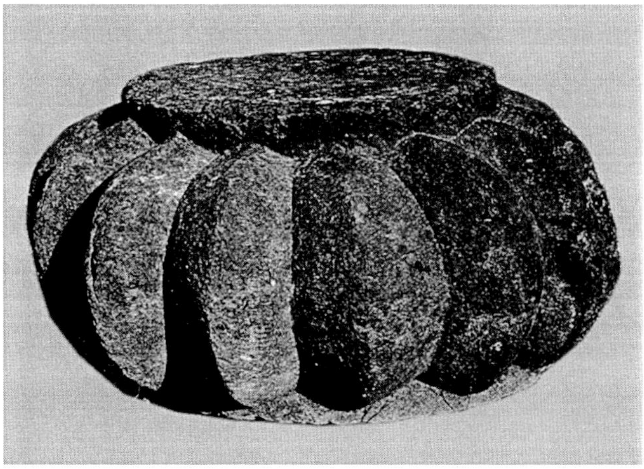

Plate 10.8. Deogaṛh, Madhya Pradesh. Gupta Temple
āmalaka, *ca.* AD 500-25

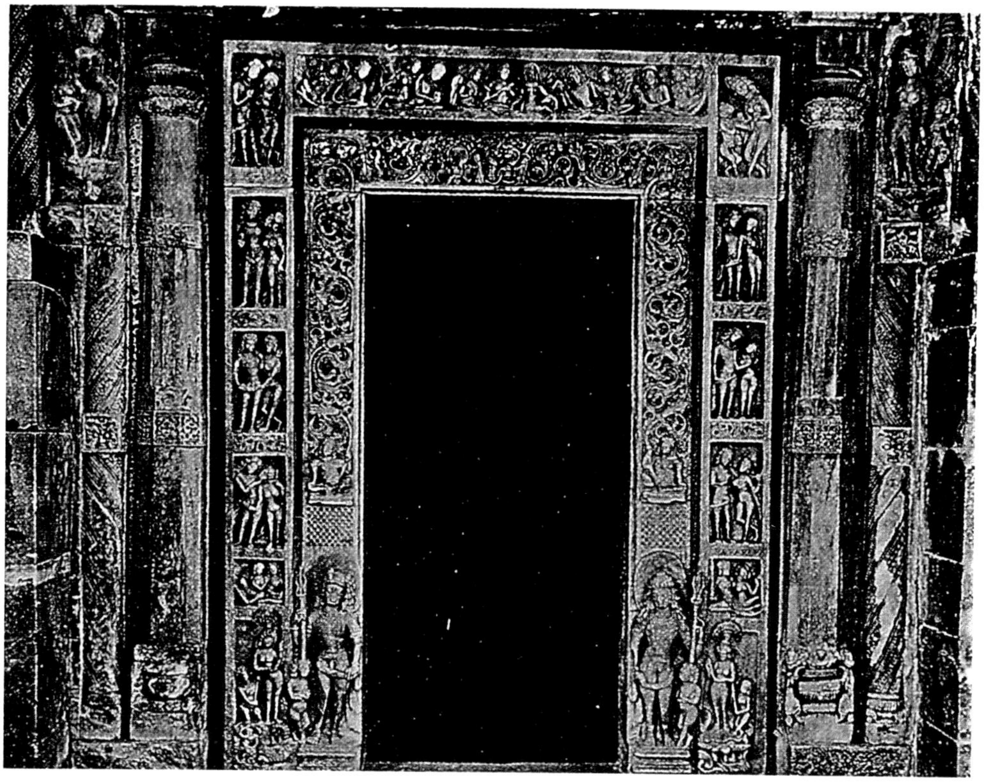

Plate 10.9. Nachna, Madhya Pradesh. Pārvatī Temple, *ca.* AD 450-75. Sanctum doorway

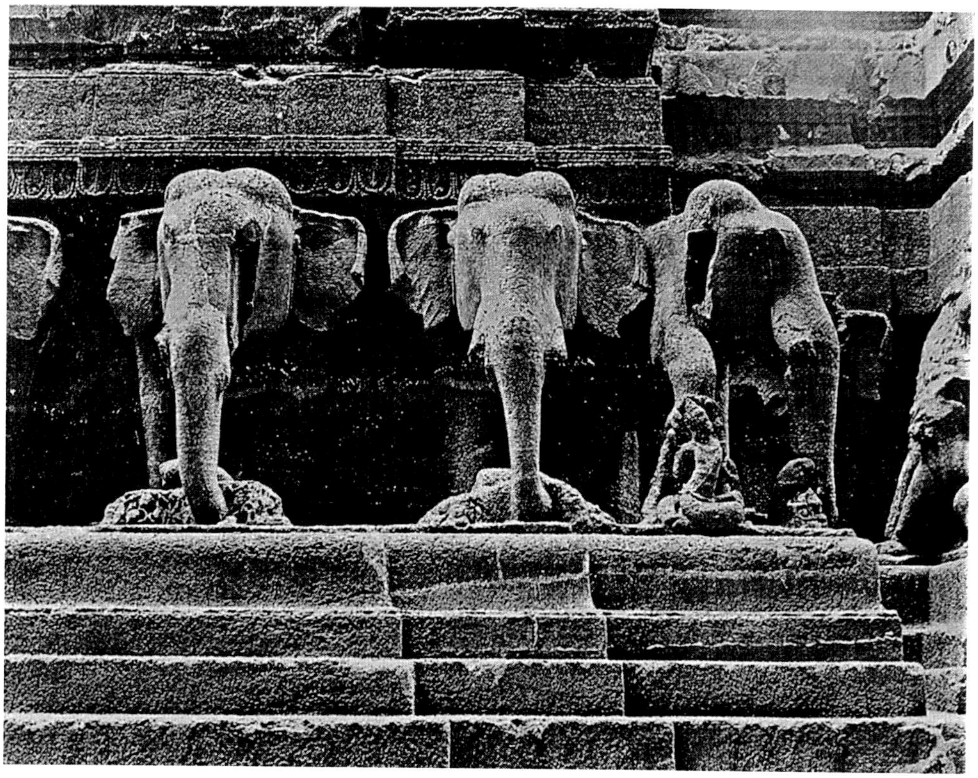

Plate 10.10. Ellorā, Maharashtra. Ellorā Kailāsa Temple, *ca.* AD 750-75. Elephants on *upapīṭha*

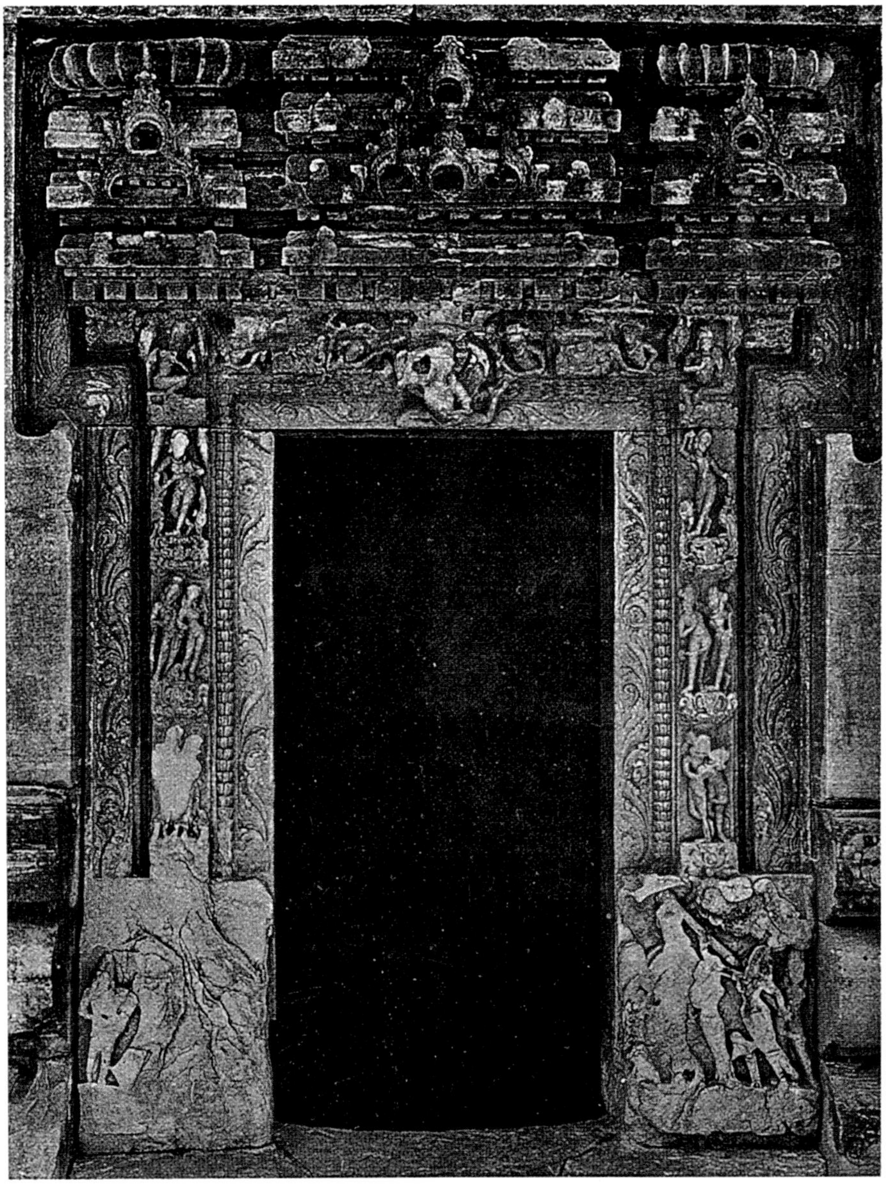

Plate 10.11. Amrol Madhya Pradesh. Rāmeśvara Temple, *ca*. AD 700. Doorway on east

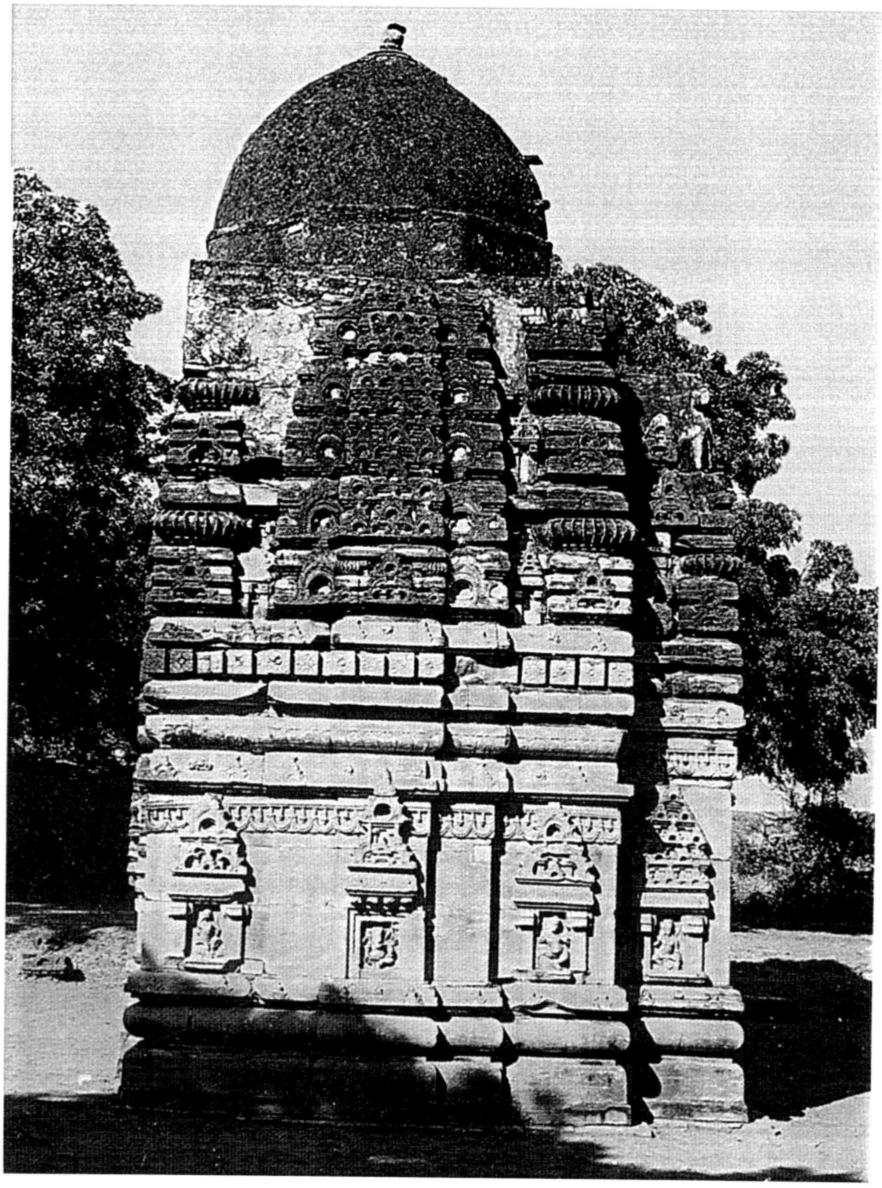

Plate 10.12. Amrol, Rāmeśvara Temple from south

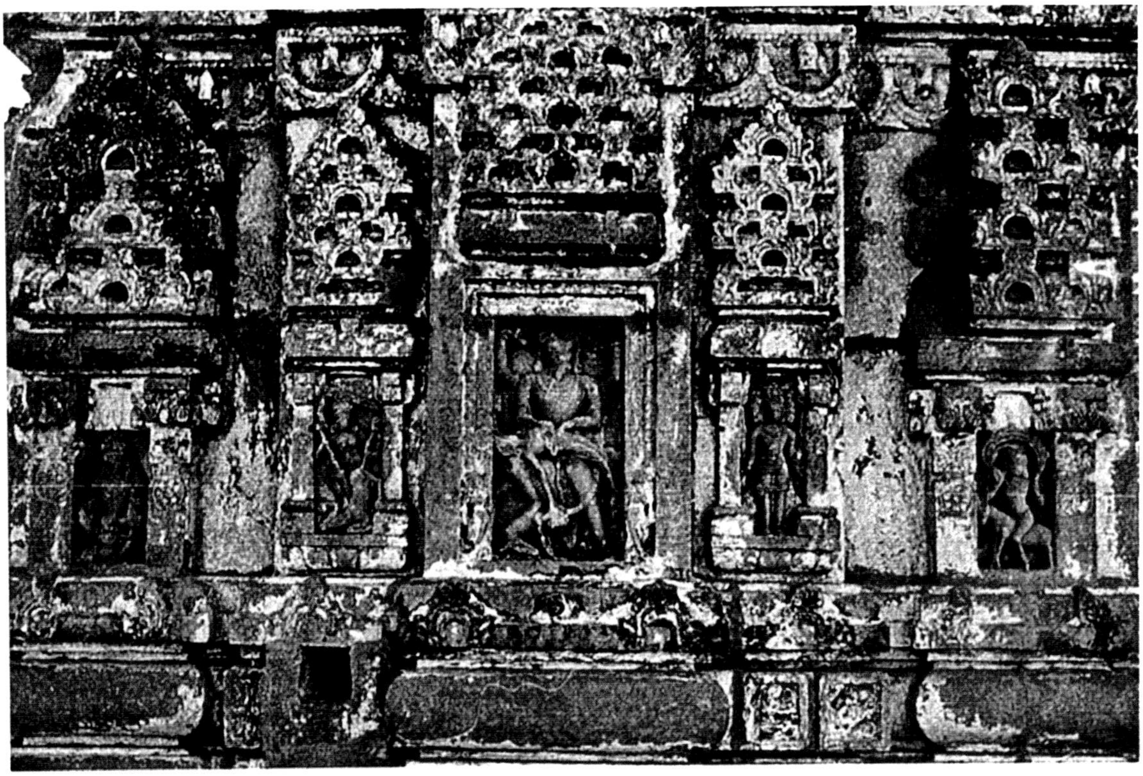

Plate 10.13. Osian, Rajasthan. Harihara Temple no. 1, *ca.* AD 725-50. North wall, images of Kubera, Mahiṣamardinī, Narasiṁha, Brahmā, and Vāyu

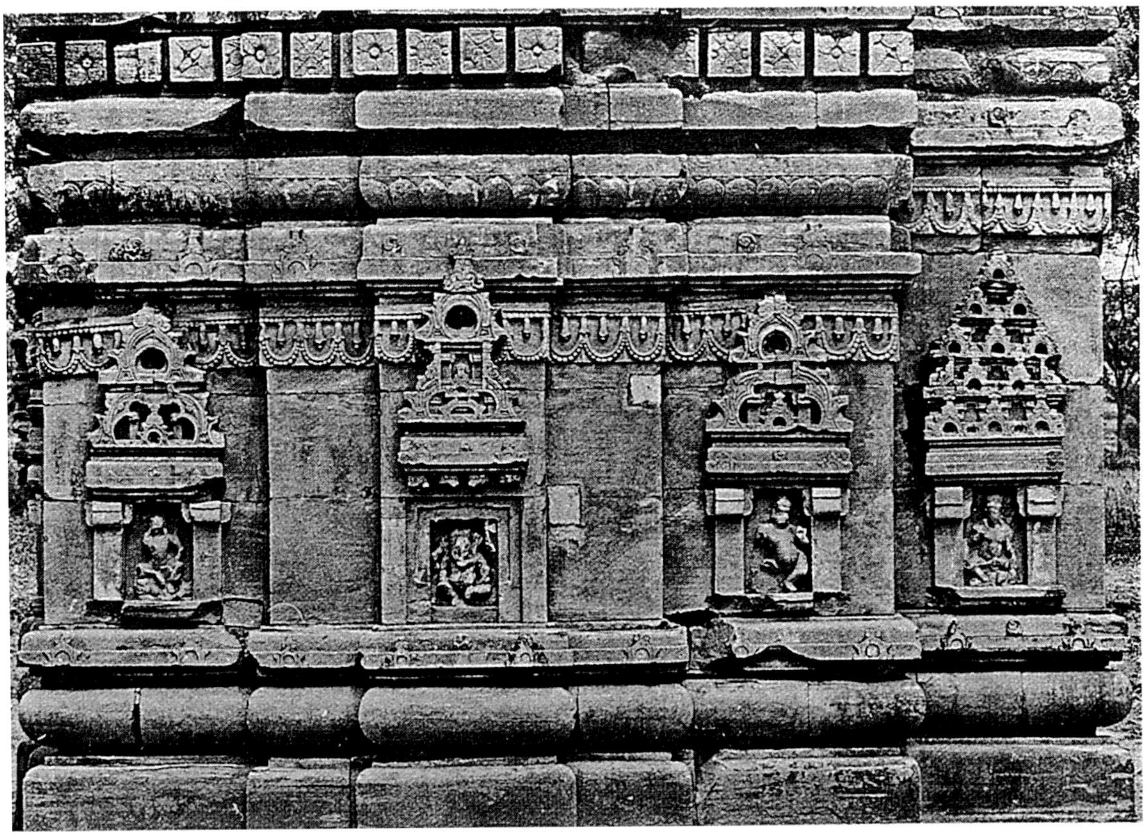

Plate 10.14. Amrol, Rāmeśvara Temple. South sanctum wall, images of Yama, Gaṇeśa, and *Pramatha*; south Kapilī wall image of Agni

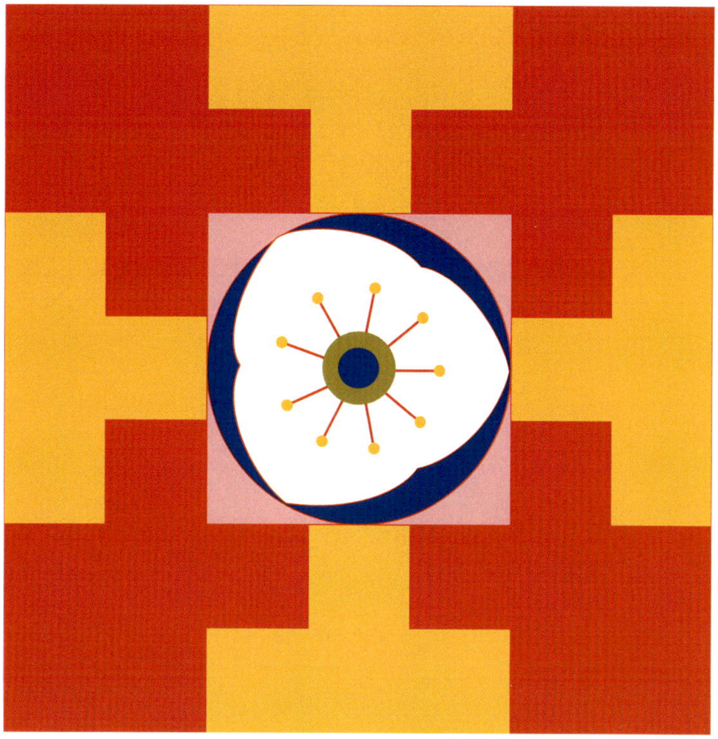

Plate 1.1. Sarvatobhadra Maṇḍala

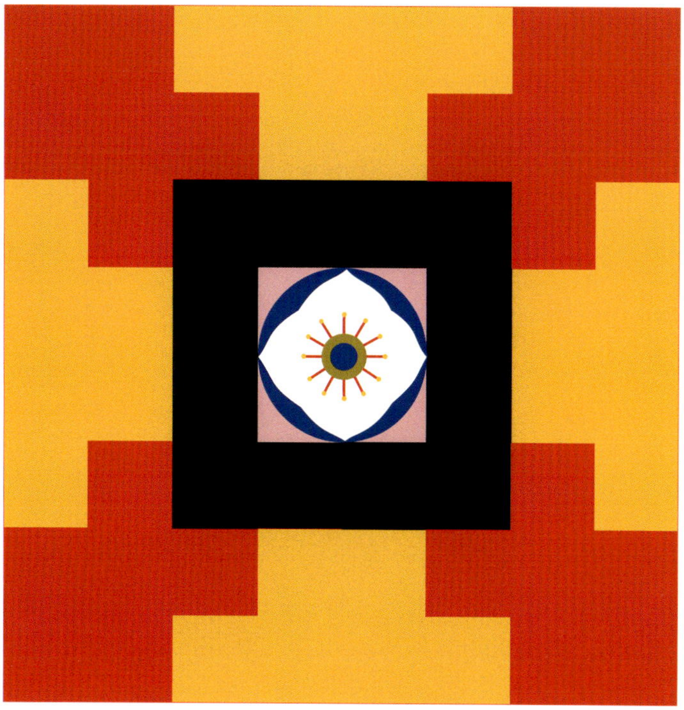

Plate 1.2. Aghanirmocana Maṇḍala

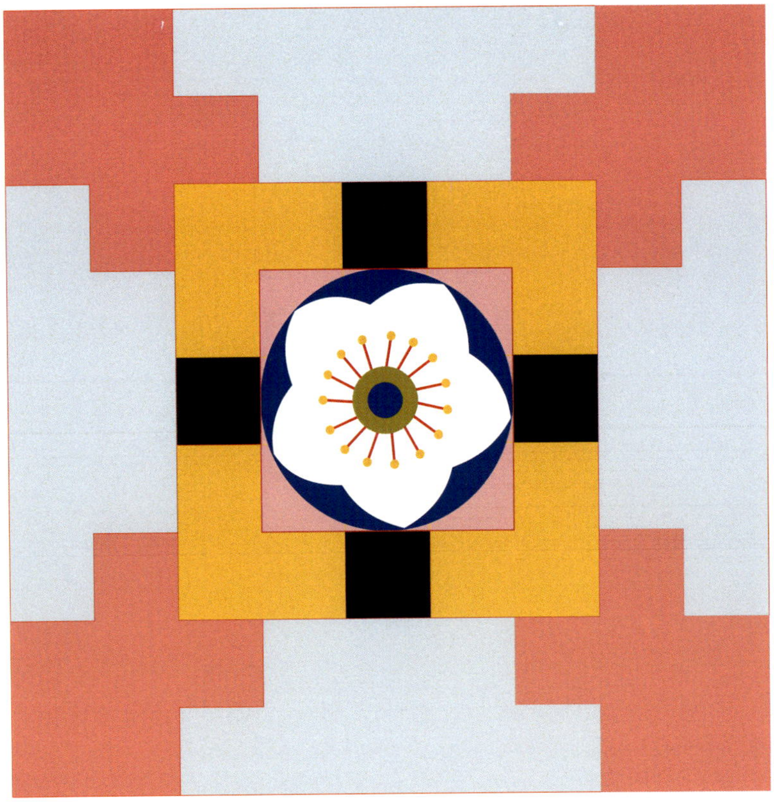

Plate 1.3. Ṣaḍadhva Maṇḍala

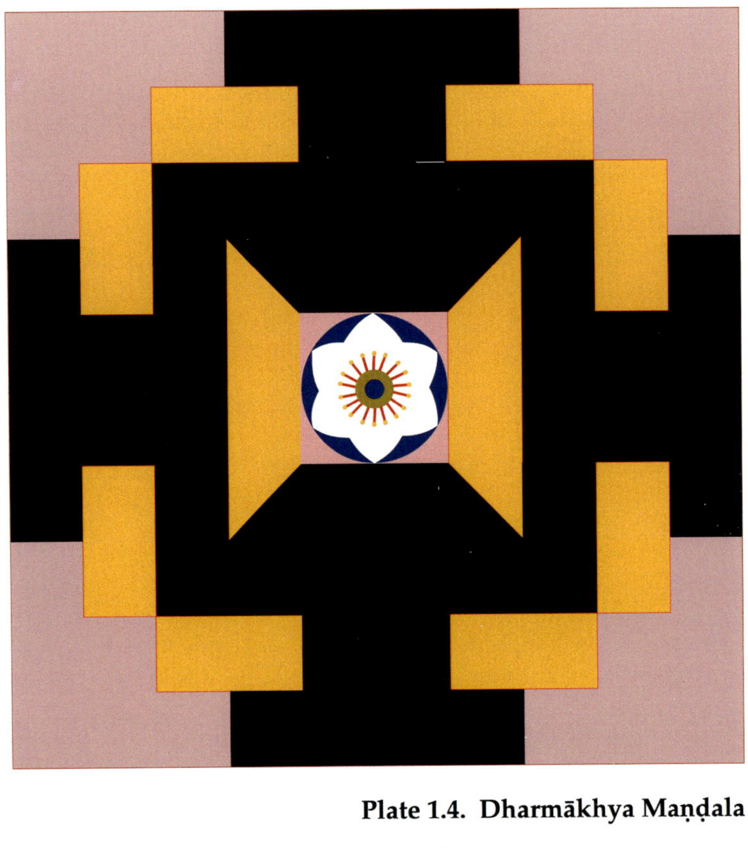

Plate 1.4. Dharmākhya Maṇḍala

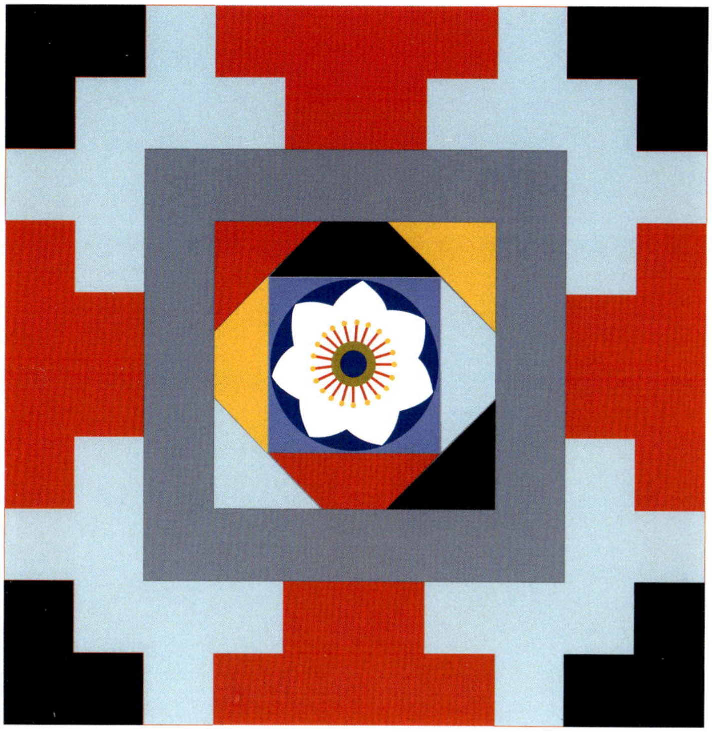

Plate 1.5. Vasugarbha Maṇḍala

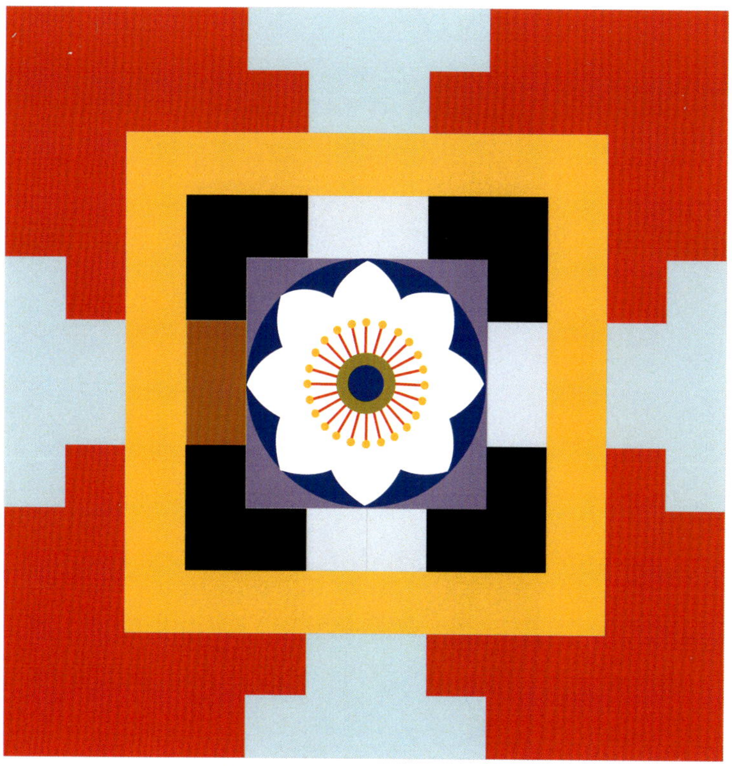

Plate 1.6. Sarvakāmaprada Maṇḍala

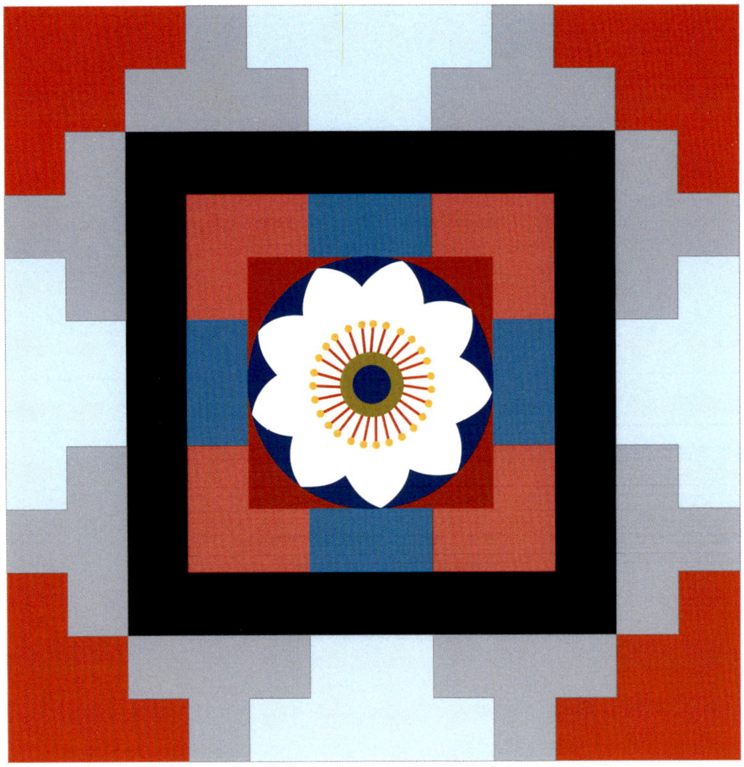

Plate 1.7. Amitraghna Maṇḍala

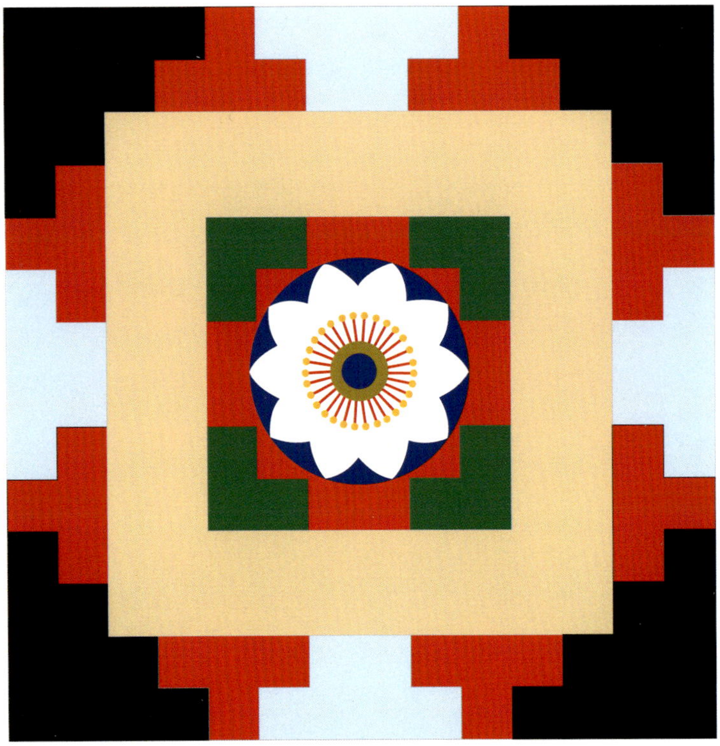

Plate 1.8. Āyuṣya Maṇḍala

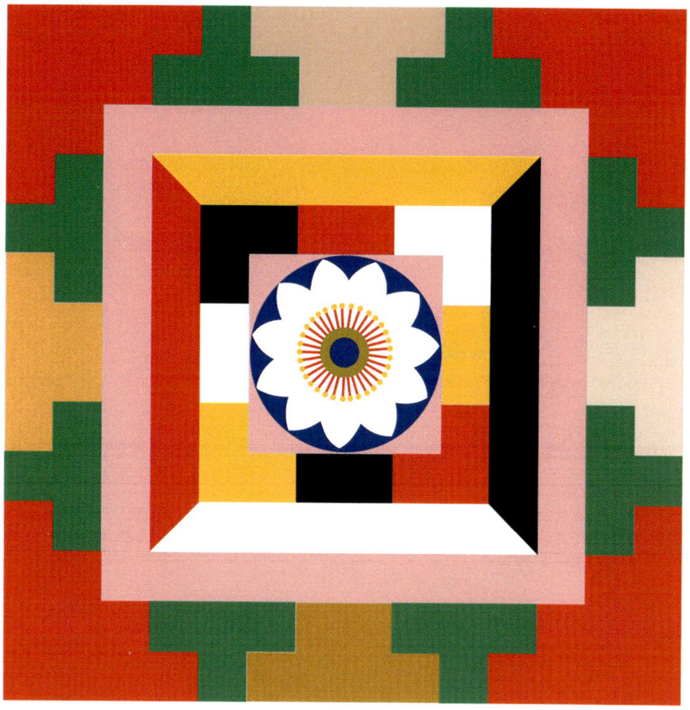

Plate 1.9. Balabhadra Maṇḍala

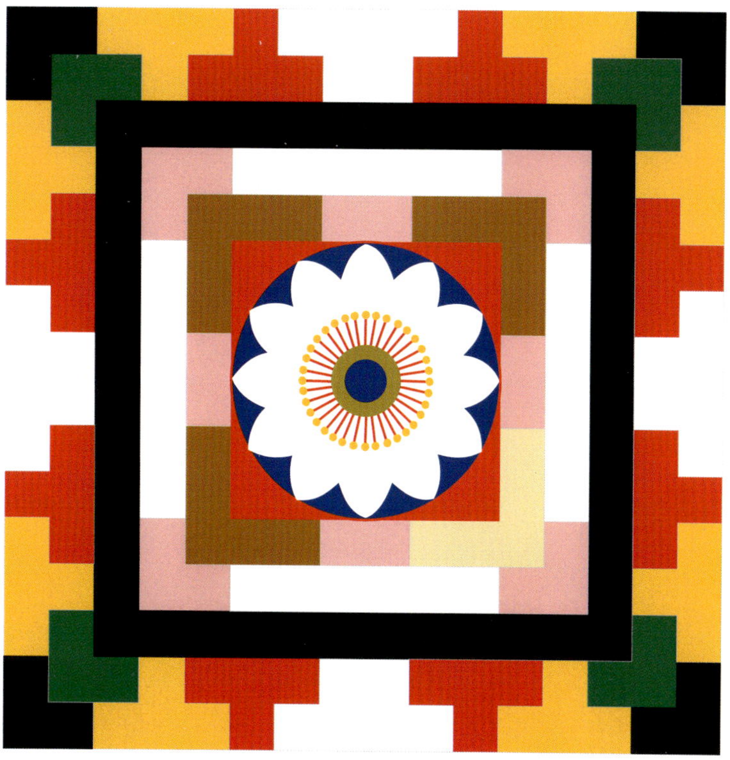

Plate 1.10. Pauṣṭika Maṇḍala

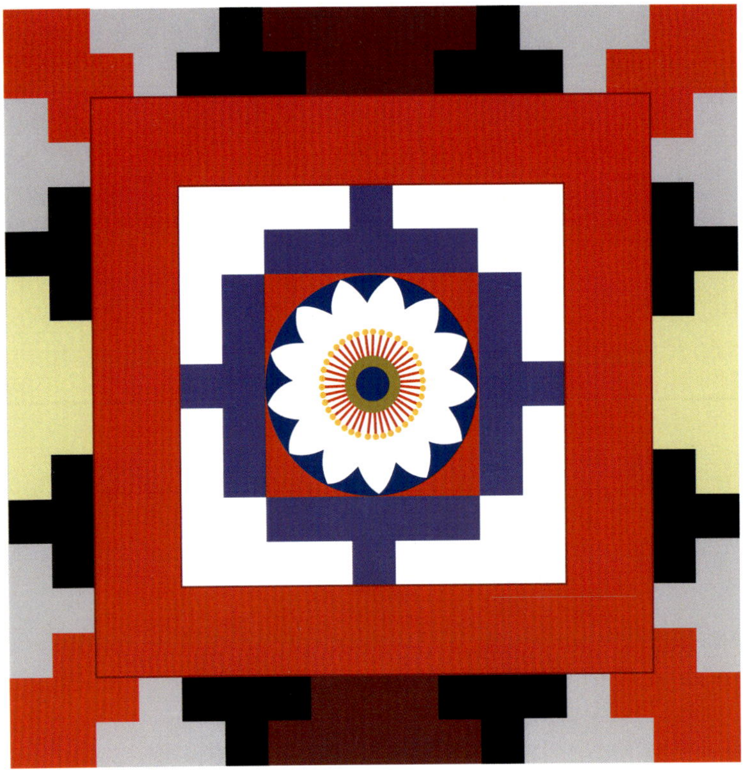

Plate 1.11. Ārogyaprada Maṇḍala

Plate 1.12. Viveka Maṇḍala

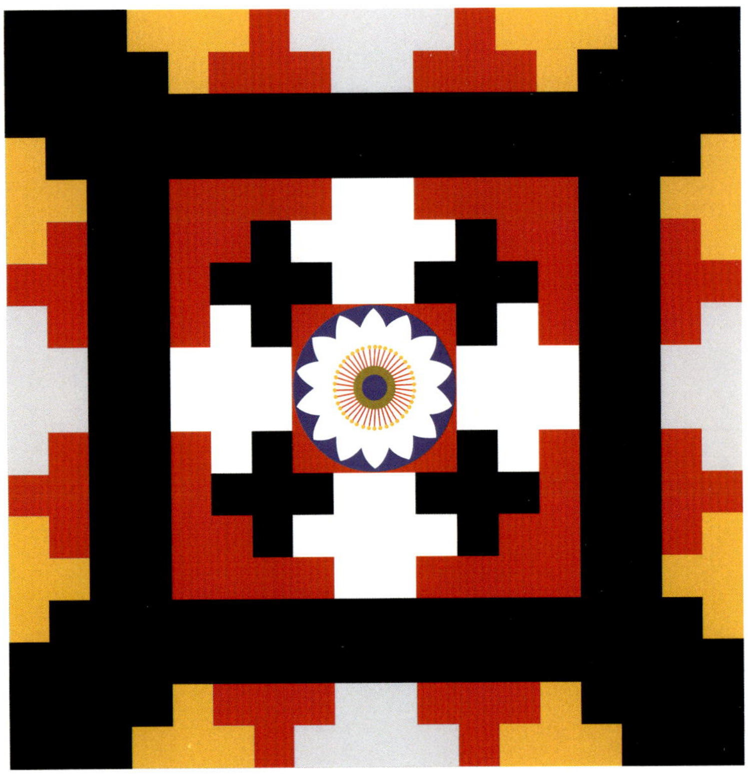

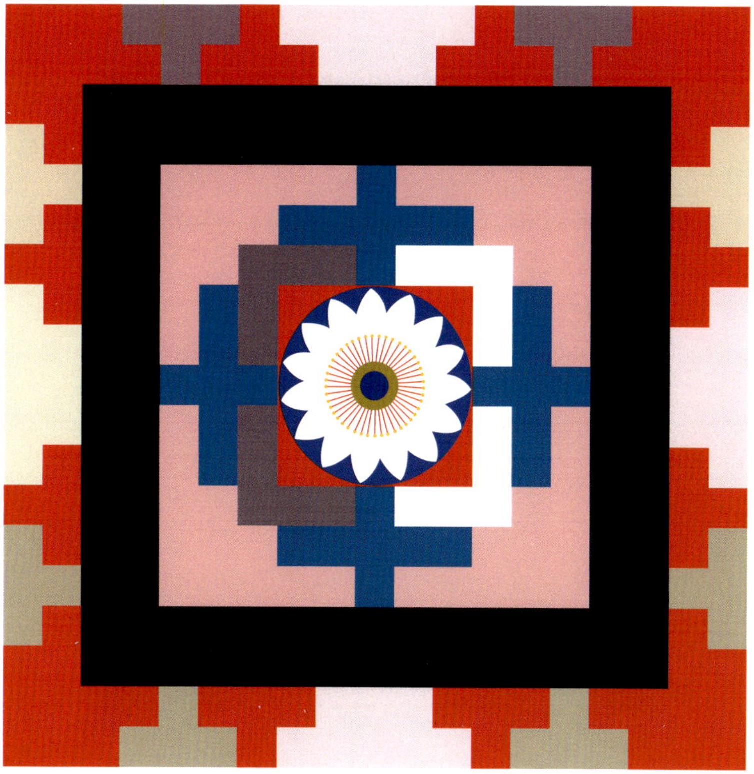

Plate 1.13. Vāgīśa Maṇḍala

Plate 1.14. Mānasa Maṇḍala

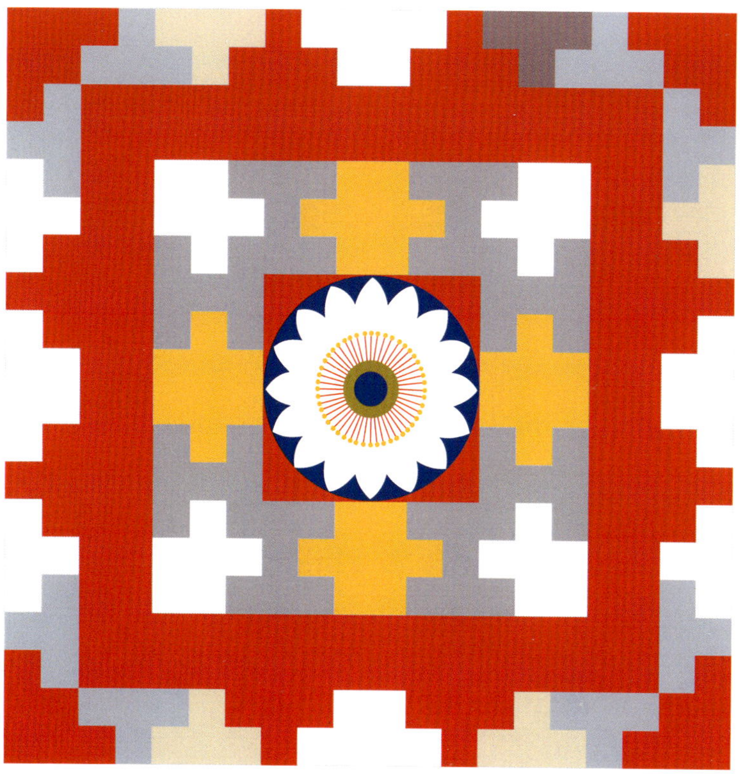

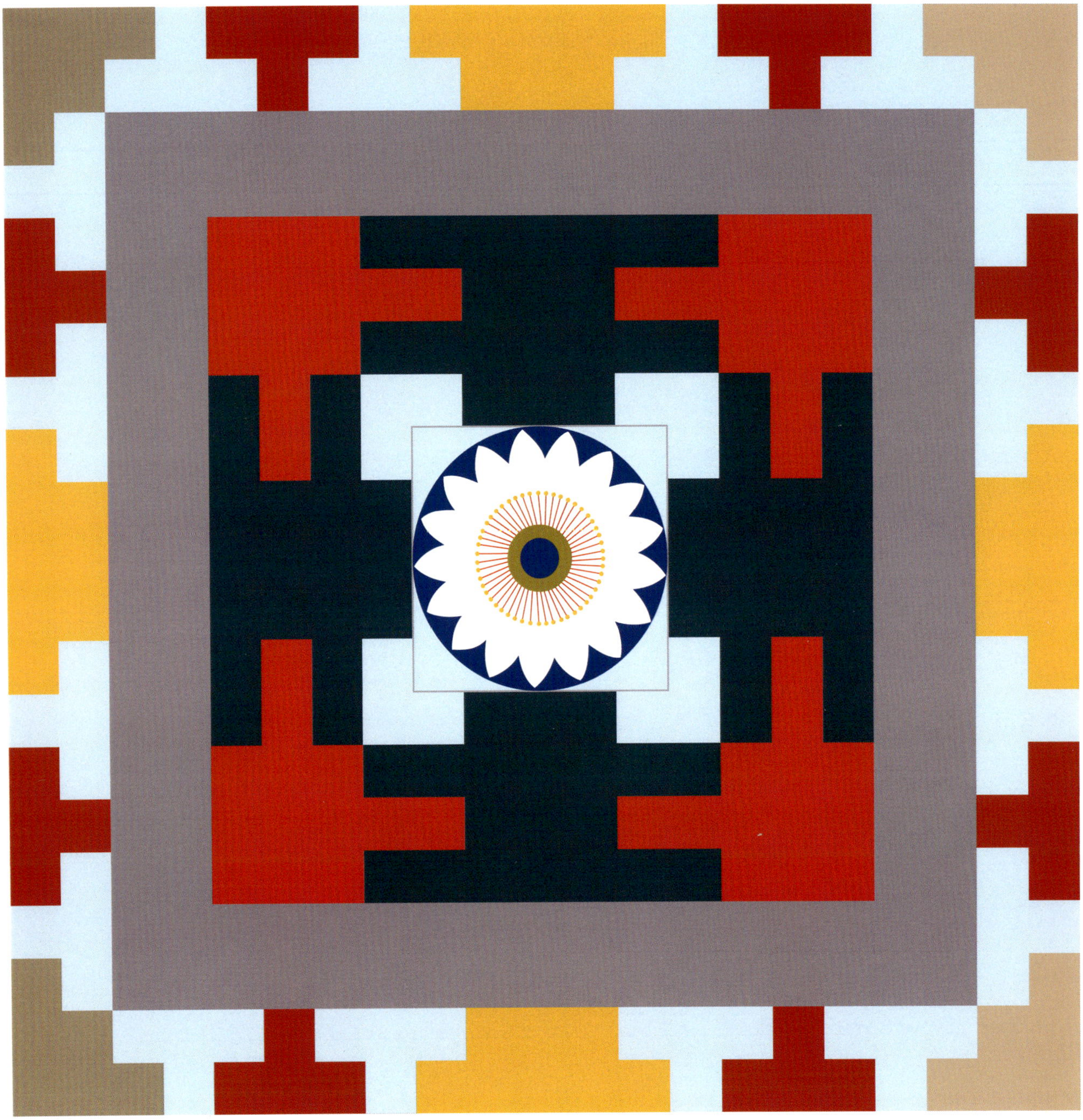

Plate 1.15. Jayākhya Maṇḍala

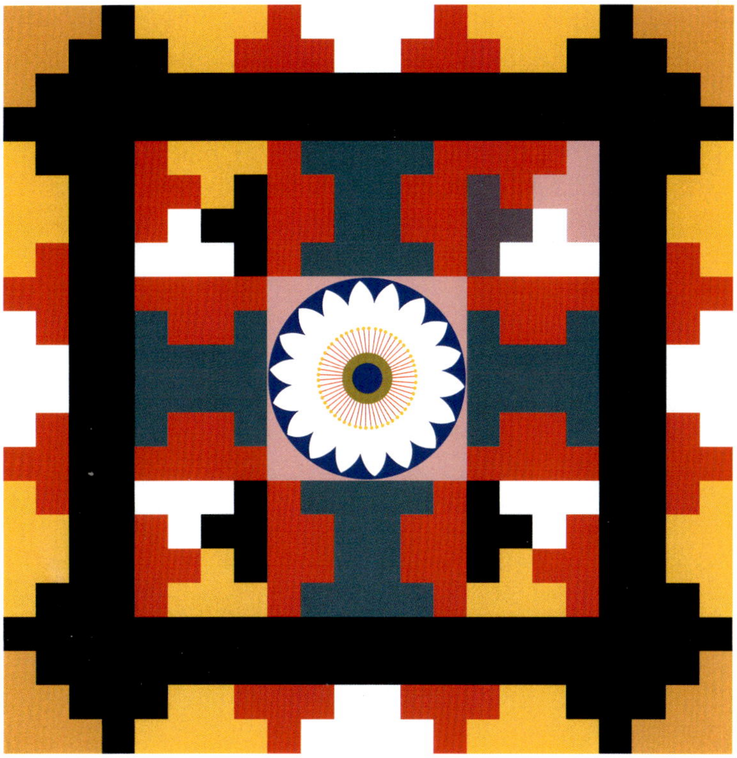

Plate 1.16. Svastika Maṇḍala

Plate 1.17. Ananta Maṇḍala

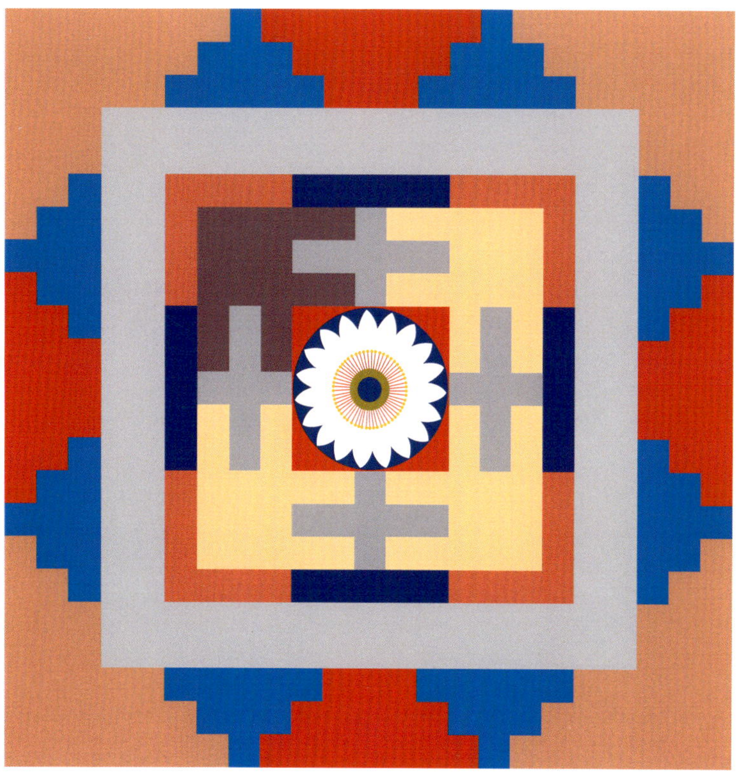

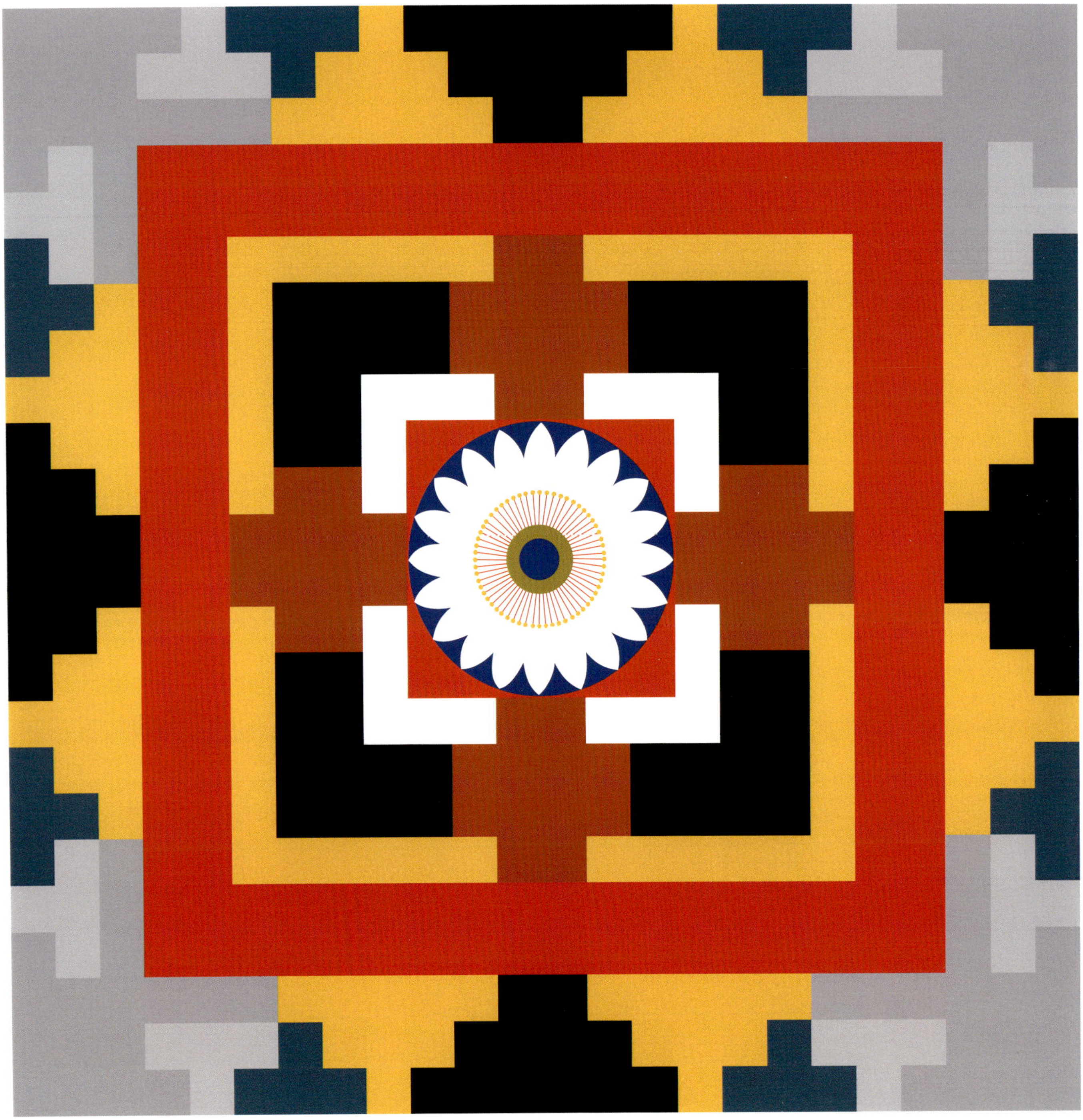

Plate 1.18. Nityākhya Maṇḍala

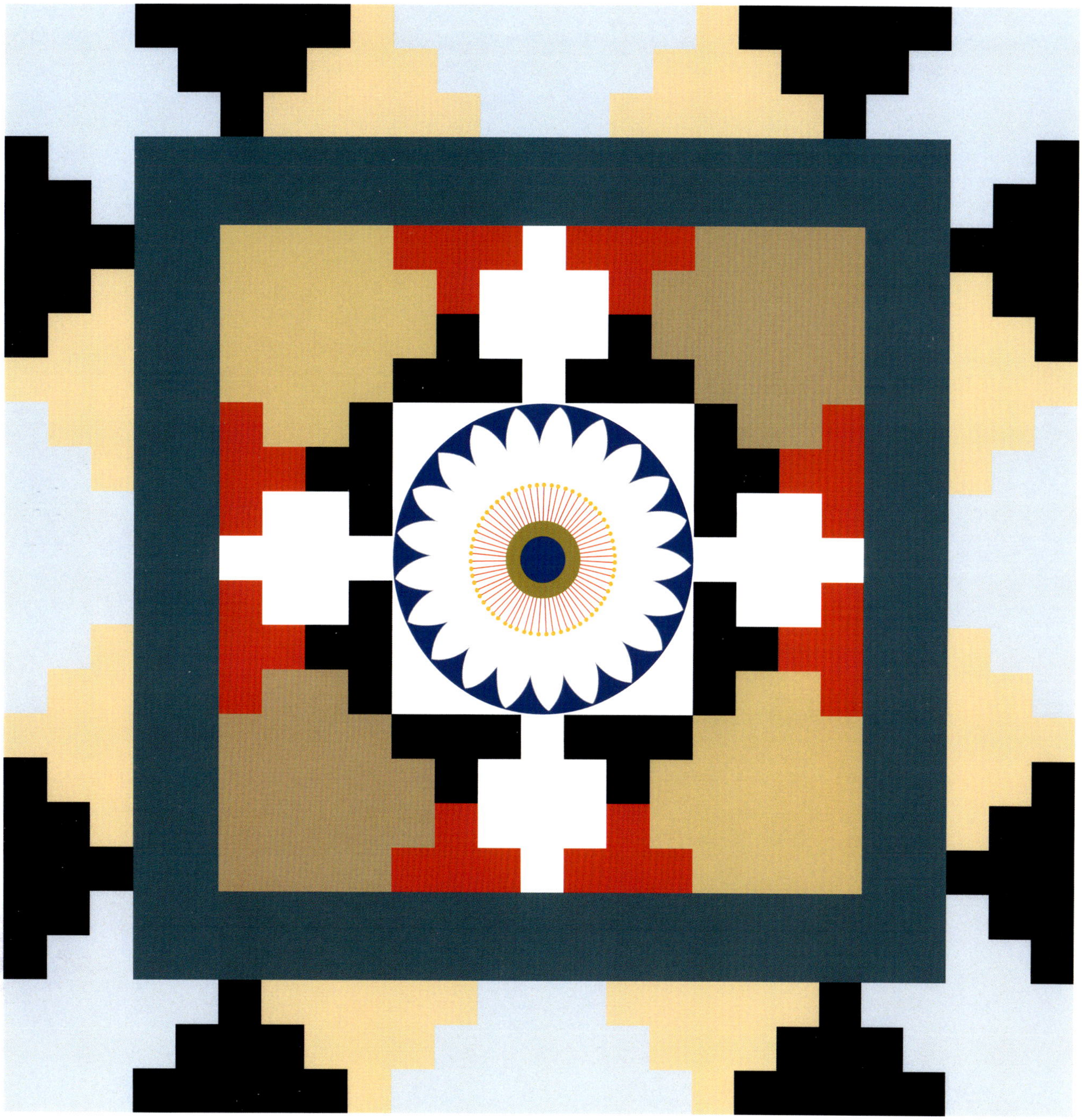

Plate 1.19. Bhūtavāsa Maṇḍala

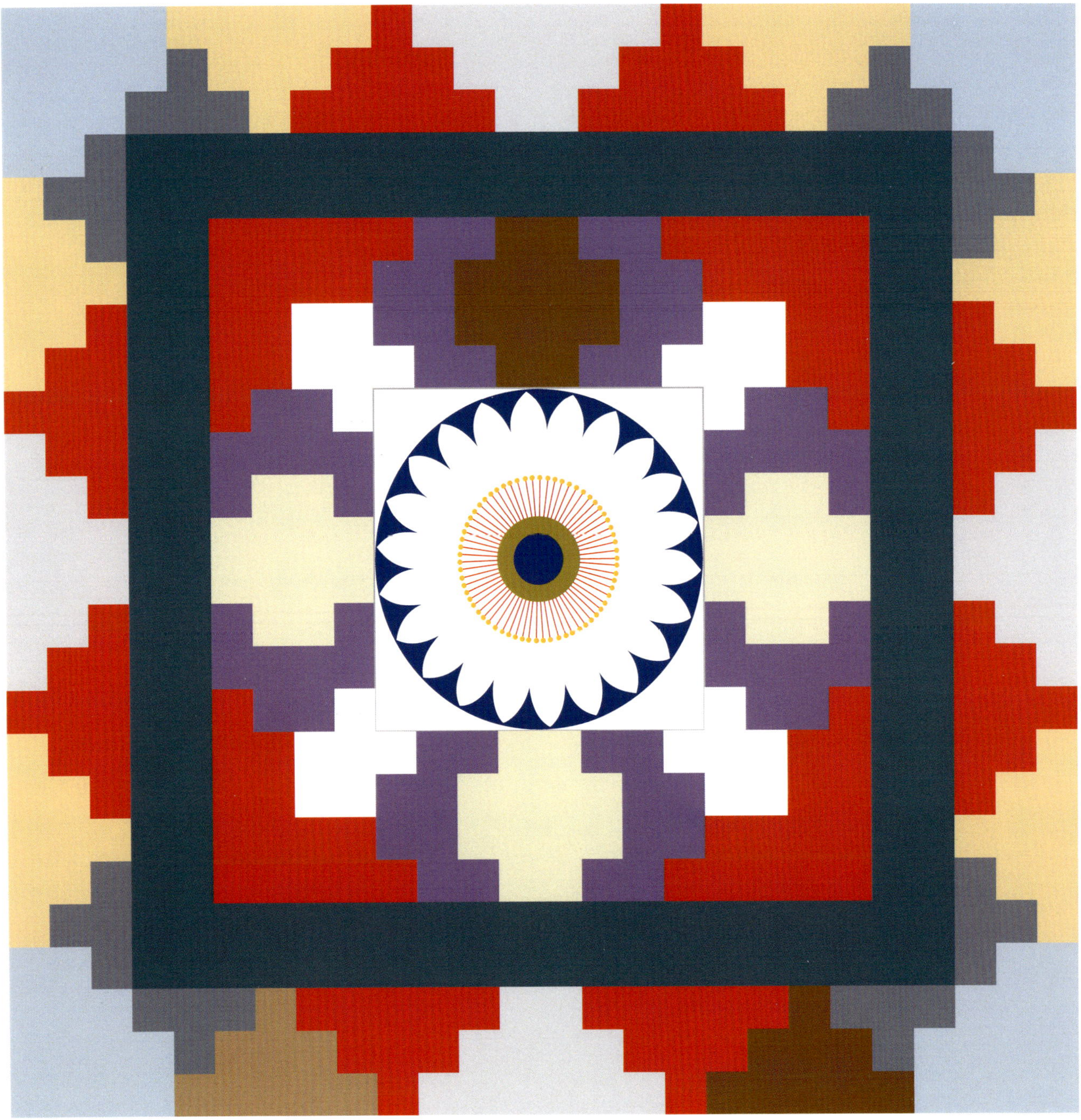

Plate 1.20. Amogha Maṇḍala

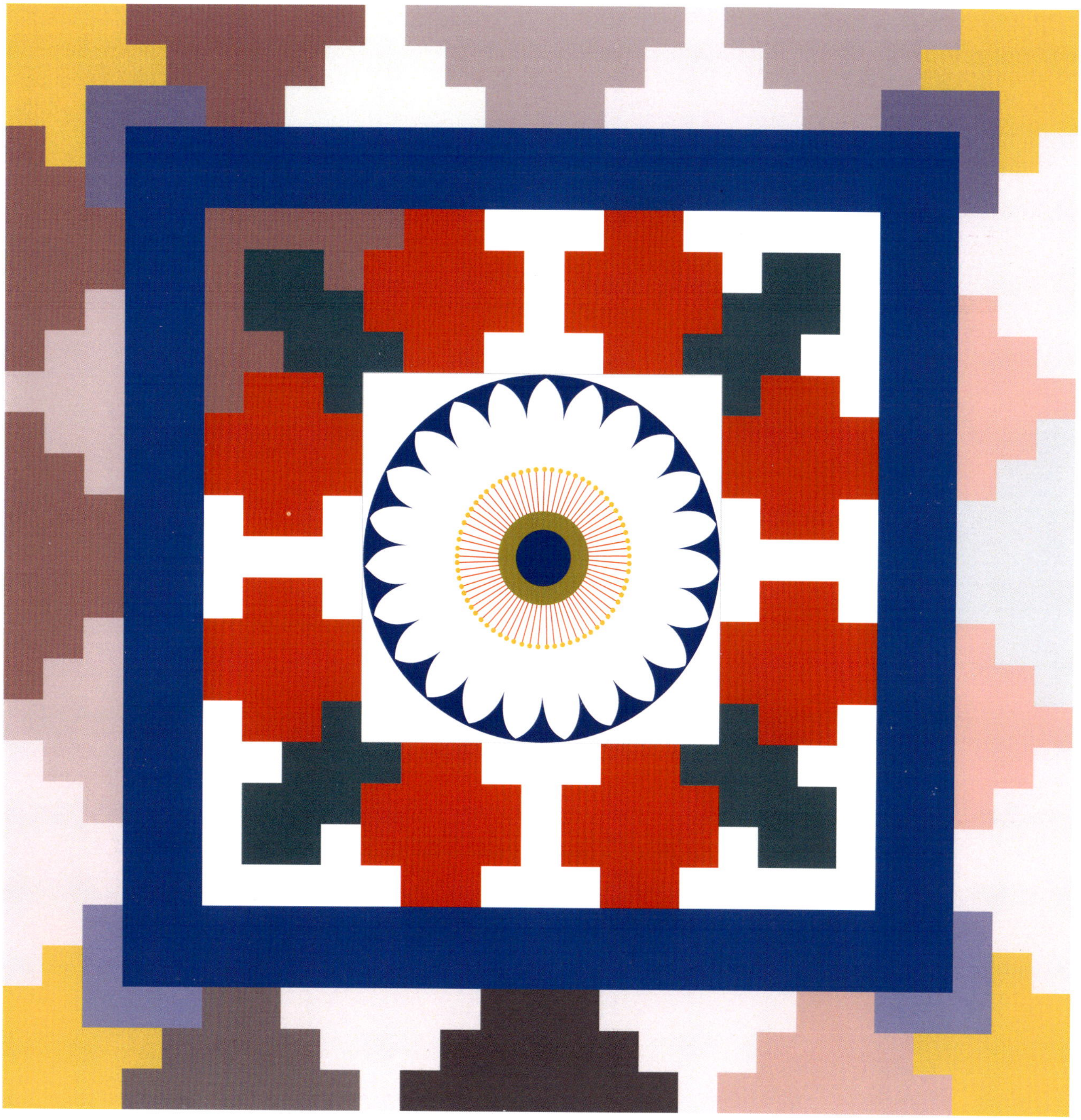

Plate 1.21. Supratiṣṭha Maṇḍala

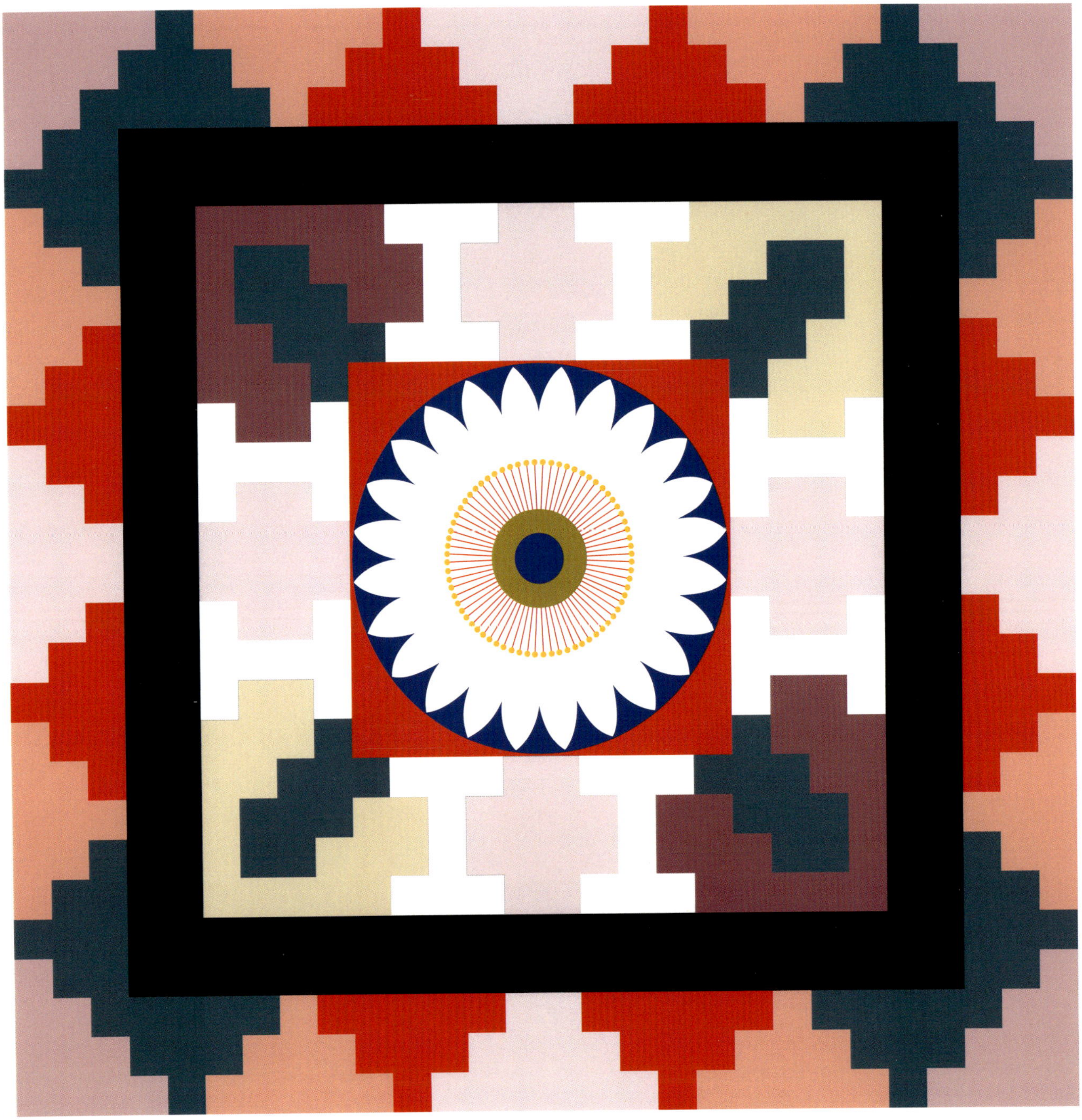

Plate 1.22. Buddhyādhāra Maṇḍala

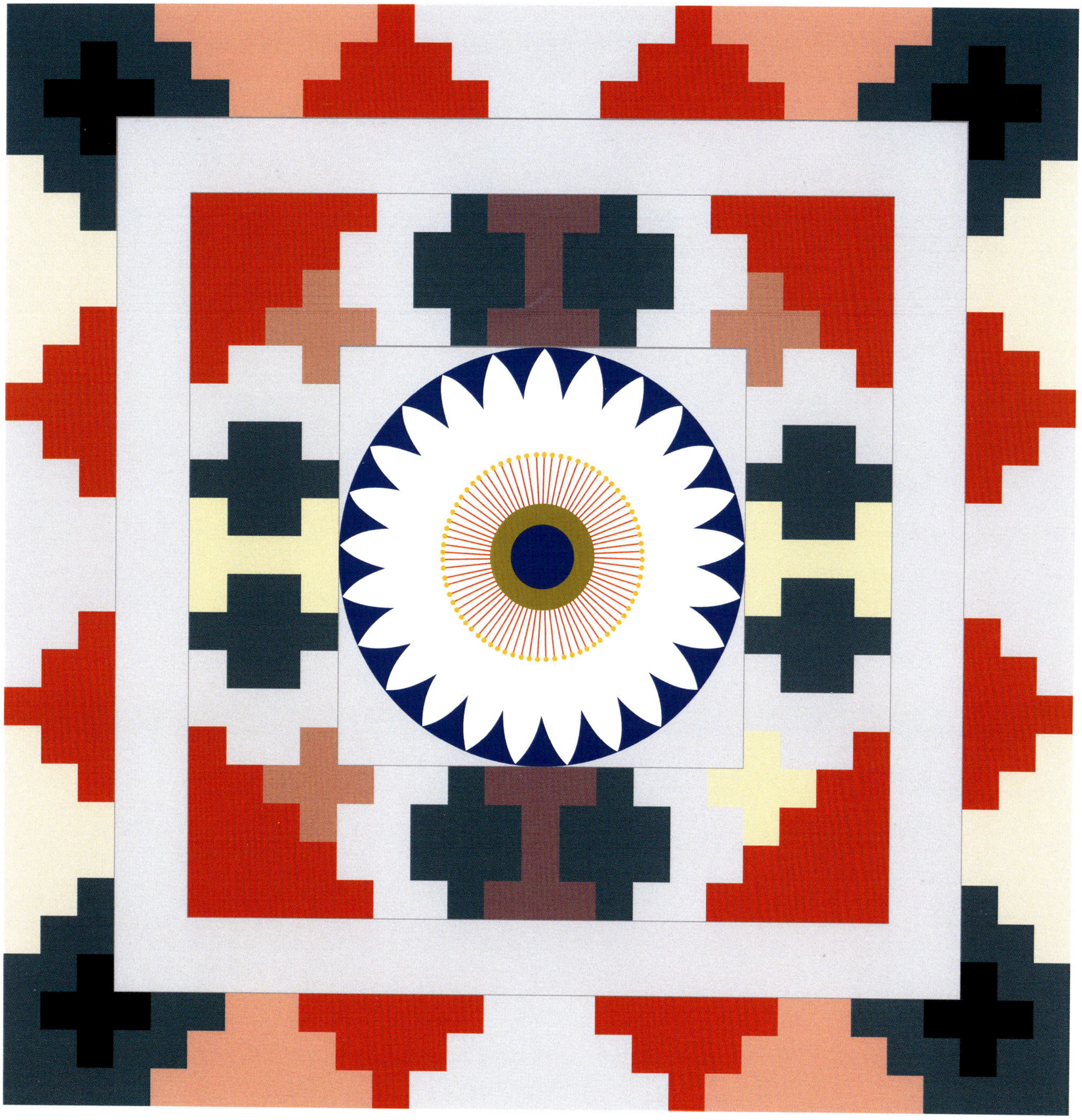

Plate 1.23. Guṇākara Maṇḍala

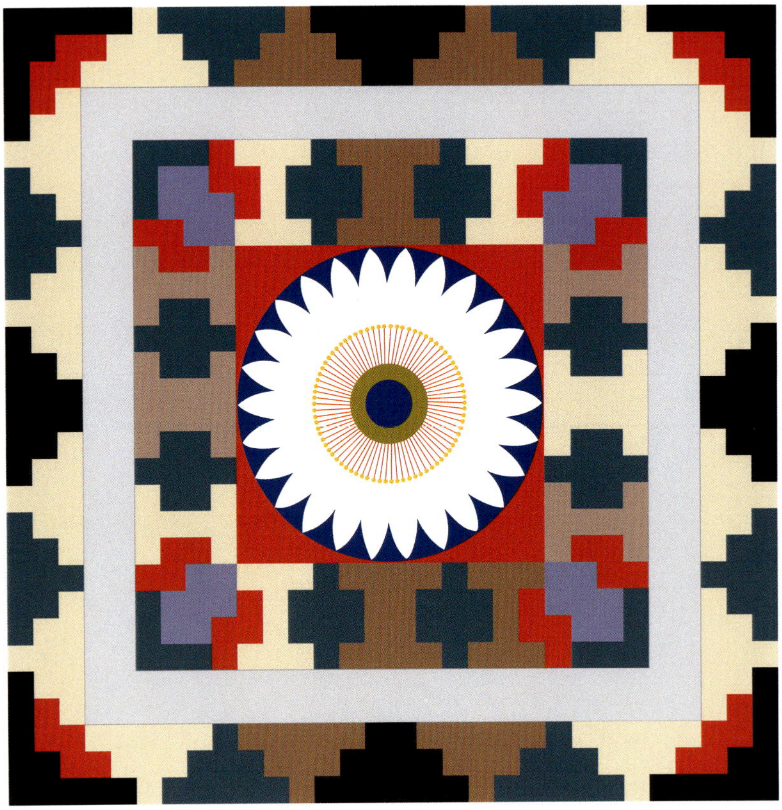

Plate 1.24. Dhruvākhya Maṇḍala

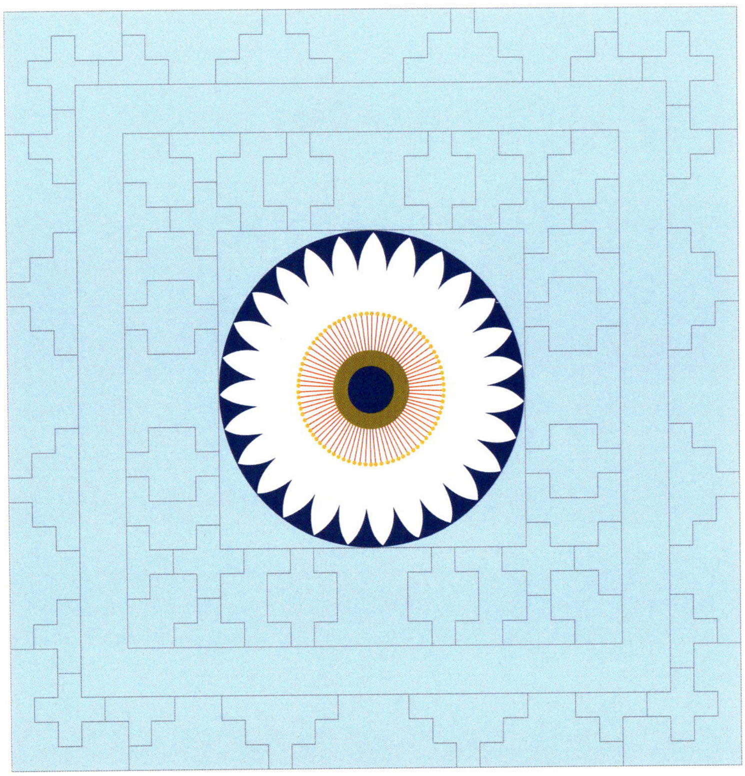

Plate 1.25. Paramānanda Maṇḍala